PLAYING
THE FIELD

PLAYING

THE FIELD

The story of the Edmonton
Folk Music Festival

ROD CAMPBELL

B. Evan White Publishing, 1994

Canadian Cataloguing in Publication Data

Campbell, Rod 1952-
  Playing the field

Includes bibliographical references and index.
ISBN 0-9698357-0-1

  1. Edmonton Folk Music Festival—History. 2. Folk music—History and criticism. I. Title.
ML38.E24E24 1994   781.62'0079'712334   C94-910569-4

B. Evan White Publishing
Box 52106 8210 109th Street
Edmonton, Alberta
Canada T6G 1T5

Printed and produced in Alberta, Canada

For Jan and Maghan and my mother and father,
Hilda and Murdo Campbell.

I *asked professors who teach the meaning of life to tell me what
is happiness.
And I went to famous executives who boss the work of thousands of
men.
They all shook their heads and gave me a smile as though I was
trying to fool with them.
And then one Sunday afternoon I wandered out along the Desplaines
River
And I saw a crowd of Hungarians under the trees with their women
and children and a keg of beer and an accordion.*

— Carl Sandburg, *Happiness*

Table of Contents

Acknowledgements

Without the generous and invaluable assistance of the staff and volunteers of the Edmonton Folk Music Festival, it would have been impossible to write this book.

I am especially indebted to Terry Wickham, Roberta Magnusson, Richard Davis, Vicki Fannon and Don Snider, all of whom patiently shared their personal experiences, provided openhanded access to the festival's archives, corporate files, wonderful photos, and were a constant source of encouragement throughout.

My gratitude also to former festival employees — Loro Carmen, Andy Laskiwsky, Holger Petersen, Kate Carey and Don Whalen — for their considerate cooperation, insight and guidance. Likewise veteran volunteers Agnes and Jim Brennan, Peggie Graham, Silvio Dobri, Percy Odynak, Tom Coxworth and Andy Donnelly.

Estelle Klein, Mitch Podolak and Richard Flohil deserve a salute from all of Canada for their invaluable contributions to folk festivals across the country. I'm extremely grateful to them for the consideration and understanding they extended while sharing their experiences.

Performers Amos Garrett, Stewart MacDougal, James Keelaghan, Sylvia Tyson, Mairi MacLean, Allan Stein, Del Cocks, Bob Remington and Mike Sadava are due much appreciation for providing numerous colourful anecdotes from their unique vantage point. The same must be said about journalists Alan Kellogg, Tom Elsworthy, Peter North and Graham Hicks.

I particularly want to thank Bruce White, my publisher, for providing me with the opportunity to write this book and for his frankness and patience throughout its gestation. Elizabeth Pogue's acute observations as editor helped immeasurably in cutting the lean from the fat from the first several drafts. Cheryl Purdey's valuable experience helped polish the manuscript. Researchers Karen Unland, Shona Dippie, Vanessa Rist and Rosa Jackson were remarkably understanding and ingenious under pressure. Debbie Kulcsar transcribed hours and hours of interview tapes with constant good humour and perceptiveness. And warmhearted Kathy Fisher went above and beyond the call of duty when it came to the use of her university library card.

Finally, I owe individual debts to several long-standing friends who didn't contribute directly to this text but influenced it nonetheless. Thanks then to Doug Swanson for giving me my first break as a writer; Rick McConnell for his contagious interest in good writing; Jim and

Jeanette MacLachlan for all these years of brilliant music; and the Wee Malkies — Jim Connor and Richard Janeczko — where this all really began. *Slainte*.

Credits

Cover art: original water color by Edmonton artist Dean Tatam Reeves

Cover Photographs: Courtesy of the Edmonton Folk Music Festival, except k.d. lang, courtesy of The Riz Photographs. The festival photographers were: Frank Gasparik (Tuva Ensemble), Joe Rizzuto (Spirit of the West), Thomas W. Turner (crowd in the rain), Wayne Stiles (Jane Siberry) and Murray Gallant (Odetta).

Black and White photography: Courtesy of the Edmonton Folk Music Festival, except where noted.

Happiness from CHICAGO POEMS by Carl Sandburg, copyright 1916 by Holt, Rinehart and Winston and renewed 1944 by Carl Sandburg, reprinted by permission of Harcourt Brace & Company.

This Land Is Your Land, words by Woody Guthrie. TRO — © Copyright 1956 (renewed), 1958 (renewed) and 1970 Ludlow Music, Inc., New York, NY. Used by permission.

Pretty Boy Floyd, by Woody Guthrie. © 1958 (renewed) by Fall River Music Inc. All rights reserved. Used by permission.

The Times They Are A-Changin' Copyright © 1963, 1964 by Warner Bros. Music. Copyright renewed 1991 by Special Rider Music. All rights reserved. International copyright secured. Reprinted by permission

The Manchester Rambler. Copyright Ewan MacColl. Reprinted with permission.

Foreword

Through fifteen turbulent years, the Edmonton Folk Music Festival has developed its tastes and infrastructure to become the premier event of its kind in North America. From the regal poise of Odetta to the apocalyptic mayhem of the Violent Femmes, it has presented some of the most powerful, emotional and vital folk and roots acts in the world. Pioneering festivals like Newport and Mariposa rode to glory on the coat-tails of the folk revival between 1957 and 1965. Edmonton, on the other hand, started out in 1980 as folk music in the U.S.A. and Canada wallowed in a mire of derisory cliches. Abroad, though, talented young musicians and singers — Celts, Africans and rogues such as Billy Bragg, The Pogues and The Men They Couldn't Hang — seized the initiative and approached the music with a new spirit of open-minded determination. And folk was reborn. The foresight to adapt to these changes turned Edmonton into the top-drawer attraction it is today — notwithstanding the valuable contributions of the festival's staff and thirteen-hundred or so adept volunteers.

In *Playing The Field*, I have attempted to show the development of the various strains of folk and roots music that influenced, inspired or were introduced by the various acts performing at the festival over the years. The only exception is world music. To provide a detailed background of all the diverse international talent presented in Gallagher Park would make this book prohibitively long, disjointed and repetitive. Instead, I concentrated on the individuals and organizations in Europe who publicized, promoted and eventually made world music available in Edmonton.

Despite the incredible standards set by this festival, it is not unique. The format had been established long before the festival's inception, so I have traced the lineage that directly affected Edmonton. While I've endeavored to make this a thorough account of the festival and its music, it is not intended to be scholarly. I make absolutely no attempt to define folk music. Why isolate it and restrict its boundaries? It should breathe and prosper. There are no footnotes to interrupt the concentration of the reader. Instead, all secondary sources are listed in a bibliography. Countless hours of interviews with staff, volunteers, fans, musicians, journalists and folk-roots personalities of various stripes took place through the winter of 1993 and into the late spring of 1994. The opinions expressed about the various performances are mine alone unless stated, and are drawn from every festival I attended as either a fan or a reporter between 1982 and 1993.

To increase the enjoyment of reading *Playing The Field*, I have included a brief discography with each chapter. The catalogue numbers were kindly provided by Mark Davis of Blackbyrd Records, 10918 88th Avenue, Edmonton. Naturally, Mark would be delighted to order any of these records for you. Finally, if this book causes you to go out and watch live folk-roots performers, or buy one of their records, then it has more than served its purpose.

Rod Campbell
Edmonton, Alberta,
May 31, 1994.

The people, music and festival

1

Singing In The Rain

■Mary's having a ball ■'This festival is
unsurpassed' ■Music for money
■Highland fling ■Stan Rogers: Canadian
legend ■Roots and rhythms■

"Me guitar player, Dick Farrelly, was crying on the way home. For us, for musicians, there was much more appreciation. They treated us like gods over there."
— IRISH SINGER MARY COUGHLAN, AFTER PERFORMING AT THE 1993
EDMONTON FOLK MUSIC FESTIVAL

A COLD DAMP RAIN TURNS THE NATURAL amphitheatre of Gallagher Park into a chaotic web of quivering plastic sheets. To the west, a spectacular backdrop of city skyline inherits the last light of the day. As darkness conceals the lush North Saskatchewan River valley, a ripple of indifferent applause greets Mary Coughlan as she waltzes onto the main stage at the 1993 Edmonton Folk Music Festival. Coughlan cannot walk the streets of her native Dublin without fans clamoring for her autograph. Here she is an unknown entity. In spite of the horrendous downpour, she appears relaxed and assured. Her powerful, provocative voice cradles an intoxicating blend of topical and sensual jazz and folk songs. For the best part of an hour, Coughlan and her vacuum-tight, five-piece band flatter and cajole the ten thousand spectators. Finally they abandon their makeshift sanctuaries and stand and sway to the rhythm of the rain.

As Coughlan concludes, a surge of adrenalin rips through the crowd. Two stark spotlights wash over the hill; with growing intensity the crowd calls out for more. Encores are the exception here due to tight scheduling, but Coughlan prevails. "Thank you Edmonton! I'm having a ball. And I hope to have a couple more before the night's out," she cackles before making her exit, dismembering *These Boots Were Made For Walking*.

The following afternoon Mary Coughlan sat backstage in the festival's hospitality tent, exhausted but thoroughly delighted with herself. A trip to the world's largest shopping mall produced several irresistible bargains, the merits of which she openly discussed with complete strangers. As she relaxed over a hot meal and a cold beer, the conversation ranged from the draconian abortion policies of the Irish government to the merits of Roddy Doyle's novel, *Paddy Clarke Ha Ha Ha*. As the first woman to go on national television in Ireland and say that marijuana should be decriminalized, Coughlan's not one to shy away from controversy. So when asked how Edmonton compared with other folk festivals, she swept back a mass of rampant red hair and looked her inquirer straight in the eye. "It's fuckin' brilliant," she offered in finest Galway patois. "Festivals back home, the bastards exploit you. They just want you for your name as a draw. They don't give a shite about the performers as long as they make money. Not here. Here, they treat you like a king. It's unbelievable!"

Frank Gasparik (EFMF)

Mary Coughlan at the 'brilliant' 1993 Edmonton Folk Music Festival

And with that, Coughlan and her band reluctantly left to catch a plane. The next night they would perform fifty-five-hundred miles away in Letterkenny, Donegal, Ireland, but Coughlan continued to sing Edmonton's praises. "It was amazing," she told the *Irish Press* newspaper. "Me guitar player, Dick Farrelly, was crying on the way home. For us, for musicians, there was much more appreciation. They treated us like gods over there." Coughlan also raved about the city's shopping and architecture. As the headline summed it up: "Even the skyscrapers are nice in Edmonton, says Mary."

♪   ♪   ♪

Rolling Stone magazine gave Edmonton its first real international nod of approval in a 1987 Summer Music Guide supplement. "Canada's biggest festival just may be the hippest of the summer," the same publication said a year later as it saluted the booking of such diverse acts as Richard Thompson, Jane Siberry and Lyle Lovett. Six years later Dirty Linen, the North American folk-roots flagship from Baltimore, still found Edmonton agreeable. "This festival is unsurpassed for organization and musical adventure," it said. Even the national perspective looked undeniably rosy. The *Globe And Mail* reckoned, "The Edmonton Folk Music Festival is the best folk festival in the country . . . head and shoulders above the competition."

Because of its relatively small population and isolated location, Edmonton does not attract a year-round parade of folk or roots acts. Absence makes the heart grow fonder, true. But this isolation creates a worldly innocence. Of the sixty or so acts on each festival bill, many like Mary Coughlan are unknown locally. Almost half of each lineup features fresh faces. Rarely are singers or musicians now booked for more than two years in a row. This constant turnover of talent requires a great leap of faith on behalf of the festival audience — a trust that has produced such startling rewards as Terry King and Bobby Evans, The Oyster Band, Fatala and Solomon Burke. Acts with widespread name recognition — Donovan, Ry Cooder, Randy Newman, Kate and Anna McGarrigle — draw the uninitiated to Gallagher Park. Such celebrities are booked sparingly, though, due to budget restrictions. At any rate, prominent names don't guarantee prominent performances, as witnesses to the John Sebastian debacle of 1987 will attest.

Since the first festival in 1980, total weekend attendance has risen from 7,000 to 45,000 in 1992. While these figures are inflated with complimentary tickets, they still indicate a considerable increase in interest in the festival — much of which stems from its outdoor ambiance. "I'm a complete sucker for it," says Stacey McCue, a relatively new convert. "I'm too poor. I can't afford to go anywhere. It's like a fifty-dollar vacation." For four nights and two days in early August, she can blister under the sun or catch pneumonia in a monsoon to the wanton pulse of world music, reggae, or rhythm 'n' blues. Outlandish concession stands and a popular beer garden take care of basic bodily needs. Eighty-eight Handi-Cans look after the rest . While decent craft stalls and a well-stocked record tent invariably wreak havoc on delicate bank accounts, the festival does offer a safe environment for children. A variety of diverse daily activities frequently wear the little tykes out so they nod off in a warm sleeping blanket just as the nightly main stage concerts grow interesting. Parental bliss.

Anita Maloney (EFMF)

Top-name artists, such as Randy Newman in 1993, help to draw large audiences to Gallagher Park

Few similar international events consistently book as many accessible top-drawer acts for such low ticket prices, treat their performers, audiences and guests with such respect, or run as efficiently in such a class location as Edmonton. Not Vienna, Austria. Not Tonder, Denmark. Not Falun, Sweden. Not Cambridge, England. Not Edinburgh, Scotland. Not Newport, U.S.A. Not Mariposa, Canada.

Yet there's an amazing paradox at play here. While Edmonton has developed one of the finest folk festivals in the world, it has done so in a community with a diminishing interest in the music's grassroots. Small folk music venues are starved for fans. Picking and singing in parlors or on porches remains only marginally more popular here than cricket. I just wish I had a dollar for the number of talented friends I've watched start an after-dinner song only to stall as the faces of their guests cloud over with bewilderment.

Loro Carmen grew up in a Metis community in central Alberta in the fifties. "There was always music in the home, because many members of the family played an instrument," says Carmen, general manager of the Edmonton folk festival in 1989 and 1990. "There was always a fiddle, banjo, piano, guitar, going most of the time. It was part of our culture, part of our social fabric in the community. Large families: you couldn't afford even to think about collecting the children and going to concerts. There just wasn't the money. So we made our own music at home. I don't see it anymore; I don't see it in the next generation coming up."

As A.L. Lloyd wrote in *Folk Song In England,* "The mother of folklore is poverty." The discovery of oil near Leduc in 1947 created the first real flush of prosperity in northern Alberta. Then OPEC pushed the world price of oil from around $3 a barrel in 1973 to $35 in 1979 and turned the province into the wealthiest in Canada with the highest per-capita income. This financial windfall coincided with the electronic revolution that brought everything from VCRs to PacMan into the home. As a result, family entertainment grew more and more passive. Instead of making music, this consumer society headed for the mall and bought it — as cassettes, compact discs and concert tickets.

Even the influx into Alberta between 1975 and 1981 of almost ninety-thousand adults and children from such spirited cultural turf as Quebec and the Atlantic provinces did little to stir the pot. Unlike the migrant workers of the past — the lumberjacks, the miners and the navies — these contemporary roughnecks created few new folk songs. Part-time Calgary songwriter and roustabout Cal Cavendish came up with *I'm A Rig Pig*. But the only enduring songs from the vast social upheaval created by the oil boom were written by professional musicians such as Stan Rogers (*The Idiot* and *Free In The Harbour*) and James Keelaghan (*Boom Gone To Bust*).

♪ ♪ ♪

Some of my warmest memories of a childhood spent in the North of Scotland come from family ceilidhs held at my grandmother's croft on New Year's Day. She spoke Gaelic fluently but used only English in front of her nine children. She considered her native tongue a social handicap. At the croft (a small farm), my father and his brothers would sit for hours and play their accordions and mouth organs as my mother, aunts and cousins danced and sang in front of a roaring fire. More often than not, we children fell fast asleep — bellies full of lemonade, trifle and dumpling — long before the last toast to the future.

In the summer of 1993, my nine-year-old daughter Maghan and I returned to visit family and friends. It was a trip planned to coincide with The Highland Traditional Music Festival in Dingwall. Held in various pubs and hotels throughout the town, it featured the likes of Michaela Rowan of Mouth Music, Billy Jackson of Ossian, and many local musicians and singers. Late Saturday night at the National Hotel, a solo Fred Morrison strolled casually on stage to close with a set of bagpipes. Morrison was utterly, utterly exquisite. But just as important, the full house held on to his every note with breathless reverence. Twenty-four hours later, Manus Lunny of Capercaillie joined Gerry O'Connor of Four Men And A Dog and aroused grey-haired adults to pogo to jigs and reels performed on a bouzouki and tenor banjo. Mayhem. And each night as the formal concerts concluded, musicians and singers of various ability sat around and graciously swapped songs and tunes until long after sunrise.

When Maghan and I enjoyed meals with friends, the visits inevitably began with the tuning of guitars. And to borrow a line from Stan Rogers, "we sang and laughed like fools." Often raw and emotional, the songs dealt mainly with local topics as diverse as the social impact of North Sea

Rod Campbell

A ceilidh outside the Caledonian Hotel in Dingwall, Scotland, during the 1993 Highland Traditional Music Festival

oil and the rearing of buffalo herds in the Highlands. Surely this is the essence of all folk music. It's people singing about their community. Voices raised with a clear sense of purpose, pride and pleasure. As the music and the odd dram of *uisge-beatha* (whiskey) flowed, our children played around us — curious but too reserved to participate. One day this tradition will belong to them. What they do with it only time will tell, but at least they have the option.

♪   ♪   ♪

Although Canada lays claim to such song writing icons as Joni Mitchell, Neil Young and Leonard Cohen, nobody wrote about this great, sprawling land with more insight and sensitivity than Stan Rogers. A cantankerous giant of a man with a glorious baritone, he profoundly understood the lives of working people, their dreams, their desires and their despair. Without Rogers — who died in an airplane fire in 1983 — James Keelaghan, Spirit of the West, Grievous Angels, and for that matter his brother Garnet Rogers, might never have found the confidence or the voice to write some of their finest lyrics.

His mother Valerie was born and raised in Hazel Hill near Canso, Nova Scotia. She married a Pictou country boy and together they left in 1948 to seek their fortunes in Hamilton, Ontario. "When I was born, she took me 'home' to show me to the folks," wrote Stan in the liner notes of his debut album *Fogarty's Cove*. "Mum's brothers most of them, anyway, played or sang or both, and I guess it naturally followed that one of my earliest memories would be of my uncles sitting around my grandparents' kitchen, 'half shot', playing guitars (some of them home-built) and singing old tear-jerkers by Wilf Carter, Hank Snow and Hank Williams, with Aunt Jane and Mum and all the rest joining in, in more-or-less harmony, while Dad looked on, smiled and played referee."

Stan Rogers earned his spurs around Hamilton, where at the age of fourteen, he made his debut at the Ebony Knight coffee house in 1963. The owner paid him five dollars and a cheap bottle of wine for a two-hour set. In the same venue later that winter, he sat mesmerized as three professional musicians sat and traded songs, stories and guitar licks. "My first store-bought guitar sat forsaken in my lap, and I was too young and impressed to open my mouth," he wrote in the 1981 Calgary Folk Festival program booklet. "But it was wonderful. I remember at the time thinking that someday I'd get a chance to share music that way." He had to wait almost fifteen years.

While he made a couple of novelty singles for RCA in the early seventies, and cut the odd track for the CBC, he recorded nothing of significance until 1974. That fall he put together a demo tape of his own songs with Daniel Lanois, a budding young Hamilton producer, who would go on to make albums for the likes of U2, Bob Dylan and The Neville Brothers. The tape they made found its way to Mitch Podolak, the artistic director of the Winnipeg Folk Festival. Suitably impressed, Podolak not only booked Rogers for Winnipeg, but also started Barn Swallow Records to release *Fogarty's Cove*.

Until his appearance in Manitoba in 1975, Rogers' support lay mainly in Southern Ontario and in pockets of the Maritimes. A consistently powerful and spirited performer, he knocked Winnipeg on its ear and earned his first national recognition. The following year he released *Fogarty's Cove* — an album inspired by Scottish traditional singers Archie Fisher, Ian Robb, and Tam Kearney as well as veteran Canadian balladeer, Alan Mills. Flush with historical and personal Maritime vignettes, it kick-started a national folk song revival that still shows no sign of abating.

♪   ♪   ♪

While most modern musical trends have a shorter shelf life than brie, folk reinvented itself as roots in the mid-eighties. From the North Shore of Vancouver to the East End of London, brash young bands with immaculately deranged hair began to assail the entrenched conservatism that dogged folk for decades. Against all expectations, folk-roots sud-denly became fashionable. And its appeal still endures as Terry Wickham,

P. Hanington (EFMF)

Gallagher Park on a hazy 1989 evening . . . a natural amphitheatre with a stunning urban backdrop

the current producer of the Edmonton folk festival, found out in a little pub in Dublin in April, 1994.

He had gone along to hear traditional fiddler Maire Breathnach. When her first set ended, rock waif Sinead O'Connor got up and sang a couple of *a cappella* songs. Then Liam O'Maonlai of Hothouse Flowers followed her before Breathnach returned to complete her second set. Nobody batted an eyelid.

"Roots is probably to the eighties what Fairport Convention were to the late sixties," Ian Keary of the trailblazing Oyster Band explained in a 1987 interview with the *Gateway*. "Bands like Fairport came out of the rock scene and moved towards folk. Bands like ourselves came out of the folk scene and are moving towards rock.

"Folk-rock in the past has been pretty nostalgic. It was looking at world that never was. The pretty milkmaids and plough-boys, green England — that time never existed. If you look at traditional songs a lot of them are very bitter. They can be an alternative to the view you get in history books. It's a look from underneath — a very cynical one. We are more in common with what punk was originally in terms of the aims. It was a view from underneath, not the official view that's written about. I think that's what folk music has been and should be."

♪   ♪   ♪

Three decades before the emergence of roots, a great urban folk revival shifted traditional songs from the backwoods and industrial plants onto the concert stages of the world. And folk music became famous. As its popularity spread, it created a slew of new North American folk festivals from which Edmonton evolved. This great awakening began in earnest in the Oklahoma and Arkansas dust bowl of the Dirty Thirties. A wiry, weather-beaten, contrary cuss no bigger than a fence post gave it the first prod. Went by the name of Guthrie — Woody to his friends.

Selected recordings

Stan Rogers: Fogarty's Cove (FCM 1001)
   Northwest Passage(FCM 004)
   Between The Breaks (FCM 002)
Mary Coughlan: Tired And Emotional (WEA International 2292-420942)
Dougie MacLean: Whitewash (Dunkeld 010)
Archie Fisher: Will Ye Gang Love (Green Linnet 3076)
Patrick Street: Patrick Street (Green Linnet SIF 1071)
Hothouse Flowers: People (London 828 101-1)
Dick Gaughan: Handful of Earth (Green Linnet GLCD 3062)

2

Bound for Glory

- The Grapes of Wrath and the Rapes of Graft ▪ Woody Guthrie and the rambling life ▪ Talking Dust Bowl ▪ Pete Seeger hits the road with Woody ▪ Un-American Activities ▪ The 'college circuit' is born ▪

"Pete and me aim to put the word Hootenanny on the market."
— WOODY GUTHRIE

MARCH 3, 1940. BROADWAY LAY cleansed after a day of rain and sleet. Backstage at the Forrest Theatre on 49th Street, Woody Guthrie, Leadbelly, Pete Seeger, Aunt Molly Jackson, Burl Ives, Josh White, and Alan and Bess Lomax tuned guitars and banjos. The aroma of spilled whiskey and damp sawdust rose with the room temperature. Some of America's greatest folk singers were there to perform a New York benefit for the thousands of migrant workers from Oklahoma and Arkansas who were by this time destitute in California. These Dust Bowl refugees inspired John Steinbeck's acclaimed novel, *The Grapes of Wrath*. And Steinbeck wanted to raise funds to ease their suffering. Actor Will Geer smiled with satisfaction at the full house. At 8:30 p.m. it was time to introduce the first act, Aunt Molly Jackson.

Jackson, who had been driven out of Kentucky for her union activity during the 1932-39 Harlan County coal wars, sang about the deprivation and oppression faced by the miners back in the Appalachian Mountains. Woody Guthrie sauntered out next in a cowboy hat, boots and blue jeans. Sorely needing a shave, he tossed out a casual "Howdy," mumbled about being pleased to perform at a Rapes of Graft benefit, then introduced himself through several of his Dust Bowl ballads. "His voice bit at the heart. A low, harsh voice with velvet at the edges, the syllables beautifully enunciated, the prose flowing with a professional writer's balance of sentence and with the salt of a folk wit," Alan Lomax wrote in the liner notes for the *Woody Guthrie: Library of Congress Recordings.* "He made us see the people he spoke of and his rawhide wit lashed us into laughter."

By the time Guthrie concluded with *Why Do You Stand There In The Rain* — a seething condemnation of President Roosevelt's growing involvement with the Second World War — twenty-year-old Pete Seeger stood stunned in the wings. Introductions had to wait, though, until after Seeger made his debut as a performer. "I was a bust," Pete later confessed to biographer David Dunaway. "You see, I didn't know how to play the five-string banjo. I tried to do it too fast and my fingers froze up on me. And I forgot the words. It was the *Ballad of John Hardy*; I got a polite applause for trying and retired in confusion."

Disappointed and dejected, Seeger arrived at the post-concert party where Lomax introduced him to Guthrie. "Go back to that night when Pete first met Woody Guthrie. You can date the renaissance of American folk song from that night," Lomax told Dunaway. "Pete knew it was his kind of music, and he began working to make it everybody's kind of music. . . . It was a pure, genuine fervor, the kind that saves souls."

Lomax then invited Guthrie to Washington D.C. to record for the Library of Congress Archives of Folk Song. Only 23 years old at the time, Alan supervised the Archives for his father, John Avery Lomax, who spent most of his time collecting and recording in rural areas. His discoveries included such treasured cowboy songs as *Home On The Range, I Ride An Old Paint, The Old Chisolm Trail* and *Sam Bass.*

♪ ♪ ♪

John took Alan on his first field trip in the summer of 1933 — to the prisons in the Deep South, where the black inmates chanted their work songs into John's 350-pound Presto tape recorder. While the teenager began this trip reluctantly, he was soon captivated by the raw intensity and beauty of the music they heard. In the Louisiana State Prison Farm in Angola they made their greatest discovery: forty-nine-year-old Huddie Ledbetter, known to his cell mates as Leadbelly. His stunning ability on the twelve-string guitar, striking voice and overwhelming charisma left the Lomaxes thunderstruck. A decade earlier, while serving a thirty-year sentence for murder in Texas, Leadbelly's playing and singing earned a pardon from Governor Pat Neff. Jailed again for ten years for assault with intent to murder, Leadbelly's musical talents now earned him a second reprieve: John Lomax successfully pleaded to Governor O.K. Allen for clemency. Freed several months later, Leadbelly became John's chauffeur and travelling companion.

Until that eventful summer, Alan, like many students his age, had been a radical at the University of Texas. Now he saw folk music as a potential weapon in the class struggle. After all, the voices of the ill-treated black prisoners he recorded often reflected the anguish they felt as victims of an unjust, racist legal system. By recording their protests, he could give them a voice. At the same time, he hoped to launch a folk music revival — a viable alternative, he reckoned, to the

Canapress

Woody Guthrie, a born wanderer from Oklahoma, was America's greatest songwriter during the Dust Bowl years

day's trivial, corporate pop sung by the likes of Bing Crosby. That idealistic notion appeared a lot more attainable when Woody Guthrie walked into Alan's life. Lomax recorded Woody March 21, 22 and 27 in Washington. These recordings, which are still available, captured Guthrie's *Dust Bowl Ballads* and long conversations about his colorful past — a unique period in American history.

♪   ♪   ♪

Woodrow Wilson Guthrie was born in Okemah, Okfuskee County, Oklahoma, on July 14, 1912, the third child of Charles Edward Guthrie and Nora Belle Tanner. Charley Guthrie, a Texan, was a man of many talents — pioneer, prize fighter, banjo and guitar player for several cowboy bands. But his prosperity came from selling real estate as the first oil boom struck Oklahoma. Nora's family was also musical. She sang Irish, Scottish, Mexican, Spanish and Negro songs to her children —

Roy, Clara and Woody. And so her youngest son grew up surrounded by music.

"Okemah was one of the singingest, square dancingest, drinkingest, yellingest, preachingest, walkingest, talkingest, laughingest, cryingest, shootingest, fist fightingest, bleedingest, gamblingest, gun, club and razor carryingest of our ranch and farm towns, because it blossomed out into one of our first Oil Boom Towns," Woody recalled in Henrietta Yurchenko's *A Mighty Hard Row: The Woody Guthrie Story*. But the boom brought high-powered land speculators into the game, who ate small-timers like Charley Guthrie for breakfast. By the beginning of 1923 he was broke.

The Guthries' upheavals continued. Since their first home burned down in 1909, Nora had developed behavioral problems, her moods fluctuating between chronic depression and fits of rage. Mysterious fires broke out in their various homes over the next decade. One morning in 1919, Clara's dress inexplicably caught fire. Woody watched her die from her terrible burns. Nora grew more and more unstable. Eight years later she poured kerosene on Charley and set him alight. She was committed to the State Asylum at Norman where doctors diagnosed Huntington's chorea — a genetically transmitted degenerative disorder of the nervous system. Charley survived but returned to his family in Texas to convalesce.

Woody remained in Okemah with Tom Moore, a family friend who played fiddle and knew many old church songs from Tennessee. Most evenings he and Woody would sit for hours making music. The teenager played harmonica, Jew's harp and bones, danced jigs and had an uncanny knack for adding hilarious, off-the-cuff verses to traditional songs. He revelled in performing in front of audiences, whether in the parlor at home, at school, on a local street corner or in front of the local Rotarians, who tipped him the phenomenal sum of $60 in coins for one performance.

The oil boom had subsided by 1928 and Tom Moore figured greener pastures lay in Arizona. He went west and Woody hitch-hiked south to the Gulf of Mexico to visit friends around Galveston, Texas, "doing all kinds of odd jobs, hoeing figs, orchards, picking grapes, hauling wood, helping carpenters and cement men, working with water well drillers." Eventually he ended up in the bustling, frontier town of Pampa, where Charley now ran a boarding house. Charley's brother Jeff — one of the finest fiddlers on the Texas panhandle — taught his nephew to play the fiddle and guitar.

While the collapse of the New York Stock Exchange in 1929 threw one in four Americans out of work, the Great Depression made little initial impact on Woody. He made a comfortable living painting signs on storefronts, drawing caricatures of bar room patrons, and playing music. Popular radio stations broadcasting out of distant cities like Chicago and Nashville had just reached southern rural areas. These stations made household names of country pioneers like Jimmie Rodgers and The Carter Family and sparked a resurgence in the old time fiddle and guitar music favored by Woody and his band, the Corncob Trio. In his spare time, he read everything he could about psychology, religion and Eastern philosophy at the local library. He also courted and married Mary Jennings, who gave birth to their first daughter Gwendolyn Gail in November 1935. They called her Teeny. Life was good, at least for a while.

By the spring of 1935, no rain had fallen on the Texas and Oklahoma panhandles in four years. In April, winds of up to 70 miles per hour whipped the dry topsoil into ferocious dust clouds and destroyed millions of acres of arable land. A Washington journalist called the region a Dust Bowl, and the name stuck. Families fled in droves — almost 500,000 Okies moved to California between 1929 and 1939. While they inspired some of Woody's greatest songs — *So Long It's Been Good To Know You, Dust Bowl Refugee, Talking Dust Bowl, Dust Can't Kill Me* — the migrants passing through Pampa stirred his wanderlust. Leaving Mary and Teeny, he began drifting around the Southwest. There he saw the human cost of the Great Depression — thousands of homeless, broken, desperate men cluttered the roadsides and railroad freight yards. Their suffering stirred Woody's radical spirit. He flirted with the militant International Workers of The World (IWW or Wobblies), who wanted to organize all skilled and unskilled labor into "One Big Union." Their astute use of humor in songs to express anger inspired Woody to make his own lyrics simpler, funnier and more hard-hitting.

Mary was pregnant again when Woody left to visit his relatives in California in the spring of 1937. In Los Angeles, he ran around with his cousin Jack "Oklahoma" Guthrie. Jack nurtured ambitions of becoming a cowboy singing star like the popular Gene Autry or The Sons of the Pioneers and talked KFVD Radio into broadcasting *The Oklahoma and Woody Show*. Neither of them received a red cent; they performed just for the publicity. With no money to feed his family, Jack returned to construction work and Woody took over the show with family friend Maxine Crissman, whom he renamed "Lefty Lou from ole Mizzoo."

Their stirring harmonies and Woody's homespun philosophizing quickly built up a huge following. At their peak, Lefty Lou and Woody received 1,500 fan letters a month. Such popularity brought a base salary of twenty dollars a week each, plus fifteen for each additional advertising sponsor they attracted. With his first paycheque, he sent for Mary, Teeny and his new daughter Sue, now four months old.

Performing two shows a day, five days a week, took its toll. Maxine grew anemic and Woody became restless and irritable. In June 1938, they took a sabbatical. Woody returned to his wandering — mostly in California. In the squalid migrant camps he saw starving children with bloated bellies, running sores, dysentery, lice and worms living next to orchards overflowing with fruit. Whole families in the bountiful San Joaquin Valley might earn three dollars a week picking fruit or cotton. Woody responded to their plight with his bitterest song to date, *Ain't Got No Home In This World Anymore* — a feisty parody of the Baptist hymn *This World Is Not My Home*.

In August, Guthrie had returned to KFVD without Lefty Lou. Ed Robbin, a journalist with the *People's World* — a West Coast communist newspaper — now worked at the station and he and Woody became close friends. Robbin acted as Woody's agent and took him to his first Communist Party rally. He also introduced Woody to an old college friend and political ally — Will Geer, a Broadway actor. Geer — best known today as the grandfather in the television series, *The Waltons* — moved to Los Angeles in July 1938 to make a film about childbirth for the U.S. government. A pregnant-for-the third-time Mary Guthrie appears in it. Geer found Woody a kindred spirit and they travelled throughout the countryside most weekends, performing in make-shift camps for the migrant workers or raising funds for them at Hollywood parties. John Steinbeck had published *The Grapes of Wrath* that April, bringing national attention to the injustice and inhumanity faced by the Okies. Sympathetic Hollywood celebrities manned the picket lines as the cotton and fruit pickers fought for better wages. And Woody would sing them songs like *Pretty Boy Floyd*:

> *Now as through this world I ramble,*
> *I see lots of funny men,*
> *Some will rob you with a six-gun,*
> *And some with a fountain pen.*
> *But as through this life you travel,*
> *And as through this life you roam,*

You won't never see an outlaw
Drive a family from their home.
(Reprinted with permission)

Woody loved hearing the workers sing his words, loved seeing them used as weapons in a strike. It made him feel useful.

♪ ♪ ♪

Neither Will Geer nor Woody Guthrie joined the Communist Party, although both shared many of its ideals — as did many Americans who were looking for alternatives as the misery of the Depression increased. By the mid-thirties, most of the socialist, communist, liberal and progressive groups on the American left had merged into an alliance known as the Popular Front. This coalition campaigned for Franklin Roosevelt's re-election to the presidency in 1936. In return, Roosevelt's New Deal included legislation that supported the growth of trade unions, many of which were led by Communist Party members. The Popular Front, meanwhile, created The American Music League to collect, study and popularize American folk music. As a result, singers like Leadbelly, Aunt Molly Jackson and her stepsister Sarah Ogan gained recognition in the left-wing hotbed of New York City. On August 23, 1939, the Soviet Union signed a non-aggression pact with Nazi Germany and the Popular Front screeched to a halt. Woody, however, grew even more vocal in his support for the communists. They were the only group helping the poverty-stricken Okies and Arkies organize themselves.

In early November, Will Geer returned to perform on Broadway. Woody and Mary grew homesick for Pampa and shortly before Thanks-giving, packed the kids and all their belongings into an old Plymouth and headed east. Within days of returning to Texas, though, Woody wanted to move on. And in the first week of 1940, he sold the Plymouth for thirty-five dollars, and hitch-hiked north to join Geer in New York. Everywhere he went that winter he heard Irving Berlin's patriotic pop tune *God Bless America*. Its smug patriotism troubled him deeply. So in a run-down hotel near Times Square in New York, he wrote his own song, titled *God Blessed America*, to the tune of the Carter Family's *Little Darlin', Pal of Mine*. The Carters had already taken the melody from an old Baptist hymn, *Oh My Lovin' Brother*. The first of Woody's five verses started:

This land is your land, this land is my land
From California to the New York Island

From the Redwood Forest, to the Gulf Stream waters
God Blessed America for me.

Once completed, he forgot about it. Typical Woody. Nobody really knew how many songs he actually wrote. Estimates range upwards from a thousand. These were the ones he took the trouble to write down. "It wouldn't include the songs that slipped away in the dusty wind, the ones that vanished in the clank and rattle of a fast freight train crossing through the hills in the darkness," wrote Millard Lampell, his future singing partner. The main body of *God Blessed America* turned up next in 1944 during a mammoth recording session for Moses Asch — the visionary owner of the fledgling Asch Recording Company and later founder of the highly influential Folkways Records. Woody had renamed it *This Land Is My Land*, and had changed the last line of each verse to read, "This land was made for you and me." In time, it was known in every school in the U.S. thanks to Pete Seeger.

Canapress

Pete Seeger eventually brought folk music to new heights of commercial success

♪ ♪ ♪

Unlike Woody Guthrie, Pete Seeger came from a privileged, New England background. His grandfather made a small fortune refining sugar in Mexico. Pete's father Charles Seeger studied classical music at Harvard, conducted the Cologne Opera and became the youngest full professor at the University of California, Berkeley. Charles married Constance de Clyver Edson — a debutante raised and educated in Tunisia and Paris — in 1911, the same year he accepted tenure at Berkeley.

Charles initially scorned politics until he witnessed the appalling living and working conditions of the farm workers in the San Joaquin Valley. He then threw his support behind the I.W.W.'s attempts to organize all workers in the state. Furthermore, when the U .S. entered the First World War, he registered as a conscientious objector. All but fired from the university for his political activities, Seeger took a permanent leave of absence, returning with Constance to his parents' estate near Patterson, 50 miles north of New York City. There Pete was born on May 3, 1919. His childhood was traumatic. At age four, Charles and Constance sent him to boarding school. Three years later they separated. Until Pete turned seventeen, he saw his parents only during holiday breaks. If nothing else, his upbringing taught independence.

Pete showed little interest in any form of music as a teenager until his father took him to the Ninth Annual Folk Song and Dance Festival in Asheville, North Carolina, in the summer of 1936. There he discovered the five-string banjo — an instrument that had all but disappeared with the passing of the turn-of-the-century Negro minstrel shows. He entered Harvard that fall, aiming to become a journalist, but devoting most of his spare time to the banjo. He was able to borrow recordings of old time players — like Uncle Dave Macon, Wade Ward and Buell Kazee — thanks to his father. Charles was transcribing field recordings for John and Alan Lomax.

In his sophomore year, Pete developed an interest in politics. He joined the Young Communist League, started a radical paper, *The Harvard Progressive*, and raised funds for the Loyalist brigades fighting fascism in Spain. His marks suffered as a consequence. Not that he cared. Academia had lost its allure. Pete moved to New York in 1938 and tried to find a job as a reporter, but newspapers were not hiring college dropouts, not even from Harvard. To make ends meet he occasionally busked on Park Avenue or performed at folk dances organized by his aunt Elsie Seeger. He even took a job as a porter at the 1939 World's Fair, sweeping up cigarette butts.

Alan Lomax, on his frequent visits to New York, introduced Pete to singers and musicians like Aunt Molly Jackson and Leadbelly — Pete worshipped Leadbelly and his songs *Irene, The Midnight Special, Rock Island Line* and *The Bourgeois Blues*. Lomax also gave the young Seeger a job at the Archives of Folk Song in Washington, where Pete remained until Woody Guthrie arrived for his first serious recording session. Pete attached himself to Woody in Washington and they spent two months compiling a book of political songs for Lomax. Woody typed the lyrics and notes and Pete transcribed melodies. Finally, they produced *Hard Hitting Songs for Hard Hit People* . No publisher would touch its political content for twenty-six years.

With their task completed, Woody easily talked Pete into discovering America. They left New York in June and drove to Texas. Everywhere they went they sang and played for anyone who would listen. Leadbelly had taught Pete the importance of rhythm. Woody now taught him to how to sway the emotions of an audience by manipulating the tempo of their tunes.

While Woody stayed on in Texas with his family, Pete hitch-hiked back to Washington. He continued to wander for the rest of the year, reaching as far west as Butte, Montana. All this travelling and singing sharpened his musical abilities. With the arrival of winter, he settled down in Greenwich Village. There he met Lee Hays, a former teacher, playwright, songwriter, song leader and cook at the radical labor college in Commonwealth, Arkansas, that was guided by Claude Williams, a leftist Presbyterian minister. There, Hays adapted Negro spirituals into such secular songs as *We Shall Not Be Moved* and *Roll The Union On*. He and Pete first performed together in December 1940. Then they added Lee's roommate, writer Millard Lampell and developed a solid repertoire. They called themselves the Almanac Singers.

By many accounts, the Almanac Singers were the first urban folk group. In early February 1941, they made their debut at an American Youth Congress rally in Washington and by the end of May had performed in front of twenty thousand ecstatic Transport Workers in Madison Square Gardens. Even by New York standards, the Almanacs led an unconventional lifestyle. They held rent-raising parties in their loft, and packed in a hundred people at thirty-five cents each and sold beer for ten cents a cup. All the money they made from performing and recording, they shared. They even raised the sink in the kitchen so their tall banjo player could wash the dishes in comfort. With their popularity in left-wing circles increasing, the Almanacs made an album of songs opposing America's growing involvement in the European war. *Songs For John Doe* was released in March of 1941. The *Atlantic* magazine described it as "strictly subversive and illegal." Then, three months later, Germany invaded the Soviet Union. How could The Almanacs sing songs like *Franklin D. You Ain't Gonna Send Me Across the Sea* when socialism was fighting for its life and needed defending?

Their success at Madison Square Gardens led to a national tour of Congress of Industrial Organizations (CIO) union halls from Philadelphia to Los Angeles. Just before they left, Woody turned up from Oregon, where he had written twenty-six songs in thirty days for a documentary about building hydro dams across the Columbia River. They included *Jackhammer John*, *Hard Travelling* and the brilliant

Pastures of Plenty. Woody joined the Almanac Singers in time to record two not particularly memorable, non-political albums: *Sea Shanties* and *Sod Busters.* The tour was a tremendous success and inspired dozens of makeshift songs. Most enjoyed a shelf life of about a week, but one song, *Pittsburgh Is A Smoky Town,* became a kindergarten classic.

As America prepared for war in 1941, unemployment dwindled and labor unrest grew. More than two million workers went on strike that year, the most since 1919. Where large confrontations took place, the Almanac Singers performed. They inspired thousands of workers to sing such songs as Florence Reece's *Which Side Are You On* or Woody Guthrie's *Union Maid* ("Oh, you can't scare me, I'm sticking to the Union . . . "). For Woody, the Almanacs' performance in San Francisco for longshoremen was particularly memorable. As he told the *Minneapolis Daily Worker:* "One of the longshoremen says to me, he says, 'Hell, I thought you was gonna sing us some a these sissified cowboy songs, but you boys talk our language. That's us.' That's why the workers like our songs. . . . This damn Hollywood stuff, the stuff about champagne and flowers, it don't talk a worker's language." By then, Guthrie's guitar bore the legend, "This Machine Kills Fascists."

Having reached Los Angeles in early September, Lee Hays and Millard Lampell headed home. Hays, a hypochondriac, claimed to suffer from tuberculosis. Lampell simply missed his girlfriend. Mary Guthrie showed up, but she and Woody then separated for good. Guthrie and Seeger returned to New York by the scenic route — up the coast to Washington, then across the northern states. In Seattle they performed at a fund raising party for a progressive alliance — the organizers called this event a hootenanny. Woody wrote in a scrapbook: "This was mortally a blowout and one of their most successful hoots. Pete and me aim to put the word Hootenanny on the market."

The Almanac Singers were on the verge of breaking up by the time Guthrie and Seeger reached New York. But they all agreed to rent "Almanac House" on Tenth Street and Sixth Avenue. Now they called their rent parties hootenannies. Leadbelly often showed up, as did bluesmen Sonny Terry and Brownie McGhee, Aunt Molly Jackson and numerous left-wing intellectuals. The Almanacs continued to perform but replaced the lethargic Lee Hays with the bass voice of Art Stern (a local teacher), the accordion of Sis Cunningham (a communist from Oklahoma) and the guitar of Bess Lomax (Alan's sister).

On December 7, 1941, Japan bombed Pearl Harbor and the U.S. entered the Second World War. Popular outrage at Japan and their own hatred of Hitler led the Almanacs to shift their focus from peace to war topics. Critics had called their peace songs propaganda; their war songs were dubbed patriotic art. Soon major labels like Decca Records wanted to release their albums and the prestigious William Morris Agency offered to manage their affairs. At the peak of their popularity, they performed for nearly thirty million listeners coast to coast on *This Is War*, a national morale booster broadcast on February 14, 1942, on all four of the major radio networks. Three days later, a headline in the *New York World-Telegram* read: "Singers On New Morale Show Also Warbled For Communists." The *New York Post* followed with "Peace Choir changes Tune." Swept up in a patriotic fervor, America had no time for radicals disturbing the war effort. Even the unions co-operated to guarantee victory for the Allies. Few dates now came the way of the Almanac Singers. They continued for another year, but most of their members — including Seeger — were in the armed forces by the end of 1943.

♪ ♪ ♪

Woody Guthrie, meanwhile, wrote his autobiography, *Bound For Glory*. The critic for *The New York Times Book Review* compared him with Irish playwright Sean O'Casey. *The New Yorker* called him "a national possession like Yellowstone or Yosemite." Such compliments elevated Woody to celebrity status.

In April of 1944, between stints as a merchant seaman, he recorded 132 traditional and original songs for Moses Asch. These cuts featured various combinations of Leadbelly, Bess Lomax, Sonny Terry, Brownie McGhee and Cisco Houston — a would-be actor, part-time singer and occasional sailor who became Woody's constant companion. This turned into one of the most memorable series of recording sessions in the history of American folk music as Woody unveiled *This Land Is Your Land*.

Meanwhile on the South Pacific island of Saipan, Pete Seeger conceived of the notion of People's Songs Inc.: "A loosely knit organization, some structure where people could get together to exchange and print songs." Founded by Seeger in 1946, it built up a library of protest songs for unions and progressive groups. Many of these were published in the *People's Songs Bulletin* — an infrequent newsletter that Seeger edited. He also helped form a roster of musicians to perform on picket lines and at political rallies. At the first board of directors meeting, Lee Hays and Seeger amused themselves by passing a sheet of paper back and forth, happily collaborating on what became *If I Had A Hammer*. People's Songs soon boasted one thousand paid members in twenty states. It formed its own booking agency, People's Artists, and organized branches in Los Angeles, San Francisco, Chicago and Boston.

Hootenannies sprang up everywhere. Within months these hoots outgrew Seeger's basement and moved to Irving Hall, which held an audience of a thousand. Other folk singers like Burl Ives and Josh White started appearing in night clubs in Greenwich Village. The seeds of a potential folk song revival began to develop serious roots. But international political events again caught up with Pete Seeger and his colleagues. On February 9, 1946, Stalin predicted a war against capitalism was inevitable within the next decade. A month later Winston Churchill responded with his Iron Curtain speech, and the Cold War began in earnest. American communists and socialists were immediately purged from the major unions. Stoked by Cold War propaganda, tolerance of radical thinking gave way to bigotry and right-wing violence.

Now seen as a radical organization, People's Songs no longer received union sponsorship. And with Seeger out on the campaign trail for months at a time with Progressive presidential candidate Henry Wallace (who finished a distant fourth), business matters fell into disarray. People's Songs filed for bankruptcy. Devastated, Seeger retreated to the country to lick his wounds. It was becoming increasingly dangerous to hold left-wing views. After performing solo at an outdoor concert with Paul Robeson in Peekskill, New York State, on Labor Day 1949, Pete Seeger and members of the audience were attacked by rock-throwing anti-communists who lined the roads leading from the venue. The State Troopers either stood back and watched or contributed to the senseless beatings.

Harmonizing on old folk standards with Lee Hays and his student friends, Freddy Hellerman and Ronnie Gilbert, brought Seeger out of his funk. They made their debut as The No-Name Quartet on WNYC Radio.

The No-Name Quartet renamed themselves The Weavers, after a militant play by the German socialist Gerhart Hauptmann. More polished and less strident than the Almanacs, the Weavers opened at the Village Vanguard nightclub Christmas week 1949 singing carols. Soon they were packing the place with folk enthusiasts and music industry executives, who were impressed with the band's sound and curious about its commercial prospects. Eventually they signed with Decca and released a song from Israel, *Tzena, Tzena*, with Leadbelly's *Irene* on the flipside. With references to morphine removed and the title extended to *Goodnight Irene*, it turned into the most popular song of 1950. Folk music, Alan Lomax reckoned, had finally reached the masses. Not quite the way he had envisioned, but "through the back door, as the idiot — 'novelty' — stepchild of pop music," wrote Guthrie biographer Joe Klein. "It was greasy smooth and harmonious, very different from the surging anguished cry he had fallen in love with in the prison camps of the South."

The Weavers followed *Goodnight Irene* with a string of hits: *On Top Of Old Smoky, Wimoweh, Kisses Sweeter Than Wine, When The Saints Go Marching In, So Long It's Been Good To Know You.* Because of their popularity, they made frequent appearances on national radio and television. Such exposure added further momentum to the folk revival triggered by People's Songs. On any given weekend in New York City, dozens of young musicians now congregated in Washington Square Park picking guitars, plucking banjos and singing traditional songs.

Woody Guthrie also benefited from the commercial success of the Weavers. Royalties from *So Long It's Been Good To Know You* exceeded $10,000. He needed the money. For most of the latter part of the 1940s, he had been writing a long, fragmented novel, *The Seeds Of Man*, which he couldn't market. Meanwhile, he had also fallen in love and married Marjorie Mazia, a New York dancer, with whom he had two children, Cathy and Arlo. Despite his literary failure, his songwriting continued at the usual frantic pace with *Deportees* his most notable. Inspired by a crash at Los Gatos airport that killed a plane load of deported Mexican migrant workers, it was the last great song he wrote.

A ruptured appendix almost killed him in 1951. While he lay in hospital recuperating, a kid by the name of Buck Elliott, the son of a Brooklyn doctor, came to visit. He had heard Woody on the radio, and then saw him perform at a hootenanny in Greenwich Village.

When Guthrie returned home, Buck, who changed his name to Ramblin' Jack, soon followed. "Woody used to say, 'Just watch me and steal it'," Elliott recalled in a 1993 interview with *Folk Roots* magazine. "So for three years, I just watched him play from every angle. I went through a period of imitating Woody for about ten years, where I sounded so much like him that it became annoying to his personal friends."

Woody by then was drinking heavily and acting strangely. His friends dismissed his irrational behavior as alcohol-induced. Marjorie knew better, but could do nothing as his life disintegrated. At one point, he lived in a rancid hotel on New York City's skid row. In July 1952, Marjorie checked him into Brooklyn State Hospital to see a specialist. The diagnosis: Huntington's chorea, the disease that killed his mother.

♪ ♪ ♪

With the Korean War (1950-53), communist baiting became a lucrative activity. Three former FBI agents started *Counterattack*, a half gossip, half newsletter that netted hundreds of thousands of dollars annually by listing suspected communists in academic, entertainment and business communities. They also published a pamphlet *Red Channels: Communist Influence on Radio and Television*. It listed Pete Seeger as a communist. While not a crime, such an allegation could end his right to perform in public. Seeger had actually left the party by then. But Harvey Matusow, an ambitious informer who infiltrated People's Songs Inc., lied to the House Un-American Activities Committee that most of the Weavers were Communists. Lee Hays, Matusow reported under oath, had quit the party. Later in his autobiography, *False Witness*, he admitted committing perjury and conspiring with U.S. attorneys to give false testimony. For his troubles, he received five years in Lewisburg Penitentiary. No charges were laid against The Weavers, but they were covertly black-listed and unable to earn a living. They finally broke up in the spring of 1953.

Moses Asch kept Pete Seeger's music alive, releasing no fewer than twenty-nine of his albums by 1955 on his Folkways label. In 1988, such contemporary rock superstars as U2, Bruce Springsteen, John Mellencamp, and Brian Wilson of the Beach Boys eulogized Asch and Folkways Records by recording *A Vision Shared* — a tribute album of Woody Guthrie's and Leadbelly's greatest songs. Still, Seeger needed gigs to feed his family — his Japanese-American wife Toshi Ohta, whom he married in 1944, and their three children, Mika, Danny and Tinya. So he toured outposts that still knew him as a singer rather than a red menace. As his admirer Don McLean, author of *American Pie*, later explained: "Pete went underground. He started doing fifty-dollar bookings, then twenty-five dollar dates at schoolhouses, auditoriums, and eventually college campuses. He definitely pioneered what we know today as the college circuit." Everywhere he went, he encouraged students to pick up a guitar or a banjo and make their own music. Inevitably, he would talk about the best songwriter he ever met. And through Woody's songs, he showed them how music could be used to rail against social and political wrongs.

In 1955, Seeger was ordered to appear in front of the congressional House Un-American Activities Committee as a suspected communist. That August, he waived his right to invoke the Fifth Amendment and refuse to answer questions. Instead, he adamantly defended his right to free speech and loyalty to America. In the process, he was charged with

Murray Gallant (EFMF)

Sonny Terry and Brownie McGhee, at Gallagher Park in 1981, were frequent guests at the Almanac Singers' New York hootenannies

ten counts of contempt of Congress and faced ten years in jail. Freed on bail, it took seven more years before the Court of Appeals ruled that his indictment was faulty and dismissed his case on May 18, 1962. Throughout the long battle, Pete Seeger's enthusiasm for folk music remained unshakable. Harold Leventhal, Seeger's manager, orchestrated a Weavers reunion in Carnegie Hall at the end of 1955. That concert sold out months in advance, and the group continued to tour. Seeger also maintained a hefty solo schedule. On the way to one of his gigs he wrote his best known song, *Where Have All The Flowers Gone?* His 1957 album, *Favorite American Ballads*, was also popular.

The following summer, the Kingston Trio — three well-scrubbed college kids from San Francisco — recorded an antiseptic version of the traditional folk ballad, *Tom Dooley*. It sold a staggering 2.6 million copies and sparked countless imitators from The Limelighters to Peter Paul and Mary. Like The Kingston Trio, most of them covered the songs of Woody Guthrie and The Weavers. By 1961, folk had become so popular that the editors of *Webster's Third International Dictionary* described hootenanny as: "a gathering at which folk singers entertain." Guthrie's prophecy was fulfilled. But while the world finally uncovered his glorious treasures, he lay immobilized in Greystone Hospital, a mental institution near Morristown, New Jersey. Then in January 1961, a young kid from Minnesota dropped by for a visit. His name was Bob Dylan.

Selected recordings

Woody Guthrie: Dust Bowl Ballads (Stony Plain CD-01040)
  Library of Congress Recordings (Stony Plain CD-01041)
Pete Seeger: Essential Pete Seeger (Vanguard VCD 94/8)
  Greatest Hits (Columbia WCK9416)
  American Industrial Ballads (Folkways 40058)
Leadbelly: Sings Folk Songs (Stony Plain CDSF 40010)
Sonny Terry and Brownie McGhee: Sonny and Brownie
  (A&M CD69886)
The Weavers: Greatest Hits (Vanguard VCD-15/6)
Ramblin' Jack Elliott: Essential Ramblin' Jack Elliott (Vanguard 89)
Kingston Trio: Best of the Kingston Trio (Capitol CCM48435)

3

Blowin' In The Wind

- The incredible folk boom
- Greenwich Village scene ▪ Newport
Folk Festival ▪ The blues of Mississippi
and Chicago ▪ Civil rights movement
▪ Robert Allen Zimmerman

"The boy's got it! He sure as hell's got it!"
— WOODY GUTHRIE PRAISES THE YOUNG BOB DYLAN.

THE FOLK BOOM ARRIVED JUST AS THE FIRST flush of rock 'n' roll soured with scandal. Jerry Lee Lewis married his thirteen-year-old cousin. Chuck Berry faced two years in jail for statutory rape. Payola scandals rocked radio stations. Influential disc jockeys such as Alan Freed received hefty fines for accepting bribes to play songs. Elvis joined the army. 'Sweet' Gene Vincent left the U.S. to live in England. Little Richard found God. Buddy Holly, Ritchie Valens and the Big Bopper all died in the same plane crash. Tainted and uninspired, rock 'n' roll grew passe.

Aroused by the stunning commercial success of the wholesome Kingston Trio, the music industry now saw folk as a viable, inoffensive alternative. Numerous Ivy League imitators — The Chad Mitchell Trio, The New Christy Minstrels and Peter, Paul and Mary — were courted and promoted by record companies. Like the hula hoop, folk singing soon grew into an international craze as songs like *Lemon Tree, Michael Row The Boat Ashore, If I Had A Hammer* became radio staples. As former Kingston Trio member John Stewart told Robin Denselow, author of *When The Music's Over:* "The Trio started everybody singing folk. Before that, folk music was something that communists did in basements." By 1961, so many weekend revellers poured into the streets of Greenwich Village looking for hootenannies that police erected safety barricades. Barkers patrolled club entrances, vying to steer people inside. "We've got what you've been reading about!" they shouted. "Authentic folk singers, right inside!" Traffic backed up for blocks.

As more and more worried men sang worried songs — and altogether too many bales of cotton were picked — hootenannies grew stale. "It almost became a study in excesses, where clapping along to shaky or non-professional performers became the order of the day. The integrity of folk song was assailed," wrote music critic Robert Shelton in the *Electric Muse*. Many veteran folk enthusiasts shared his views.

Almost from the outset, the revival split into three camps. Purists relished authenticity: anything less than rough-voiced approximations of native singers, white or black, was a disservice to the origins of the music. Populists respected traditional sources but added commercial spit and polish to appeal to city audiences. And pretenders performed hootenanny: "folkum — tawdry, imitative music," as Ian and Sylvia described it on the liner notes for their second album, *Four Strong Winds*. This was a view shared by a second wave of revival folk singers set to ascend from the coffee houses.

No neighborhood in the world has produced more literature than Greenwich Village. Authors as diverse as Edgar Alan Poe and Norman Mailer have called it home. Abandoned by New York's aristocracy in the late 1890s, its stately homes and elegant row houses provided cheap and attractive accommodation for the city's young writers, artists, musicians and political rebels. Here American bohemian culture developed and provided an audience for poetry, jazz and later folk. During the hootenanny boom, every dilapidated nook and cranny zoned for commercial in the Village became a venue for folk music. As the groups that laundered hootenanny ran out of steam, young talented, solo musicians took over the hole-in-the-wall coffee houses. These no-frills joints — with such colorful names as Cafe Wha?, Gerde's Fifth Peg, The Third Side and The Bitter End — hosted an ever-revolving lineup of singers and musicians. Performers started around 7 p.m., and changed virtually every half-hour until dawn. Few venues had a public address system and fewer paid their acts. Compensation came from wicker baskets passed for pocket change. The more ambitious performers played half-a-dozen houses a night and collected as much as $200 a week.

These places were the bottom of the show-biz scale. Noisy, small and poorly lit, they were crammed with tiny tables and sold unappetizing, over-priced food and gritty coffee. Yet this sorry ambiance actually attracted people. It was an adventure to catch a glimpse of the beatniks and folk singers written about in magazines and newspapers — certainly, something to talk about back in squeaky-clean homes in the suburbs of New Jersey and Long Island. "They didn't want to hear us; they wanted to see us... Until the last drunken fireman was shovelled into the street, folk singing was one hellish ordeal," remembered Dave Van Ronk, the rough, gruff Village denizen who specialized in reworking jazz and blues tunes. Under these adverse conditions, though, folk singers quickly developed a seasoned professionalism that other performers took years to perfect. Judy Collins, Buffy Sainte-Marie, John Sebastian, Ian and Sylvia, Phil Ochs, Peter (Yarrow), Paul (Noel Stookey) and Mary (Travers), Maria Muldaur, Richie Havens, Tom Paxton, Tiny Tim, Bob Dylan — all served their apprenticeships on the Village "basket-house" circuit.

Greenwich Village did not have a monopoly on coffee houses, though. All across America, such little establishments had flourished, offering jazz and beat poetry until the arrival of Tom Dooley. With folk music's ascendancy, many new venues opened, especially around college campuses. Nightclubs such as The Ash Grove in Los Angeles, the hungry i in San Francisco, the Bohemian Embassy in Toronto, and The Gaslight in New York started to book folk acts exclusively. College and university campuses launched folk festivals, beginning in Oberlin, Ohio, in 1957 and the University of California, Berkeley, in 1958. From this academic environment evolved the concept of "workshops," where performers and academics would sit on small, intimate stages and discuss and demonstrate various aspects of folk music. Like a school class or seminar, the audience contributed. These casual gatherings soon matured into a standard feature of all North American folk festivals.

The most influential of these festivals began in 1959 at Newport, Rhode Island, as an offshoot of the city's annual jazz festival, which had run for the previous five years. Co-produced by George Wein (of the jazz festival board) and Albert B. Grossman (an economist and co-owner of the Gate of Horn folk club in Chicago), the first event sold a modest 13,000 tickets. Those in attendance heard nearly sixteen hours of performances and discussions by about seventy-five musicians and scholars. Wein and Grossman, as much taste-makers as producers, booked such sure-fire draws as The Kingston Trio, Pete Seeger and Odetta — a brilliant, husky-voiced African-American folk singer who performed a sublime blend of traditional ballads and urban blues — to finance lesser-known performers like Earl Scruggs, The Stanley Brothers and New Lost City Ramblers.

That weekend an eighteen-year-old Joan Baez took her first serious steps towards international fame. Baez had dropped out of Boston University to sing in local coffee houses. Her reputation spread. Established folk singer Bob Gibson invited the breathtaking soprano to sing *Jordan River* and *Virgin Mary Had One Son* with him at Newport. "The two songs were religious, and I looked and sounded like purity itself in long tresses, no makeup and bible sandals," Baez wrote in her autobiography *And A Voice To Sing With*. " No wonder the press labelled me 'the Madonna' and 'the Virgin Mary' the next day." Within a year, she had rejected offers from several major labels and released her acclaimed self-titled debut with small, independent Vanguard. The follow-up, *Joan Baez II*, went gold without the benefit of a hit single. Despite her commercial success, she shunned show business. Unlike her peers, she performed in her street clothes, limited her personal appearances and turned down offers of TV shows, movies and nightclub stints. In 1962, a *Time* magazine feature on the folk revival put Baez on the cover. Now she was, inhale, the Queen of the Folksingers, exhale. While her repertoire consisted of traditional British and American ballads, Baez took an active role in political and social issues from the start of her career. Bob Dylan was the first to criticize this apparent contradiction between her beliefs and her art. As Dylan told Baez's brother-in-law, Richard Farina: "Take Joanie, man, she's still singing *Mary Hamilton*. I mean where's that at? She's walking around on picket lines, she's got all kinds of feelings, so why ain't she stepping out?" Although Dylan's songs eventually changed her mind about recording contemporary material, her main focus had turned to politics by 1965 and she grew more and more preoccupied with U.S. involvement in Vietnam.

♪   ♪   ♪

While Newport had run successfully in 1959 and 1960, a riot at the town's jazz festival in 1961 suspended folk activities for the next two years. When it resumed in 1963, it operated as a non-profit organization guided by a board of directors that included Pete Seeger, Alan Lomax, Albert Grossman, Judy Collins, Ralph Rinzler, Jean Ritchie, Peter Yarrow and Ronnie Gilbert. All musicians would now perform for union scale, and any profits went towards the advancement and research of folk music. Under the guidance of this new board, the audience grew from 40,000 to 80,000 in three years. These figures truly reflect the growing popularity of folk music. And Alan Lomax, as always, had his part to play.

Lomax had returned to the U.S. in early 1959 after eight years overseas, a self-imposed exile sparked by Senator Joseph McCarthy's witch-hunts. In Britain, he developed the notion that the parameters of folk music should expand to accept such contemporary forms as rock 'n' roll, as long as its practitioners remained faithful to their cultural environment. No cross-pollination. American rock 'n' roll bands experimenting with Irish jigs and reels amounted to an artistic obscenity in his book. Lomax produced "Folksong '59 " at Carnegie Hall. The bill included Ozark country singer Jimmy Driftwood, Chicago-based electric bluesmen Muddy Waters and Memphis Slim, Virginia's Earl Taylor and the Stoney Mountain Boys bluegrass band, the Southern Selah Jubilee Singers gospel choir, and an anonymous local rock 'n' roll band. One reviewer described the event as a musical milestone; others saw it in less flattering terms. Nonetheless, all agreed that the Stoney Mountain Boys stole the spotlight. It was a significant achievement. Until then, bluegrass appealed mainly to a southern country audience and had made only marginal converts among folk enthusiasts.

Bluegrass had evolved from traditional English, Irish and Scottish ballads and dance tunes preserved in the mountains of the southeast states. Early American string bands, consisting mainly of fiddle, banjo and guitar, developed indigenous instrumental variations of this mountain music. Through time, gospel and country influences were added. Eventually, Kentucky singer and mandolin player Bill Monroe refined this whole concoction in the late 1940s. Critics now called it bluegrass after Monroe's band, The Blue Grass Boys. Through the various formations of The Blue Grass Boys passed most of the music's influential stylists, most notably Lester Flatt and Earl Scruggs. In time, this pair would form their own trail-blazing Foggy Mountain Boys. Yet for all of the formidable talent of those Southern virtuosos, it took a Yankee — Mike Seeger, Pete's banjo-picking step-brother — to provide bluegrass with widespread recognition.

Like his father before him, Mike considered himself a conscientious objector and refused to fight in the war in Korea. Instead, he was sent to work at Mount Wilson State Hospital in Baltimore. He quickly discovered the Baltimore-Washington area fostered a thriving bluegrass community made up of migrants from the mountains. There he and other young enthusiasts perfected their banjo picking, and family friend Moses Asch suggested he recruit several performers to record *American Banjo Scruggs Style*, for Folkways. As producer, Mike hired such friends as Eric Weissberg and Ralph Rinzler to play on it. Released in 1956, that album played a key role in introducing Scruggs' virtuosity to New York folk audiences.

While Weissberg went on to record the international hit *Duelling Banjos*, Rinzler would discover Doc Watson in North Carolina, manage

Wayne Stiles (EFMF)

Bill Monroe and band at the 1988 festival . . . a whole style of mountain music was named after Monroe's Blue Grass Boys

Bill Monroe, and help direct the Newport Folk Festival. In 1959, both Weissberg and Rinzler performed with the Greenbriar Boys, one of the two most important northern bands to promote bluegrass and old-time stringband music on the coffee house and folk festival circuit. The other was Mike Seeger's New Lost City Ramblers. That summer, Mike produced another landmark album for Folkways, *Mountain Music Bluegrass Style*. This disc came with a detailed, twelve-page history of bluegrass and its musicians. It also included information on musical instruments, a list of mail-order record labels and details of radio stations broadcasting bluegrass. As musicologist Neil Rosenburg noted: "This album with its notes served as a primer and guidebook for the young folk revivalists who were beginning to take notice of bluegrass and reinforced the idea that it was a separate, distinctive form."

No doubt inspired by the success of Earl Taylor and The Stoney Mountain Boys at "Folksong '59" and Earl Scruggs's triumph at Newport the same year ("he bears about the same relationship to the five-string banjo that Paganini does to the violin," declared the *New York Times*), Alan Lomax increased his efforts to promote bluegrass. In the October 1959 edition of the popular magazine *Esquire*, he described it as "folk music with overdrive" as he endorsed the mighty talents of Flatt and Scruggs as well as The Stanley and Osborne Brothers. He also arranged for United Artists, a major label, to make *Alan Lomax Presents Folk Songs from the Blue Grass — Earl Taylor and His Stoney Mountain Boys.* Ralph Rinzler did his bit, too. In 1960, he organized the Friends of Old Time Music, a club in New York that sponsored concerts by such rediscovered stars as Clarence Ashley, Mother Maybelle Carter and Almeda Riddle. In the months that followed, Rinzler and the Green-briar Boys recorded with Boston's Joan Baez. Chauvinistically touted as the new "Queen of Folk," Baez had developed a close relationship with Earl Scruggs at Newport in 1959, and recorded numerous bluegrass-based songs on her first three albums. All this groundwork paved the way for a breakthrough. In the summer of 1961, folk festivals as far apart as Mariposa in Ontario and Berkeley in California included bluegrass acts on their bills.

♪　♪　♪

Country blues performers, on the other hand, benefited immediately and immensely from the folk revival. "Its chief appeal," as blues historian Peter Guralnick noted, "was its unassailable purity." Developed from the field holler, a plaintive chant slaves brought from West Africa to ease the pain of back-breaking labor, it combined with European folk forms to provide the basic ingredients for country blues. Undoubtedly, no region in the U.S. produced more influential country bluesmen than the Mississippi Delta. The flat, fertile plains of the Delta have long been associated with cotton harvests and the black laborers who worked in the cotton fields, first as slaves and later as sharecroppers. It was a life of grinding poverty, and thousands left to seek work in cities in the northern states. Most of those who left took the Illinois Central Railroad, which ran from New Orleans to Chicago in just 24 hours. The fare from Memphis in 1940 was $11.10.

Many musicians took that train to the Windy City. One was McKinley Morganfield, better known as Muddy Waters. He was still working on a plantation near Clarksdale when Alan Lomax visited the Delta in the summer of 1941. Lomax and his assistant, John Work, were searching for country bluesman Robert Johnson who, in 1936 recorded forty-one extraordinary tracks for Ernie Oertle and Don Law of the American Recording Company. These included *Sweet Home Chicago*, *Dust My Broom* and *Love In Vain* — some of the most influential blues songs ever written. Repackaged as a boxed set in 1991, Johnson's initial (and only known) recordings for Oertle and Law sold five hundred thousand copies and earned Johnson a posthumous Grammy. John Hammond, the talent scout who signed such acts as Billie Holiday, Count Basie, Aretha Franklin and Bob Dylan to Columbia Records, was among the first to recognize Johnson's phenomenal talents. Hammond tried to book the "King of the Delta Blues Singers" for his landmark concert series, From Spirituals To Swing, in Carnegie Hall in December of 1938. These recitals were among the first to present black performers in a formal setting. Hammond hired Oertle to return to the dusty back roads of the Delta to seek out Johnson. Oertle went, only to learn that Johnson had died in August after swallowing whiskey spiked with poison. Oertle sent Hammond Big Bill Broonzy instead.

Although Alan Lomax never located Johnson, he did record Johnson's mentor, Son House, and the moonshiner and tractor driver Muddy Waters. In 1942, Lomax returned to Mississippi and made extensive recordings of Waters. These records persuaded Muddy that he sounded as good as any of the popular blues artists heard on jukeboxes. Ambitious and determined to escape the ever-deteriorating social conditions on the plantation, Muddy boarded the train for Chicago in Clarksdale in May 1943, and rode it all the way to world-wide fame.

While the electric guitar made its debut on blues records in the late 1930s, it was still a novelty when Muddy got his first one in 1944. Although he didn't enjoy it as much as his acoustic models, it helped cut through the noise in ghetto taverns. Settling down in the city's South Side, his reputation on guitar soon spread through the neighborhood. At first, he performed for friends, then moved into local clubs. By 1949, he fronted his own electric band that included harmonica player Little Walter Jacobs from Helena, Arkansas; drummer Baby Face Leroy from Mobile, Alabama; and second guitarist Jimmy Rogers from Greenwood. While Chicago had developed its own blues stars and styles throughout the twenties, thirties and forties, by the early fifties, amplified Delta blues dominated the city, and Muddy and his bands set the pace. Like Bill Monroe's Blue Grass Boys, Muddy's bands provided an important apprenticeship for most of the up-and-coming musicians who played modern Chicago-style blues. Buddy Guy, Willie Dixon, James Cotton, Otis Spann, Junior Wells, Walter Horton, Hubert Sumlin, Earl Hooker: all played in Waters' bands at one time or another.

By the fifties, there was still considerable activity in Mississippi, but Chicago now produced the most popular blues recordings. Young musicians back in the Delta began to duplicate the music Muddy and his band recorded for Chess Records, and the great acoustic country blues performers of the South lost ground. Many disappeared, only to be unearthed, rediscovered — and relabelled "folk blues" — in the early sixties.

The folk revival rekindled an extraordinary interest in the old blues masters. Inspired by scavenged original recordings and reissues from The Library of Congress, Folkways or Riverside Records, as well as such seminal books as *The Country Blues* by Samuel Charters, *Negro Folk Music USA*, by Harold Courlander or *Blues Fell This Morning* by Paul Oliver, young blues and folk enthusiasts across America took it upon themselves to trace their heroes. Guitar prodigy John Fahey found Bukka White in a Memphis boarding house. Ann and Samuel Charters tracked Sleepy John Estes — blind, emaciated and destroyed by poverty — to a broken-down sharecropper's cabin near Brownsville, Tennessee. Still others located Son House in Rochester, New York; Skip James in Dallas, Texas; Mance Lipscomb in Navasota, Texas; and Furry Lewis in Memphis. The greatest of them all, though, came to light in Avalon, Mississippi.

Mississippi John Hurt was born in Teoc, Carroll County, March 8, 1892, but grew up in Avalon. His music absorbed influences from both the black transient field hands and the white Scottish settlers who pioneered the area. He was first discovered in 1928 by Tommy Rockwell, director for New York's Okeh Records. Hurt recorded eight songs for Rockwell, two of which — *Frankie* and *Nobody's Dirty Business* — sold particularly well. Rockwell brought Hurt to New York for a second session, which included *Candy Man, Stagger Lee, Louis Collins, Spike Driver Blues* and *Avalon Blues*. The Depression, however, soon devastated the record market and Hurt returned to Avalon to work as a farm laborer. In 1952, Folkways released *Frankie* and *Spike Driver Blues*.

Eleven years later, Tom Hoskins, a young blues musician from Washington, D.C., borrowed an original recording of *Avalon Blues* and decided to find its author. The first verse of the song offered a clue to his whereabouts: "Avalon's my home town, always on my mind." But no Avalon showed up on road maps printed in the early sixties. Undeterred, Hoskins found an atlas from 1878 that showed the town on a secondary road between Greenwood and Grenada, Mississippi. It took him two days to drive there. Unbelievably, the first person he talked to at the local general store gave him directions to Hurt's house. Bingo! With Hoskins' support John travelled to Washington to record and play a few dates in folk clubs. The response was extraordinary. Features about his incredible story ran in Washington and New York newspapers as well as in *Time* and *Newsweek* magazines. All this publicity produced a booking at the Newport Folk Festival in July of 1963. There, he made such an impression that fans mobbed him backstage. At age 71, a star was reborn.

♪   ♪   ♪

Of all the diverse and compelling music stemming from black American culture, gospel provided the folk revival with its strongest impetus.
Modern gospel dates back a mere eighty or so years, but it continues a
tradition of singing, preaching and shouting familiar to generations of
black people. While it sprang from such sacred sources as the old hymns
and Negro spirituals sung in Southern churches, it took Mahalia Jackson
to add the energy and influence of jazz and blues. Born in New Orleans
in 1911, the daughter of devout Baptists, she grew up idolizing and
imitating acclaimed blues singers Ma Rainey and Bessie Smith. This
combination of sacred and secular truly defined Jackson's unique voice.
"Her style and manner became the stuff of mimicry and legends. She has
a characteristic vocal habit of combining slurs and blue notes in a
disembodied soprano. It's a weird, ethereal sound, part moan, part failed
operatics," wrote Anthony Helbut in *The Gospel Sound*.

Jackson made her recording debut at the age of 24 in Chicago, having
moved there eight years earlier to work as a domestic and then a nurse.
A talent scout for Decca Records discovered her singing at a funeral. She
actually recorded little with Decca before moving on to Apollo, the small
New York label, in 1947. *I Will Move On Up A Little Higher*, her third
single there, sold over a million copies. Naturally, it became her
signature piece. In the early fifties, Studs Turkel, the respected Chicago
journalist, frequently featured Mahalia on his local television show.
From this exposure she acquired a cult following among jazz aficiona-
dos. Invitations from jazz festivals soon followed. Similar offers to
perform at folk, gospel and blues events developed later. By the early
sixties, "she so defined her field that to use the words 'Mahalia Jackson'
and 'gospel music' in the same sentence was to risk redundancy."

Meanwhile, the revered Mahalia became active in the Civil Rights
Movement led by Dr. Martin Luther King Jr. Indeed, she would sing
Precious Lord at King's funeral. The movement got its initial momentum
in Montgomery, Alabama, in December 1955, when a black housewife
was arrested and fined for refusing to give up her seat on a bus to a white
passenger, as local custom dictated. As the movement gathered momentum, gospel music and its variations developed into a unifying force for
black activists. Like the Wobblies before them, Dr. King's followers
created their "freedom songs" from traditional sources. Take the old
spiritual:

Go down Moses,
'Way down in Egypt's land,

Tell old Pharaoh, To let my people go.

Rewritten it now read:

Go down Kennedy
'Way down in Georgia land,
Tell old Pritchett,* To let my people go.

(*Old Pritchett was Chief of Police Laurie Pritchett of Albany.)

Old songs set to new words were used at mass meetings, demonstrations, prayer vigils, on Freedom Rides, in jails and sit-ins to protest segregation. "These songs give the people new courage and a sense of unity. I think they keep alive a faith, a radiant hope in the future, particularly in our most trying hours," said Dr. King.

While the Civil Rights Movement blossomed in the southern states, it found a natural ally in the northern folk community. Raised on the dictum "black and white unite," Pete Seeger could hardly sit on the sidelines. After all, his words to *We Shall Overcome* became the movement's *Marseillaise*. As a pacifist, Seeger sympathized with its non-violent tactics. Music, he maintained, would transform society. While singing at a benefit for the Student Non-violent Co-ordinating Committee (SNCC) in Atlanta in 1962, he passed that belief on to a young singer "with a voice like a cannon," Bernice Johnson. Today, she's better known as Bernice Reagon, leader of the mighty *a cappella* sextet Sweet Honey In The Rock. Seeger encouraged Reagon to form a group of SNCC singers, who could spread freedom songs the way the Almanacs stumped for the trade unions. Within weeks, she had quit college, formed the Freedom Singers, and recruited the highly efficient Toshi Seeger as their manager. Thereafter, this quartet performed numerous concerts throughout North America and raised thousands of dollars for the SNCC. Just as important, though, the Freedom Singers exposed young audiences to a music whose primary function was to convey a stirring message. For many raised in the cultural dark of the Cold War, this was a novel concept.

♪   ♪   ♪

As the Civil Rights Movement coincided with a growing awareness and abhorrence of American military activity in Vietnam, poignant "protest" songs began to emerge from Greenwich Village coffee houses. The initial trickle turned to a flood after Peter, Paul and Mary placed Pete Seeger's peace anthem, *If I Had A Hammer*, high in the national pop charts in 1962. Brought together by Albert Grossman, they became the first political artists since the Weavers to be embraced by the mass media. While their soft, easy-on-the-ear harmonies hardly radicalized their pop audiences, they did play an invaluable role publicizing obscure writers whose songs they recorded. Certainly, they opened the door for the relatively unknown Bob Dylan to walk out of the coffee houses into the international spotlight.

Born Robert Allen Zimmerman in Duluth, Minnesota, on May 24, 1941, Dylan grew up in the mining town of Hibbing. There, his father Abe Zimmerman owned a furniture and appliance store. Nobody would call Abe and his wife Beatrice rich, yet their son Robert wanted for little. His early life was unremarkable. His high school marks remained respectable if unexceptional. His real education, however, came from the radio. Depending on the reception, he could pick up stations as far away as Tallahassee and Denver. Sometime in 1955, he pulled in a station from Little Rock, Arkansas, that played the most wild, wanton, music driven by throbbing electric guitars, a swaggering piano and screeching saxes - something the announcer called rock 'n' roll. Bob fell under its spell. His ambition, he noted in his high school graduation year book, was "to join Little Richard."

Young Bob was single-minded about two things: breaking into the music business and leaving town. Throughout high school, he fronted several rock 'n' roll and rhythm and blues garage bands. He even took a stage name: Bob Dylan. While he never specifically acknowledged taking it from Dylan Thomas, it did coincide with his discovery of the Welsh poet. In the fall of 1959, he left Hibbing to enrol in the liberal arts program at the University of Minnesota. An arts degree wasn't exactly a top priority, and he dropped out after three semesters. Most of his time he spent in Dinkytown, the small, bohemian centre of Minneapolis. Status there was measured in terms of social awareness of such burning issues of the day as the Cuban revolution, the Cold War, civil rights and the politics of sexual enlightenment. Music too, defined one's standing in Dinkytown. Initially, jazz was cool, until it grew too esoteric. Wholesome, white choirboys such as Frankie Avalon, Bobby Darin and Paul Anka sanitized rock 'n' roll. So, like the young elsewhere in America, the middle-class students who haunted the local coffee houses gravitated towards folk music, drawn by its radical, missionary appeal. "Bob Dylan," says his biographer Bob Spitz, "got involved with folk music because it was the only game in town." Certainly he traded in his electric guitar for an acoustic one soon after his arrival in Minneapolis. At first he learned the usual folk standards — *Jack O' Diamonds, Johnny I Hardly*

(EFMF)

Dave Van Ronk, right, with John Bayley at the 1982 Edmonton festival . . . remembers that playing Greenwich Village was at times an ordeal

Knew Ye, Jamaica Farewell — but as his tastes developed, he became an apostle of Odetta. He also discovered country blues singers Bukka White, Blind Lemon Jefferson and Lonnie Johnson, as well as Leadbelly and Woody Guthrie. His fascination with Guthrie turned into an obsession after he read *Bound For Glory*. It was as if Dylan found God. As he later told BBC Radio in England: "I was completely taken over by him. By his spirit, or whatever. You could listen to his songs and actually learn how to live, or how to feel. He was like a guide . . . I didn't know if he was dead or alive, but by now I was trying to find out where he was."

Dylan left Minneapolis for New York in January 1961. On his arrival, he went to visit Woody at the Greystone Park State Hospital in Morris Plains, New Jersey. On weekends, Woody stayed with friends, and on Sundays, such folk singers and old colleagues as Pete Seeger, Alan Lomax, and Ramblin' Jack Elliott regularly dropped by to pay their respects and sing for hours. Dylan, too, turned up frequently. And in time, he became Woody's favorite. "The boy's got it! He sure as hell's got it!" Woody would cheer.

Meanwhile, Dylan polished his craft in the Village coffee houses. From imitating Woody, he gradually developed his own way of interpreting traditional songs. As his confidence grew, so did his reputation. In April of 1961, Gerde's Folk City booked him to open for veteran

Canapress

Times certainly were a-changin' in folk music once Bob Dylan appeared on the scene in the early sixties

bluesman John Lee Hooker. It was the first of only two paid performances Dylan ever gave in the Village. His second, also at Gerde's, came in September, when he opened for the Greenbriar Boys. That night the eminent Robert Shelton sat in the audience and wrote Dylan's first review. It appeared in the *New York Times* on Friday, September 29, 1961: "A bright new face is appearing at Gerde's Folk City. Although only 20 years old, Bob Dylan is one of the most distinctive stylists to play in a Manhattan cabaret in months." Within a week, the venerable John Hammond of Columbia Records offered the "bright new face" a contract. They recorded Bob Dylan in November 1961 and released it the following March.

For the most part it received favorable reviews. Eleven of the thirteen tracks ranged from Bukka White's forlorn country blues hymn *Fixin' To Die* to the frivolous Scottish ditty *Pretty Peggy-O*. The final two songs were originals: *Talkin' New York* (a humorous, Guthriesque talking blues) and *Song to Woody* (a moving tribute to his hero). Nobody at the time, not even Dylan, thought they could get by solely on original material. But *Song to Woody* changed all that — the widespread support Dylan got from his peers buoyed his confidence.

All the same, Bob Dylan sold poorly and the euphoria he felt upon its completion quickly evaporated. Still, his affairs were now managed by the influential Albert Grossman. In April, he completed *Blowin' In The Wind*, an alluring alchemy of metaphor and poetry that asks a series of foreboding social questions without answers. Published in *Broadside #6*, a mimeographed four-page folk newsletter that circulated throughout the Village, it quickly spread beyond the local folk community into surrounding college campuses and schools.

In the meantime, the Cuban missile crisis and the civil rights movement sharpened his social conscience. The evidence appears on his
second album, *The Freewheelin' Bob Dylan* , which came out in May 1963.
Preceded by Peter, Paul and Mary's hit cover of *Blowin' In The Wind,*
Freewheelin' took on a life of its own. As critics raved and radio played it,
sales rose to 10,000 copies a day. More important, though, such original,
political highlights as *Masters Of War, A Hard Rain's A-Gonna Fall,*
Talkin' World War III Blues and *Blowin' In The Wind* established Dylan
as one of America's most imaginative folk singers and the leading
exponent of protest songs. Veteran radicals like Pete Seeger now sang his
praises (and his songs) at every opportunity, as did Dylan's more
established colleague Joan Baez. In July, he made a triumphant appearance at the Newport Folk Festival in front of 46,000 fans. His songs
received standing ovations — no matter who performed them. It was
Dylan's crowning moment. A month later, he appeared with Mahalia
Jackson, Odetta, the Freedom Singers, Peter, Paul and Mary, Harry
Belafonte and Joan Baez in front of 200,000 civil rights activists surrounding the Lincoln Monument in Washington D.C. All performers
that day, though, took a back seat to Dr. Martin Luther King Jr. as he
delivered his epochal "I have a dream" speech.

In January of 1964, Dylan consolidated his position as the crown
prince of folk music with the release of *The Times They Are A-Changin'.*
Aside from its topical anthems — *Only A Pawn In Their Game, The*
Lonesome Death Of Hattie Carrol and *With God On Our Side* — the title
track made an extraordinary, revolutionary political statement. *The*
Times They Are A-Changin' was the first clarion call for a growing
number of disaffected American teenagers to challenge the orthodox
values set by parents, politicians, philosophers and critics. The old order,
Dylan stated, could no longer cope with the increasing concerns of
young Americans. Change was inevitable. Contribute or stand aside:

> *Come mothers and fathers throughout the land*
> *And don't criticize what you can't understand*
> *Your sons and your daughters are beyond your command*
> *Your old road is rapidly agein'*
> *Please get out of the new one if you can't lend your hand*
> *For the times, they are a changin'.*
> (Reprinted with permission)

With this song, Dylan became a spokesman for a generation. At
Newport in July 1964, though, Dylan's new songs focused on the bitter

frailties of love gone wrong. These he released a month later on *Another Side Of Bob Dylan*. "There aren't any finger-pointing songs in here," he told freelance journalist Nat Hentoff in *Playboy* magazine. "Me, I don't want to write for people any more. You know — be a spokesman. From now on I want to write from inside me, and to do that I'm going to have to get back to writing like I used to when I was ten — having everything come out naturally." The following March he moved further away from politics with his fourth album, *Bringing It All Back Home*. Its sophisticated, rapid-fire lyrics, combining oral literature, folk tradition and stream of consciousness, image-laden beat poetry, elevated folk-song writing to an art form. Never-ending debates raged over the meaning of his words. Dylan's influence even changed The Beatles' approach to lyrics: *She Loves You Yeah, Yeah, Yeah* didn't quite have the same ring as *Subterranean Homesick Blues*. *Bringing It All Back Home* also departed from folk's purism. Half of the album featured Dylan backed by a rock 'n' roll band. Oh, the shock! The horror!

If his performance at Newport in 1964 raised a few eyebrows, his next appearance there made history. Artistically, Newport was extremely conservative. In 1965, electric instruments were still taboo. Ignoring this restriction, the Paul Butterfield Blues Band was loud and proud at its Sunday afternoon workshop — prompting several snide remarks from Alan Lomax. To Lomax, white college kids performing electrified, black rhythm and blues was cultural vandalism. Albert Grossman took exception and the two folk potentates traded punches. The confrontation didn't end there. During Butterfield's early evening mainstage performance, Pete Seeger threatened to take an axe to the power cables. Cooler heads prevailed, though, and Butterfield concluded with an encore. The crisis subsided. Temporarily. An hour later, stagehands set up additional amplifiers and the Paul Butterfield Blues Band returned to the stage. This time they were led by Bob Dylan sporting an electric Telecaster guitar. Predictably, Seeger and Lomax exploded. They charged the sound board, determined to stop this desecration, but scrawny Peter Yarrow delayed them long enough for Grossman to round up stagehands to protect the board. On stage, Dylan and his colleagues barrelled through *Maggie's Farm*, *Like A Rolling Stone* and *It Takes A Lot To Laugh, It Takes A Train To Cry* to a combination of jeers and cheers. Tears flowed down Pete Seeger's cheeks. Folk music would never be the same.

Selected recordings

Odetta: Essential Odetta (Vanguard VCD-43/4)
Joan Baez: Joan Baez Volume 1 (Vanguard VMD 2097)
Bob Dylan: Freewheelin' (Columbia WCK-8786)
   Times They Are A Changin' (Columbia WCK-8905)
   Bringing It All Back Home (Columbia WCK-9128)
Dave Van Ronk: Folkways Years 1956-61 (WEA CDSF-40041)
Mississippi John Hurt: Best of Mississippi John Hurt (Vanguard VCD-19)
Sleepy John Estes: Brownsville Blues (Delmark 613)
Robert Johnson: The Complete Recordings (Columbia C2K 46222)
Muddy Waters: Best of Muddy Waters (Chess CHBD-31269)
Bill Monroe: Columbia Historic Edition (Columbia 38904)
New Lost City Ramblers: Early Years 1958-1962 (Folkways 40036)
Sweet Honey In The Rock: Live At Carnagie Hall (Flying Fish FF-701606)

The Canadian scene in the sixties

4

Four Strong Winds

■Ian Tyson departs for L.A. but arrives
in Toronto ■The Yorkville coffee house
scene ■A festival for Leacock's
Mariposa ■Lightfoot and company
■Festivals for Winnipeg, Vancouver
and Edmonton■

"It was my first attempt and only took about twenty minutes to write at the time. It was real easy and I thought, 'Boy, I'll never have another hungry day in my life.'"
— IAN TYSON WRITES HIS MASTERPIECE

ACONTINENT SEPARATES PRESTIGIOUS Newport, Rhode Island, from provincial Victoria, British Columbia. Ian Tyson would make that great cultural trek in triumph.

Born in 1933, Tyson grew up on Vancouver Island before moving to the mainland to work for the provincial forestry service. George Tyson wanted more for his son and convinced Ian to enrol in a four-year course at the Vancouver School of Art in 1953. Weekends he saved for rodeos. An enthusiast since high school, he rode bareback and saddle broncs around B.C. and Alberta until he landed in a Calgary hospital with a shattered ankle. Tyson spent four months there, recuperating and experimenting with a guitar borrowed from the patient in the next bed. At art school, he'd flirted with jazz guitar but in hospital his interest in music intensified. By the time he returned, on crutches, for his final year of college, he "had really gotten the bug," he told English journalist Peter O'Brien in the British magazine *Omaha Rainbow*. "That was the year Bill Haley came out with *Rock Around The Clock* and Gene Vincent came out with *Be Bop A Lula*." Halfway through his last semester, he graduated to performing in honky tonks in Vancouver's Chinatown. "And that is how I started."

For a casual cowboy, Tyson drew inspiration from some intriguing sources — bluesmen Lightnin' Hopkins, Sonny Terry and Brownie McGhee, for instance. "[Pete] Seeger was always too political for me. That was the message that was always there and it was all very trade union oriented. I'd worked in that heavy trade union thing in B.C. — raised in it — and I always thought it was bullshit. You know, the trade unions fucked up B.C. so bad, I couldn't understand what the hell he was singing about."

Having graduated in 1957, Tyson wound up in Toronto two years later, more by chance than design. He had set off to hitchhike to California, but the first motorist to offer him a ride was heading east. "If the car had been going south, I would have ended up in L.A. It was just an accident I ended up in Toronto." His arrival there coincided with the emergence of the folk coffee house scene, centred in Yorkville — a bohemian district near the University of Toronto. Soon he was making the rounds, picking up as much as $15 in change on a good night plus a further $50 a week working as a commercial artist — a decent wage in those days. He formed a short-lived duo with a young actor and folksinger, Don Francks, but before the year ended, Ian met eighteen-year-old Sylvia Fricker.

Fricker grew up in Chatham, Ontario, and developed a love of folk music through the epic Scottish ballads she studied in poetry classes in high school. Her mother taught music, played the organ and directed the local Anglican church choir. Because she could read music, Sylvia learned traditional songs from books rather than records, thus developing a singing style free from outside influences. Restricted by Chatham's small-town values, Sylvia moved to Toronto in 1959. She worked part time in a jewelry store and sang and hung out in coffee houses at night. It was a small, intimate scene and soon she and Ian Tyson became fast friends and started casually singing duets. "It just evolved informally into what became Ian and Sylvia about a year later. It was not a planned thing," Ian told the Halifax *Daily News* in 1975. "There was just a sound the two voices made that was really unique."

Around Yorkville, singers and musicians polished their stagecraft in coffee houses and clubs such as the Bohemian Embassy, the Village Corner or the Purple Onion. As Sylvia says: "At that point there were more places to play than people to play in them. Not that they paid that much, they didn't." Later, the prestigious Riverboat coffee house would bring the elite of the folk world to Toronto: Peter, Paul and Mary, Phil Ochs, Judy Collins — almost everyone but Dylan.

At the grassroots level, The Toronto Guild Of Canadian Folk Artists provided the main platform for the city's budding folk enthusiasts. From its inception in the late fifties, the guild included folk music fans, singers and musicians, who organized song-sharing evenings and benefits for local charities. Teenagers Sylvia Fricker and Sharon Hanson (of Sharon, Lois and Bram) sang at these events, arranged by such non-musicians as Estelle Klein. Klein recruited touring musicians like country bluesmen Sonny Terry and Brownie McGhee to lead guild-sponsored workshops. "These were really workshops in the sense of teaching," she said in an interview for this book. "People obviously performed songs, but there was a real attempt to make it a two-way thing."

Klein's interest in folk music began in her youth at summer camps organized near Brampton, Ontario, by the left-wing United Jewish People's Order. She recalls performances there in the forties and fifties by socialist standard-bearers such as The Weavers, Paul Robeson and Pete Seeger. "I have always had a strong social conscience, and I have always worked with people of all backgrounds and levels. . . . The business of human relationships in folk music I'm sure is what appealed to me." Although she had no interest in performing, Klein publicized concerts, ran hootenannies and organized and negotiated with the likes of the Toronto Musician's Association to set a standard wage scale for folk artists working the local coffee houses. Before that, performers without a written contract often completed six sets a night, seven days a week, for miserable fees. Trusted and endeared by local performers, Klein became their unofficial and unpaid agent.

On visits to New York with her husband Jack, a Toronto architect, she discovered the impressive talent developing in Greenwich Village. Then there were trips to the Newport Folk Festival. "Newport had a profound influence on me," she says. "I heard a lot of British music that I hadn't heard before and I was enormously impressed . . . I had been continually broadening my interest in folk and this only added to it and confirmed for me that folk was this whole world of treasures." She eventually advised the board at Newport about Canadian talent.

Klein's proudest achievements, however, took place on the stages of Canada's first prominent folk festival: Mariposa. The fictitious town of Mariposa first appeared in 1912 in Canadian humorist Stephen Leacock's satire, *Sunshine Sketches of a Little Town*. It was clearly a caricature of the

Genia Ainsworth (EFMF)

Stan Rogers and Sylvia Tyson at the first Edmonton Folk Music Festival in 1980

summer resort community of Orillia — Leacock's latter-day residence, eighty miles north of Toronto. Orillia was also the birthplace of such creative talents as Franklin Carmichael (the youngest member of the celebrated Group of Seven painters) and Gordon Lightfoot (the most distinguished songwriter in the history of Canadian popular music). In January of 1961, the local Chamber of Commerce wanted to boost tourism. Various arts festivals flourished around the country at the time, so when local community activist and folk music enthusiast Ruth Jones suggested Orillia hold a folk festival, the town council readily agreed. As a tribute to Leacock, councillor Pete McGarvey suggested calling the event The Mariposa Folk Festival.

With the town's financial backing, the festival nominated its first board of directors: Jones president, McGarvey vice-president, Ed Cowan producer, and Ruth's husband, Dr. Casey Jones, the secretary-treasurer. While Ruth approached Newport for direction, most of her advice came from an informal advisory board in Toronto that included Estelle Klein, Edith Fowke and Ian Tyson (who designed the festival's first poster).

Three days before the gates opened, producer Cowan proudly told the local Rotary club: "Right now the name of Orillia is being flashed over Times Square in New York" on a sign promoting travel to Canada. The initial festival ran August 18 and 19 and drew six thousand fans — mostly college students — to hear an all-Canadian bill. Local lad Lightfoot failed the audition. "Ed felt that he had no reputation at that time," says Pete McGarvey. "He really wasn't the calibre they were looking for." Top billing went to Alan Mills who, along with Edith Fowke and Nova Scotia's Helen Creighton, pioneered field research in Canadian folk song. All three possessed an incredible repertoire of traditional material, which they passed on to younger musicians such as Ian and Sylvia.

Merrick Jarrett, a teacher and folk music scholar who performed at several of the early Mariposas, recalls the first event: "I especially remember Alan Mills headlining, playing with Jean Carignan, a taxi driver who couldn't make enough money playing fiddle, but who was probably French Canada's finest — the kind of fiddler that orchestra violinists would go to hear." Leon Jourard, at the time a production manager for an Ontario radio station, recalls: "The audience went there to listen and to sing and to participate." And it was easy to meet the performers. "We were in the restaurant with Alan Mills and Jean Carignan and people were square dancing in the streets. We were up in the late-night Chinese restaurant until two or three in the morning, sitting around in a banquet singing and swapping stories."

Most of the musicians that weekend performed traditional Anglo Saxon songs. "Jacques LeBrec was booed off the stage because he had overstayed his time and people just didn't want to hear French Canadian folk music," says Jarrett. Only in later years did Mariposa truly embrace diverse cultures.

♪   ♪   ♪

By the end of 1961, Ian and Sylvia had developed into the most popular act around Toronto. Outside the city, though, they remained relatively unknown. They needed a manager. At the time, only Manny Greenhill, Harold Leventhal and Albert Grossman handled folk acts and they were all based in New York City. Confident and carefree, Ian and Sylvia set off for Greenwich Village. Singing at Gerde's Folk City, their harmonies impressed Grossman, who had a hunch that folk music was more than a fad. That winter he signed Peter, Paul and Mary and, in the same week, Ian and Sylvia. Six months later he added Bob Dylan. With Grossman's help, Ian and Sylvia recorded their self-titled debut album — a mixture of traditional North American and European songs — for Vanguard Records in September 1962. Reviews were generally positive. "By far the most pleasing folk record heard in the past five years," said *The Pittsburgh Press*. Sales, however, were slow.

Then Dylan threw the cat among the pigeons by writing *Blowin' In The Wind*. Tastes now shifted from traditional to original songs. Subsequently, on a rainy New York afternoon, Ian sat down in Albert

Grossman's apartment, and wrote his classic *Four Strong Winds*. It wound up the title track of Ian and Sylvia's second album. On the liner notes he explains its motif: "Canada has many seasonal workers . . . and when the weather turns harsh they must move on and find a different type of work. Many of these people cross the country every year — from the tobacco harvest in Ontario to the wheat harvest on the prairies to apple picking in British Columbia. With the advent of fall they move on, perhaps to return in the spring."

Aside from its gorgeous melody, the clever conflict in *Four Strong Winds* — the pull of the open road versus the temptations left behind and the itinerant's inability to resolve this dilemma — makes it such an endearing and appealing song. Such diverse performers as John Denver and Neil Young later covered it. "It was my first attempt and only took about twenty minutes to write at the time," Ian said in a 1983 interview. "It was real easy and I thought, 'Boy, I'll never have another hungry day in my life.' But they get harder as you go along."

Sylvia made her own equally impressive songwriting debut in 1964 with *You Were On My Mind*, not long after her marriage to Ian Tyson. Covered by We Five, it became a chart-topper across North America. Now at their creative and commercial peak, Ian and Sylvia's albums sold an average of 150,000 copies each — a significant number at the time. Their popularity was such that they could fill New York's Carnegie Hall twice a year. And on Saturday, July 24, 1965, they made their first appearance at Newport — then, the pantheon of the folk world — alongside such aristocrats as Pete Seeger, Odetta, Joan Baez, Bob Dylan and Peter, Paul and Mary. Gordon Lightfoot also performed at there that weekend — mainly through the support of the Tysons.

♪ ♪ ♪

Ian and Sylvia first met Lightfoot in Yorkville. Lightfoot had grown up in Orillia but moved to Los Angeles in 1958 to study music at Westlake College. However, within fourteen months he grew homesick and returned to Toronto to sing and dance on the popular CBC Television show, *Country Hoedown*, which featured singer Tommy Hunter. Lightfoot was soon caught up, with many of his generation, in the excitement of the folk revival. The attraction was obvious: the music was gutsy, rhythmic and intentionally rough, so that the odd wrong chord hardly mattered. As Lightfoot's biographer Maynard Collins says: "Ian Tyson thought Lightfoot was a woefully inadequate guitar player (he might have known all of six chords and a few variations then), so he took it upon himself to teach him. They spent long hours together, working very hard, trading songs, listening to Dylan, Woody Guthrie and the Carter Family."

Laid-back Yorkville offered Lightfoot the opportunity to polish his repertoire of old cowboy and hobo songs. Growing more ambitious, he formed a duet with Terry Whalen, an old school friend from Orillia. Calling themselves the Two Tones, they cut a live album at the Village Corner before Lightfoot left to work briefly for BBC Television in London in the summer of 1963. While overseas, he wrote nearly twenty songs — which he later refined during a steady gig at Steele's Tavern on Yonge Street. Ian and Sylvia now owned a farm eighty kilometres outside Toronto and dropped by regularly. Lightfoot's new material impressed them greatly, especially *For Lovin' Me* and *Early Morning Rain*. Not only did Ian and Sylvia record *Early Morning Rain*, they also made it the title track of their fourth album released in July of 1965. "To me it was the light at the end of the tunnel," says Lightfoot. "It kind of scared me a bit too. You've got to hope that it's going to keep on happening."

The Tysons persuaded Albert Grossman to manage Lightfoot, who recorded his first album in New York in November 1964. It took Grossman more than a year to find a label to release the record, but in the meantime he placed *For Lovin' Me* with Peter, Paul and Mary and Johnny Cash, *Ribbon of Darkness* with Marty Robbins, and *Steel Rail Blues* with George Hamilton IV. Lightfoot had arrived.

♪   ♪   ♪

The first Mariposa Folk Festival was a tremendous artistic success, but financially it was a bust, losing $4,300. To cover some of the debts owed to advertisers and equipment rental agencies, Casey and Ruth Jones took out a second mortgage on their home. They were never reimbursed. There were no arts grants for folk festivals in those days, but Mariposa needed significant seed money if it was to survive. Jack Wall, a Toronto entrepreneur who owned the Fifth Peg coffee house, offered a solution. He would buy the rights to stage the next event, front the finances and clear all outstanding debts. He would also retain the original board to approve expenditures and the lineup. To quote Pete McGarvey: "We had nothing. We had run out of money. If there was going to be a second festival it would have to be done by someone of Wall's nature. Nobody else appeared." So in March 1962, Wall paid all of two dollars to take control of Mariposa.

In its second year, the festival expanded to three days with a bill that remained essentially the same as its predecessor. Lightfoot finally made his debut as a Two Tone. As the *Globe and Mail* reported: "There was a faintly reminiscent flavor of the Kingston Trio when the Tutones (sic), a pair of local boys, came on with *Fast Freight, Old Blue* . . . and several other numbers which failed to rouse an expectant audience."

The *Toronto Star* thought otherwise: "The Tu Tones (sic) were great crowd pleasers." The weekend was considered another triumph. Attendance rose modestly to 7,000. Eight months after its conclusion, however, Wall failed to produce a financial statement. Still, he assured the board all would be well. It had no option but to trust him.

♪ ♪ ♪

As the popularity of the likes of Dylan, Baez and Peter, Paul and Mary spread throughout North America, national television networks latched onto the folk boom. In the U.S.A., ABC broadcast *Hootenanny* from coast to coast, and in Canada, CBC ran *Sing Along Jubilee*. With all this exposure, Mariposa sold 8,000 advance weekend tickets that year. On opening night, the festival grounds were full , and still folk fans poured into Orillia. Rowdies, too. Attracted by the possibility of a "wild weekend," countless youths crammed into the streets, drinking and carousing. While Friday night passed without incident, by the following evening dozens of reports of vandalism, theft and minor assault poured into the local police station. "I remember Ian Tyson telling me that his mother read headlines about riots in Orillia, and his mother lived in Victoria," says Estelle Klein. These media reports were exaggerated, but sporadic mischief did occur.

Peter Sutherland (EFMF)

Ian Tyson at the 1986 festival . . . he composed the festival's anthem in a New York apartment

Leon Jourard recalls: "The third year it was too much of a success; it overran the town. The camping facility was overwhelmed. The accommodation as well as the 'sanitation facilities.' If you have three johnny-on-the-spots for 3,000, you have problems." The festival blamed local drunken louts. The town pointed its finger at the folk fans. And when the dust finally settled, it banished the Mariposa Folk Festival from Orillia for good.

To make matters worse, Jack Wall disappeared. So did an estimated $20,000 in ticket receipts. Besides that, the festival's board of directors found itself holding a further $9,000 worth of debt. Homeless as well as penniless, an undignified death appeared imminent. That prognosis looked even more of a certainty when Ruth Jones and Pete McGarvey resigned from the board the following spring. At Toronto radio station CKFH, Randy Ferris followed these events with growing concern. Ferris had grown up in Orillia and now hosted a nightly folk music program heard throughout Central Ontario. Unwilling to stand by and watch the festival sink, he approached the few remaining board members with more determination than solutions. First he asked Estelle Klein to take over as artistic director. "Oh, I was terrible to him. I said, 'You don't know anything about folk music. Why would you do this?' He just knew commercial folk music and I was a religious zealot . . . I was saying, 'No way. I don't trust you. You don't know anything.' For some reason he convinced me. I came to believe he really cared and I agreed to take it on for some minimal honorarium."

With Klein as artistic director, Mariposa dumped its all-Canadian policy. Her first bill featured the country blues of Mississippi John Hurt, Skip James, Sonny Terry and Brownie McGhee, the bluegrass of the Greenbriar Boys, as well as familiar homegrown talent like Alan Mills, Jean Carignan and Buffy Sainte-Marie. Not only that, Klein paid each act union scale plus expenses. No star rating here. For the next twenty years, all of Canada's major folk festivals used this payment guideline until Edmonton scrapped it in the mid-eighties. "There was no arguing that scale, and I never ever gave in to anyone who thought they should get more," says Klein. "I wanted to have James Taylor one year, and his manager told me that he was getting $20,000 the next week at the Hollywood Bowl. I said, 'Then he could afford to do Mariposa.' He didn't argue with that. I said, 'People come to Mariposa because they want to participate in a festival . . . they are not coming to make large sums of money . . . So, James Taylor was not available for three days; he said he'd come for one day for $78 plus his airfare and hotel. And I said, 'Great.' It turned out he showed up on the Friday unexpectedly and he just hung around all weekend. That was very common."

Before James Taylor or anyone else could perform at Mariposa, it faced a devastating legal battle in 1964. After its banishment from Orillia, a new site was found twenty kilometres west on a 176-acre farm in Medonte Township. Fearing the hooligan element that showed up at the previous event, the township sought a court injunction to halt the festival.

Twenty-four hours before the first performer was due on stage, the Supreme Court of Ontario granted a restraint. With advance box office receipts already spent on technical needs and promotion, the festival either relocated or perished. Although stunned by the court's decision, Ferris recovered quickly and booked The Toronto Maple Leaf Ball Club's stadium on Lake Shore Boulevard. Stagehands labored round the clock — right up to the moment the Greenbriar Boys opened on Friday night — to pull off a minor miracle. As Marvin Schiff reported in the *Globe and Mail*: "The high walls of the stadium and admission prices of $8 for the entire festival or $3 for Saturday night served to shut out the rest of the city and provide a magnificent setting for banjo and guitar workshops, song exchanges, impromptu songfests and an almost uninhibited enjoyment of folk music concerts."

Of course, the sudden shift of location had its drawbacks. Only 4,000 fans showed up in Toronto instead of the anticipated 13,000 at Medonte. Cold weather and sporadic rain didn't help. Neither did the non-appearance of Brownie McGhee and Sonny Terry, lost in the hinterlands of rural Ontario. To her credit, Klein pulled the Reverend Gary Davies out of a local coffee house to successfully fill their spot. Still, it all added up to a $5,000 loss. For all of these setbacks, though, Mariposa regained a lot of respect through its ability to promote outstanding music despite overwhelming odds. As the *Globe and Mail* concluded in its weekend wrap-up: "In all, it was an exceptional weekend for folk buffs, who were treated to a well-balanced program directed by Estelle Klein, in which Canadian music, quite properly, was heavily stressed."

For the next three years, Mariposa matured in the small summer resort of Innis Lake, sixty-five kilometres northwest of Toronto. Ferris cleared many of the outstanding debts and a credit line took care of the rest. At the conclusion of 1965, the festival actually made a profit. And as the crowds grew, so did the scope of the music. Workshops became more prominent. Indeed, for the first time at any North American folk festival, Mariposa brought together diverse cultures to swap songs and share their instrumental expertise. Prior to that, the accepted format consisted of bluesmen playing at blues workshops or gospel singers harmonizing at gospel workshops and the twain ne'er meeting. As its reputation spread from Innis Lake, Mariposa began to attract such veterans as Pete Seeger, Bill Monroe and Ramblin' Jack Elliott. It also provided up-and-coming songwriters, such as Joni Mitchell, Leonard

Cohen, Murray MacLauchlan, with their first major exposure. Old and new blues innovators boosted their careers performing there.

Many of these blues acts were booked on the recommendation of Richard Flohil, a Toronto journalist and concert promoter. Flohil had grown up in Britain, infatuated with Dixieland jazz, or trad jazz as it's called in the U.K. "My parents hated it. My music teacher hated it. It was cannibal music and it was, therefore, for me." But by the mid-fifties his musical tastes broadened to include blues, particularly Muddy Waters. As Flohil jokes, "I really came to Canada because I wanted to meet Muddy Waters . . . So I came to Toronto because it was the biggest city and it was the nearest one to Chicago, where Muddy was. With my first paycheque I went to Chicago to meet Muddy Waters. Very simple. Got off the train and said, 'Smitty's Corner.' And all the cab drivers told me to fuck off. It was a very memorable sort of thing." Several trips later, Flohil got to know the likes of Sleepy John Estes, Big Walter Horton and Muddy Waters. Few of these artists had agents in Canada in those days, so Flohil booked them into Toronto venues like the First Floor Club. In his spare time, he also wrote about blues in the folk magazine *Hoot*. The combination of these activities led to his increasing involvement with Mariposa — first as an advisor, then publicity director, and eventually artistic director.

While Mariposa came of age at Innis Lake, it moved again in 1968 to Olympic Island in Toronto harbor in hopes of drawing even larger audiences. As the distinguished wildlife artist Robert Bateman recalls: "It was very much a family event. It was clean and green and pleasant and very family. Just wandering around behind the scenes even, you weren't told you couldn't go here and you could sort of eavesdrop on the performers having fun talking to each other. They did seem to be having a good time, like we were doing."

For the first time, Klein booked more than fifty acts, which she spread over three full days and evenings. Under her meticulous supervision, workshops grew more and more sophisticated. Evening performances, though, still took place on a large, impersonal mainstage that faced huge, often restless crowds — hardly a suitable setting for subtler acts like unaccompanied traditional singers or solo instrumentalists. Troubled by the lack of respect accorded these performers, Klein took the controversial step of doing away with mainstage concerts altogether in 1971. Crowd problems the previous year also played a key role in this decision.

In the aftermath of Woodstock and its hippie ethos of free music, gate-crashing festivals grew into a fad. Almost 1,500 individuals broke through the turnstiles at Mariposa in 1970. To discourage such behavior in the future, name acts received little undue emphasis in a program that now consisted solely of daytime workshops and solo concerts on eight small, intimate stages. While veteran board members like Richard Flohil criticized this move, musicians like Mike and Pete Seeger supported her efforts. For a brief period, this new schedule worked on all levels. Nobody gate-crashed. Daily crowds topped 10,000. And five-hundred letters of approval arrived.

In 1971, Neil Young, Joni Mitchell, Jackson Browne and Bob Dylan turned up as unexpected guests. Such was the status of Mariposa now. Fame, though, had its drawbacks. As Dylan wandered around the site, thousands of fans trampled after him. A serious accident appeared imminent. At one point, the crowd stood pushing and shoving — eight deep — around the performers' area trying to catch a glimpse of him talking to Gordon Lightfoot. Concerned for the safety of both Dylan and his fans, a board member called for the harbor police to escort him off the Island. Of course, during all this upheaval nobody paid any attention to the scheduled performers. And that created a lot of hard feelings. Despite its best intentions, Mariposa had fallen victim to its own success.

♪ ♪ ♪

Dylan never did perform at Mariposa. He did, however, sing at the Bohemian Embassy coffee house in the early sixties. Its owners included actor Don Cullen, who worked with the CBC Television comedy duo Wayne and Schuster. Aside from folk singing, the Embassy presented chamber music, early experimental electronic music, revue theatre and poetry recitals. Margaret Atwood often read there. "In fact Bob Dylan came up there one night . . . and Bob Wilson, the guy who was running the poetry night, wouldn't let him read because he wasn't scheduled," Mitch Podolak recalled in an interview for this book. Barely fourteen in 1961, Podolak worked at the Embassy's hootenannies as a busboy — he couldn't afford the dollar cover charge — and within three years was managing the place. One night, Neil Young showed up at a hootenanny then asked for a gig. "I went 'Nah! This guy, he ain't got nothing!' At the time the songwriters were like Dylan and [Tom] Paxton — they were all into politics — and I just didn't know how to relate to him. I was just too young." Although only sixteen, Podolak had already promoted his first concert — the New City Ramblers at the Eaton Auditorium. "I lost my ass."

Podolak's calling came suddenly, like Saul's on the road to Damascus. While he was studying classical music at the Royal Conservatory in Toronto in 1960, his older sister Alice took him to a Pete Seeger concert.

"The next day I went down to the pawn shop with a $200 clarinet and traded it for a $40 banjo, and my life's been fucked ever since. It's true." It's also true that Podolak eventually became one of the most prominent folk music impresarios in Canada. His inspiration and guidance would launch the Winnipeg, Vancouver and Edmonton folk music festivals.

(EFMF)

Amos Garrett did for the Winnipeg Folk Festival in 1977 what Dylan and Butterfield had done in Newport

Podolak's initial interest in folk music developed through listening to Alice's Folkways records and their uncle Phil's three-hundred-member mandolin orchestra. Like Estelle Klein, Podolak attended the United Jewish People's Order summer camp near Brampton. Weekly radio programs hosted by the CBC's Alan Mills and Edith Fowke provided further sustenance until that fateful Seeger concert with its powerful political songs. "I found something real in the music that gave me guidance in my life. I can't think of any other bigger influence. Not the philosophers. Not the ideologues. The music."

Aside from managing the Embassy, Podolak made annual pilgrimages to both Mariposa and Newport. In 1965 he sat amid the turmoil of Dylan's electric appearance, too respectful to boo. Already a committed member of the Socialist Workers Party, he revered Dylan's protest songs. When they had met several years before at the Embassy, Dylan actually expressed interest in joining the Party's American affiliation, The League for Socialist Action. Dylan then was: "Decent. Accessible. Not fucked up . . . that came later."

As the Vietnam War picked up momentum, Podolak dropped out of the Toronto folk scene to become a full-time political activist — first in Edmonton in 1967 and then in Winnipeg a year later. There he eventually went to work for CBC Radio as a freelance documentary writer for such shows as *This Country In The Morning* and *Between Ourselves*. Then one night, as Winnipeg approached its centennial in 1974, the city ran a television advertisement. It wanted suggestions for the celebrations. "It just popped into my brain right there and then — just a flash of folk festival," says Podolak. All proposals went before a committee of prominent citizens and city officials for review. Bound by civic duty: "I went and conned this group. I got a friend of mine, Colin Gorrie, who is an architect and very British, with an Ascot accent — been in the British army in Africa, you know. He played the straight role . . . so I played the sort of intense hippie and the two of us did the Mickey, Mickey routine on everybody. It worked like a charm and it raised $100,000, which we couldn't believe. That was the seed money. That was it. We put the first one on free. Centennial project. Bang!"

The Winnipeg Folk Festival made its debut on August 9, 1974 (the day after Richard Nixon resigned the U.S. presidency). A small but vocal group of drunks threatened to dampen the opening night festivities, but a tenacious Podolak, concerned about the consequences of excessive rowdiness, persuaded them otherwise. The piece of wood he carried probably helped. "I was damned determined nothing was going to go wrong. I'd just go and talk to them very reasonably, very rationally and, if that didn't work, I'd bop them — that's all."

On stage that night, Bukka White and Bruce Cockburn cornered most of the kudos. While Saturday saw Mike Seeger, John Hammond Jr. and Murray MacLauchlan triumph, Canadian Leon Redbone turned out the undisputed star of the weekend. Redbone — a mysterious, guitar-picking throwback to country and jazz pioneers Jimmie Rodgers and Jelly Roll Morton — earned a twenty-minute standing ovation for his extraordinary solo set Sunday. All in all, an estimated 20,000 revellers made that first trip to Birds Hill Provincial Park for a top-drawer bill. "Even the raccoons, dogs and children seemed happy with the offerings of the top folk artists around," reported Chris Ladd of the *Winnipeg Free Press*. And before the last notes faded, plans were under way to make the Winnipeg Folk Festival an annual occurrence.

Podolak still knew next to nothing about running a folk festival. What he did know, he'd picked up from friends and acquaintances in the few preceding months. "The interesting thing that first year was trying to tell the American performers how to find Winnipeg. 'Yeah, you know where North Dakota is? We're just north of that. No, it's hot here in the summer.' It was just like that, too." Directions he could cope with. Guidance was another matter. First he approached Estelle Klein. "She said she'd be happy to help but she was charging a consulting fee of two hundred bucks a day. Now in retrospect, two hundred bucks a day is cheap . . . but I got offended by it." Richard Flohil, on the other hand, volunteered his services. He invited Podolak to his home in Toronto and sat him down beside the stereo with 5,000 blues albums for company. Then he dragged him off to the massive Philadelphia Folk Festival and various other gigs to further broaden his tastes. Flohil taught Podolak how to organize the large body of volunteers needed to make the festival run smoothly and also to choose and match talent for an appealing, cohesive bill. "The festival really owes a lot to him. I owe a lot to him," says Podolak.

Flohil, in turn, credits his mentor: "Everything that I learned, I learned from watching Estelle Klein. I think Estelle was years ahead of anyone else in this business. Her tastes were very wide; her knowledge was very wide." After being in existence for a year, the Winnipeg Folk Festival qualified for a number of provincial, federal and municipal grants. Other funding came from the Canadian Broadcasting Corporation, which taped a number of performances for the influential folk show *Touch the Earth*, hosted by Sylvia Tyson. With the bulk of the finances taken care of, Podolak looked at streamlining the festival. He went to Mariposa and filled three notebooks with his impressions. While he marvelled at how smoothly it ran, he found its treatment of volunteers woeful. Only those with senior positions received invitations to mingle with performers at after-hours parties. The rank and file made do with a pat on the back and a free T-shirt. "We stopped that right off the bat. We put on free booze for everyone." One year someone bought a pound of pot, rolled it up and put it out in little cups. "Can't do that anymore," Podolak says. "Too dangerous. We were kind of stupid."

Winnipeg continued to thrive. Each year it grew in size and stature, and within five years it was the largest folk festival in North America in terms of attendance and the number of featured acts. Like Mariposa and Newport before it, Winnipeg paid all of its performers a similar scale. It also prohibited electric instruments — at least until 1977 when Amos Garrett rebelled. At the time, Garrett performed a combination of acoustic blues, folk and jazz with his partner Geoff Muldaur. But part of their repertoire demanded an electric guitar.

Already bothered by the fact that post-war-era black blues artists were excluded on the account of their instruments, Garrett took a stand. After all, every acoustic instrument performed on mainstage blasted through five-thousand watts of sound system. "I pulled out my Fender Telecaster guitar and we did three or four songs with it. And Mitch came up to me at the end of the night and sort of confronted me. He was sort of pissed off. And I just said right away, 'You're excluding Muddy Waters and B.B. King and Sunnyland Slim and all this wonderful aural tradition . . . that just happens to amplify its instruments. Do you want to go public about that? ' Mitch backed off right away and the next year there were several Chicago blues bands at the Winnipeg Folk Festival."

Podolak recalls: "Amos did it without telling me. He just went up and did it on the stage. And once that happened my attitude was: Great, because now we can do whatever the fuck we want." The incident left no bitter feelings and Garrett went on to perform at Winnipeg on several other occasions.

♪ ♪ ♪

The following year Podolak took the great leap forward and launched the Vancouver Folk Music Festival — a project he'd been planning since 1974. Unsettled in Winnipeg, he and his partner Colin Gorrie wanted to move to the West Coast. It took four years to secure backing. To assist with this new venture he hired Gary Cristall, a history student at Simon Fraser University. With Winnipeg now in its fifth year, Podolak's technical expertise guaranteed Vancouver a smooth, although wet, start in beautiful Stanley Park. The same familiar, albeit talented, faces — Leon Redbone, Bruce Cockburn, John Hammond Jr., Louis Killen, Mike Seeger — turned up. Nevertheless, *The Province's* headline proclaimed: "Weekend folkfest a winner." In *The Vancouver Sun*, Podolak agreed: "I think in one year we've established one of the major festivals in Canada." He was right, of course.

While Year Two varied little from its predecessor, it did feature the great Gambian masters of the kora, a twenty-one-string gourd harp, Dembo Konte and his father Alhaji Bai. While Newport and Mariposa had staged World Music in the past, Vancouver would become its leading advocate. Not under Podolak's guidance, though. Personal problems arose and Podolak and Cristall parted ways. Podolak , in his own blunt, amiable manner, explains: "At thirty, which was how old I was then, I believed all my own bullshit. And I was an insufferable asshole to be around, you know. And I paid for it." So Cristall took over and Podolak returned to Winnipeg to lick his wounds and contemplate the future.

Vancouver continued to develop into one of the most distinctive folk festivals in North America. The overtly political Cristall scoured the world — from Nicaragua to Tuva — for performers to match his philosophical needs. No festival in North America has showcased as many songwriters from the gay rights and women's movements as Vancouver. "When people talk about political songwriting, they tend to think of the old labor songs," he told songwriter Leon Rosselson in an interview for *Folk Roots* magazine. "But politics are different now and these social movements are part of that difference; their songs express a different view of the world. So we make sure the festival is balanced in terms of its representation of women and men."

All performers still receive the same pay scale, yet Vancouver attracts such name acts as the British post-punk political songwriter Billy Bragg, American roots-revivalist Michelle Shocked and, of course, the veritable veteran Pete Seeger. "You cannot rely on so-called stars because once you do, the minute the stars don't come out at night, you're finished. So we have a policy of paying everyone the same," Cristall said.

Back in Winnipeg, Mitch Podolak had his finger in more pies than Little Jack Horner. Throughout 1978, he hounded Edmonton concert promoter Don Whalen to start a local folk festival. "I remember Mitch coming out here and saying here is what you have to do. You have to meet these various levels of government," says Holger Petersen, chairman of the board of the first Edmonton Folk Music Festival. "Mitch, bless his heart, made himself available to come here and be part of these meetings." By now, plans were underway to celebrate Alberta's 75th anniversary as a province in 1980. To mark the occasion, the oil-rich provincial government earmarked seventy-five million dollars for new cultural programs and community projects. Podolak and Whalen decided to approach Horst Schmid, the provincial minister for culture, for funding. As Podolak recalls: "We sit down across from his desk and he looks at us and says, 'Tell me boys, how much money do you want to screw out of me?' Whalen and I were going to ask for forty grand, so I said, 'Yeah, we need eighty thousand dollars.' And we got it."

With an attitude like that how could they fail?

Selected recordings

Ian and Sylvia: Four Strong Winds (Vanguard VCD-2149)
Gordon Lightfoot: Early Morning Rain (Capitol CDLL57275)
Joni Mitchell: Ladies of The Canyon (WEA CD-6376)
Leonard Cohen: Songs of Leonard Cohen (Columbia CK9533)
Neil Young: After The Goldrush (Reprise CD-02283)
Bruce Cockburn: Stealing Fire (True North TN-57)
   The Trouble With Normal (True North TN53)

The British invasion inspires folk rock

5

Monday, Monday

■We love you, Beatles ■The Byrds
take flight ■California dreamers
■Paul and Artie■

"I can remember coming out of that movie so jazzed that I was swinging around stop-sign poles at arm's length. I knew right then what my life was going to be."
— *A HARD DAY'S NIGHT CHANGES DAVID CROSBY'S LIFE*

CAPITOL RECORDS PLASTERED FIVE million posters across the U.S.A. to announce the imminent arrival of The Beatles. Beatlemania had already swept Britain; America now beckoned. Their single *I Want To Hold Your Hand* sat at Number One on the national charts as Pan Am flight 101 left Heathrow Airport on February 7, 1964, bound for New York. There, local radio station WMCA announced: "It is now 6:30 a.m. Beatle time. They left London thirty minutes ago. They're out over the Atlantic and headed for New York. The temperature is 32 Beatle degrees." At 1:30 p.m., more than ten thousand fans greeted them at Kennedy Airport, screaming and singing "We love you Beatles, oh yes we do."

Two nights later, the Fab Four made their North American debut on the *Ed Sullivan Show* as a record audience of seventy-three million watched bemused. According to local legend, not one hubcap was stolen in New York City during the entire broadcast. Within two years, The Beatles were more popular than Jesus Christ, at least according to their guitarist John Lennon. Ultimately, their music would redefine rock 'n' roll.

The Rolling Stones, The Kinks and The Animals soon followed The Beatles across the Atlantic. All of these British bands imitated and absorbed a variety of American rock 'n' roll, rhythm and blues and rockabilly to create their own refreshing sound. As they infiltrated the U.S.A., their music became known as rock rather than pop, a word associated with the commissioned songwriters of Tin Pan Alley. From Greenwich Village to Hollywood, rock grabbed young musicians the way the integrity and purity of folk once had. The fact that these performers from Liverpool and London portrayed themselves as working class lads merely added to their credibility.

The Beatles "ended the folk thing like that. After that, for our generation, it wasn't the same," Ian Tyson told the *Globe and Mail* in February 1994. "Everyone had to relearn their craft — to play electric guitar and to play with a drummer."

Joe Rizzuto (EFMF)

Roger McGuinn at Gallagher Park in 1989 . . . his electric 12-string guitar gave the Byrds their unique sound

Jim McGuinn saw the writing on the wall. As the Village folk scene collapsed, he moved to Los Angeles in early 1964 and founded the Jet Set with David Crosby and Gene Clark. Inspired as much by Bob Dylan as The Beatles, they aimed for the middle ground between the two. As a trio, the Jet Set cut one single for Electra before adding Chris Hillman and Michael Clarke. The inspiration for their recruitment came from The Beatles' first movie, *A Hard Day's Night*. "I can remember coming out of that movie so jazzed that I was swinging around stop-sign poles at arm's length," says David Crosby in his autobiography, *Long Time Gone*. "I knew right then what my life was going to be. . . .I loved the attitude and the fun of it; there was sex; there was joy; there was everything I wanted out of life, right there. They were cool and we said, 'Yeah, that's it. We have to be a band. Who can we get to play drums?'"

Michael Clarke was not much of a drummer; aside from McGuinn, they were all relatively inexperienced musicians. The Jet Set briefly renamed themselves The Beefeaters to cash in on the British invasion. Finally, they settled on The Byrds (misspelled, like The Beatles) and signed with Columbia Records in October. Sometime over the winter of 1964, McGuinn, who later changed his name to Roger for religious reasons, received a tape of a recording session that featured Bob Dylan singing new songs with Woody Guthrie's old buddy Ramblin' Jack Elliott. One song in particular, *Mr. Tambourine Man*, caught McGuinn's fancy and he set about toying with its structure, altering the lyrics of three of its four verses, slowing the tempo and adding an unforgettable opening riff on a twelve-string Rickenbacker electric guitar. The ringing of that guitar would define the sound of The Byrds.

"Roger could cop anything from anyplace, except that he didn't do it like a copyist," Crosby wrote. "He would take a thing and make it his own. That was the genius of it. He didn't just copy somebody; he'd take the essence of their idea and turn it into his idea. Synthesize something with something else and come out with something new. And he did it repeatedly. Y'see, I think that's the essence of creating new music because new music doesn't just appear out of thin air."

Only McGuinn played on the initial recording of *Mr. Tambourine Man*. Studio musicians like Glen Campbell (the future country star) and Leon Russell (the future rock celebrity) provided additional backing. Released as a single in March, it topped the pop charts in both America and Britain. Consequently, The Byrds' combination of Dylan's poetic literacy and The Beatles' melodic intensity legitimized folk-rock as a full-fledged commercial phenomenon.

For the next two years, The Byrds produced a string of artistically admirable, yet commercial, singles, including *Turn, Turn, Turn* — a passage from Ecclesiastes 3:1-8 set to music by Pete Seeger. Serious disputes over artistic direction eventually curbed their momentum and David Crosby left to form Crosby, Stills and Nash. Gram Parsons, a renegade country songwriter, took his place in early 1968. With encouragement from Chris Hillman, Parsons inspired The Byrds to establish country-rock with the release of their sixth album, *Sweetheart Of The Rodeo*. Like many pioneers, they didn't get it quite right, and although now considered a landmark recording, it took a savage beating from music critics at the time. Within a year, only McGuinn remained from the original lineup. Subsequently, the quality of each album declined (with the exception of the double album *Untitled*, released in 1970) until The Byrds flew their own separate ways in 1973.

♪   ♪   ♪

As the Jet Set experimented with folk-rock in Los Angeles, the Mugwumps did likewise in New York. The Mugwumps consisted of hootenanny stalwarts Cass Elliot, Denny Doherty, Zal Yanovsky and versatile multi-instrumentalist John Sebastian. But within a year Yanovsky and Sebastian established the Lovin' Spoonful and Elliot and Doherty left to form The Mamas And The Papas with John Phillips and his wife Michelle. While their impeccable vocal harmonies picked up where Peter, Paul and Mary left off, The Mamas And The Papas avoided the social and political protest messages of their celebrated peers. Their first two hits were unorthodox, though. As author Charlie Gillet points out in *Sounds of the City*: "*California Dreamin*" effectively carried on the West-is-best ethic cultivated by the Beach Boys, and *Monday, Monday* went back to a favorite topic of the blues." While they successfully resurrected the Five Royales' *Dedicated to the One I Love*, the autobiographical *Creeque Alley* described the group's decision to leave folk music of Greenwich Village behind and join the Byrds in the Top Ten.

Wayne Stiles (EFMF)

John Sebastian plays the Fest in '87 . . . his Lovin' Spoonful racked up twelve hit singles in less than three years

The Lovin' Spoonful, on the other hand, pursued a grittier sound that alternated between country, blues, rock and good-time jug-band music. Essentially, jug bands performed folk music fit for dancing — a legacy of the southern black bands of the rag-time era that used such diverse instruments as kazoos, harmonicas, banjos, fiddles, wash-boards, mandolins, massed guitars and, of course, jugs that were blown into. A slap-happy reply to the seriousness of the folk revival as typified by Peter, Paul and Mary, jug bands enjoyed a certain popularity throughout the early six-ties. The best of these included The Even Dozen Jug Band (which included John Sebastian), the Jim Kweskin Jug Band (whose members included Maria Muldaur), the Instant Action Jug Band (which evolved into Country Joe & The Fish, the first overtly political folk-rock group) and the Nitty Gritty Dirt Band. From jug band music, then, the Lovin' Spoonful took the happy-go-lucky spirit that heightens such songs as *Do You Believe In Magic?* Ultimately, they racked up twelve hit singles, including *Summer In The City*, in two-and-a-half years before disband-ing in 1968.

Predictably, the success of folk-rock motivated numerous imitators. The most notable was Barry McGuire (a friend and confidant of The

Mamas And The Papas) whose apocalyptic *Eve of Destruction* sold a phenomenal six million copies world-wide in 1965, despite the odd ban from radio stations peeved by its pessimistic lyrics. It was McGuire's only day in the sun and he quickly faded into obscurity.

Record companies, never slow to cash in on a popular trend, soon turned their attention to folk-rock. And none quicker than Columbia. In 1964, the New York duo of Paul Simon and Art Garfunkel recorded *Wednesday Morning, 3 A.M.* — a collection of traditional songs and Simon originals that included *The Sounds Of Silence* — under the guidance of the gifted Tom Wilson. He produced such seminal albums as Dylan's *Bringing It All Back Home*, The Velvet Underground's *White Light/White Heat* and Frank Zappa's *Freak Out*. But *Wednesday Morning, 3 A.M.* went nowhere, selling a paltry 8,000 copies between 1964 and 1965. The discouraged duo split up and Simon left America to tour and record in Britain as *Mr. Tambourine Man*, *Subterranean Homesick Blues* and *Eve of Destruction* were exploding onto the pop charts. Meanwhile, radio stations in Houston and Miami picked up on *The Sounds of Silence*. Inspired by the airplay, Wilson took the original version — recorded with just an acoustic guitar and vocals — dubbed on bass, electric guitar and drums and released it as a single. Subsequently, it went to Number One on the American singles charts. Simon promptly returned to the U.S., rejoined Garfunkel, and together they went on to record such substantial hits as *The Boxer* and *Bridge Over Troubled Water* before pursuing solo careers in 1971.

Selected recordings

The Byrds: Mr. Tambourine Man (Columbia WCK-9172)
Mamas and Papas: Sixteen Of Their Greatest Hits
   (MCA MCAD-5701)
Lovin' Spoonful: The Very Best of The Lovin' Spoonful
   (WEA BCD-68002)
Simon and Garfunkel: Greatest Hits (Columbia CK31350)

6

Dirty Old Town

- The songs of Ewan MacColl
- Trad jazz and skiffle ▪ Ban the Bomb
- Hippie bliss ▪ Fairport Convention
- Steeleye Span ▪

"The very first time I played in public I was a floor singer and Ewan MacColl was the main singer. I got up with my little guitar, and I was fifteen or something, and he sat in the front, head bowed all the way through my set; and I'm sure he just nodded off."
— ELVIS COSTELLO ENCOUNTERS A GIANT OF THE OLD GUARD

DESPITE THE ENORMOUS POPULARITY of folk-rock, general interest in folk music in North America peaked around 1965. Its audience abandoned the coffee houses for rock venues like the Fillmores East and West in New York and San Francisco. In Britain, though, folk-rock bands such as Fairport Convention and Steeleye Span helped to revitalize traditional music. Britain's developed in folk clubs rather than in coffee houses. These clubs usually flourished in upstairs rooms in pubs or in college or university common rooms that rarely held more than three hundred people. While these venues started out with an open attitude, many developed a purist format, accepting only singers who sang traditional material in a prescribed manner. At the root of the problem lay the man most responsible for the post-war urban folk resurgence in Britain, Ewan MacColl.

MacColl, born James Miller in 1915, was the son of a Scottish communist and active trade unionist. From his father William, James inherited a passion for militant politics, and a love of traditional ballads and street songs. Often blacklisted, William moved his family around a lot before he finally settled in Salford, England — the industrial slum that inspired MacColl's much-covered *Dirty Old Town*. There he grew up and left school at age fourteen to work in a wire-making factory. His recreational interests lay in acting and songwriting. At seventeen, he wrote his first important protest song, *The Manchester Rambler*. It describes a violent clash between working class hikers and the game-keepers who worked for local wealthy landowners. Like all great songs, it survives because it deals with issues far broader than a long-forgotten punch-up on the moors of Derbyshire:

He said, 'all this land is my master's.'
At that I stood shaking my head.
No man has the right to own mountains
Any more than the deep ocean bed.
(Reprinted with permission)

In other words, this land is your land, this land is my land. Like Woody Guthrie, MacColl spent a lifetime writing political songs for the moment, many of which became immortal. But theatre, more than music, enveloped MacColl's early life. He married gifted English actress Joan Littlewood, and together they founded Theatre Workshop to make drama as classless and as popular as in the days of Shakespeare. The artistic and financial struggles of keeping the company afloat in the days before government funding took its toll on their marriage and they separated in the early fifties.

Around the time his marriage disintegrated, MacColl's interest in folk songs was rekindled by Alan Lomax, who left the U.S. to collect and record folk songs in Britain for the Library of Congress. Not only did he record MacColl's parents, Alan also played MacColl his recordings of black blues artists and white American folk singers. "When Alan Lomax came along with this music that had proved popular to generations and generations, I thought, 'This is what we should be exploring!'" he told Robin Denselow, author of *When The Music's Over*. And explore, they did. Lomax introduced MacColl to A.L. (Bert) Lloyd, who had just written a social-historical introduction to folk song, *The Singing English-man*. The three of them then approached BBC Radio with the concept of documenting the connection between British and American folk song, and American folk song and jazz. *Ballads and Blues*, a series of eight documentaries, was first broadcast in 1951. It featured, as well as

Anita Maloney (EFMF)

Peggy Seeger, who performed at the festival in 1992, wrote I'm Gonna Be An Engineer and inspired The First Time Ever I Saw Your Face

MacColl, Lomax and Lloyd, American guests Big Bill Broonzy and Jean Ritchie, and locals Isla Cameron and Humphrey Lyttelton and his trad jazz band. Its tremendous success led to regular concerts at a London theatre and at London's Princess Louise pub where the Ballads and Blues Club — the first folk club in Britain — was established in 1953.

Trad jazz, or Dixieland jazz as it is known in North America, developed a highly enthusiastic cult following in post-war Britain. By the mid-fifties, trad jazz and folk began to cross paths more often. For instance, in 1954, Chris Barber's jazz band recorded *New Orleans Joy*, an album that included 23-year-old guitarist Lonnie Donegan singing Leadbelly's *Rock Island Line*, accompanied by a double bass and a washboard. *Rock Island Line* produced such an extraordinary live reaction that Decca Records released it as a novelty single in 1956. It sold over a million copies and became the first British pop song to crack the American Top Ten. This modest arrangement of jazz and folk became known as skiffle, and it provided the Glasgow-born Donegan with a further twenty-six hits over the next six years.

The sheer vitality and romantic simplicity of skiffle knocked British kids arse over tea kettle. Even the instruments were simple: cheap zinc wash-boards that took the place of drums, plywood tea chests attached to a pole laced with stout string that made a rudimentary double-bass, and a variety of ukuleles, banjos and guitars used to pound out three-chord American folk songs written primarily by Woody Guthrie, Leadbelly or Big Bill Broonzy. Not only did skiffle introduce folk songs to the masses of Britain, it also acted as a springboard for a variety of musicians later prominent in rock circles, most notably Liverpool's Quarrymen, John Lennon and Paul McCartney.

Even Lomax and MacColl formed a skiffle group. The Lomax-MacColl Ramblers included noted singer Peggy Seeger, sister of Mike and half-sister of Pete. She was on her way back from a youth festival in Moscow when she stopped over in England and met and fell in love with MacColl. She inspired his best-known song, *The First Time Ever I Saw Your Face* (later covered by both Elvis Presley and Roberta Flack). Ewan and Peggy eventually married and continued to sing and write together for the next thirty years. Peggy's considerable contributions included *I'm Gonna Be An Engineer* — arguably the first contemporary feminist folk song.

Back in 1957, though, MacColl grew disenchanted with skiffle's American repertoire. As he told Robin Denselow: "I became concerned that we had a whole generation who were becoming quasi-Americans, and I felt this was absolutely monstrous! I was convinced that we had a music that was just as vigorous as anything that America had produced." So MacColl initiated his infamous dictum: only English singers should sing English songs, only Scots should sing Scottish songs, and so on. Alan Lomax agreed and took a variation of this policy to the U.S. Today, folk-root artists scoff at such a notion. Fusion, after all, keeps the music fresh and dynamic rather than a museum curio. But with MacColl's rigid principles in place, the Ballad and Blues Club's membership exceeded 11,000 by the end of 1959. There, performers as diverse as Irish singer Dominic Behan (brother of playwright Brendan Behan) and American Ramblin' Jack Elliott held court every Sunday night. Still, only a handful of professional folk singers existed in Britain at the time and possibly only twenty clubs in the whole country for them to sing in. As skiffle faded, though, its clubs became folk and skiffle clubs, and then simply folk clubs. Twenty years later, more than 1,700 existed throughout Britain.

Meanwhile, MacColl's reputation and influence spread thanks to his ground-breaking work on the BBC documentary series, *The Radio Ballads*. Recorded between 1957 and 1964, it highlighted the everyday lives, joys and tragedies of ordinary British people — fishermen, railwaymen, miners, laborers, travelling people. Prior to *The Radio Ballads*, documentary makers had "rough dialect voices" transcribed and read by trained actors, but MacColl and his producer Charles Parker used the actual voices of those interviewed and emphasized their tales with MacColl's songs, such as *Shoals Of Herring*, *The Moving-On Song* and *Freeborn Man*. Not only did these songs boost the repertoire of the folk revival, they also provided confidence and inspiration for its young writers.

♪ ♪ ♪

Many new songs also evolved from the Ban the Bomb protests organized by the Campaign for Nuclear Disarmament. Launched in February 1958, the CND pressed for a halt in the production of nuclear weapons and their eventual elimination. To publicize these objectives, it organized an annual four-day march over Easter from the British Atomic Weapons Research Establishment at Aldermaston to London. The first march attracted a mere couple of thousand demonstrators — and a lot of publicity. By 1962, that number had swollen to over 100,000. Similar demonstrations took place all over Britain.

Just as North American folk singers allied themselves with the civil rights movement, their British counterparts aligned themselves with the Ban the Bomb campaign. At rallies and marches they wrote and sang such appropriate songs as *The Sun Is Burning*, *Old Man Atom (Talking Atomic Blues)*, and *Ding Dong Dollar*. Of course, performing in front of such large crowds not only raised a performer's profile but also provided increased exposure for folk music in general.

Folk music converts also multiplied with the arrival of the Kingston Trio and *Tom Dooley*. While unaccompanied solo singers like Louis Killen, Jeannie Robertson and Bob Davenport dominate the fledgling days of the folk revival in Britain, numerous combos soon flourished, dressed in *de rigueur* Arran sweaters. Like their North American hootenanny counterparts, British bands The Spinners, The Clancy Brothers and The Ian Campbell Folk Group relished stomping chorus songs. They all initially achieved considerable commercial success, but their style stagnated and that led to their decline.

The legacy of skiffle, though, began to pay dividends as its participants probed further into the world of folk and blues. Martin Carthy delved briefly into hootenanny with Leon Rosselson in the quartet Three City Four before exploring traditional British folk songs as a solo performer. Carthy provided the traditional tune *Lord Franklin* for Bob Dylan's *Dream* and also passed on *Scarborough Fair* to Paul Simon. While a highly influential singer, Martin's early experiments with open guitar tunings spearheaded a playing style later adopted and transformed by the likes of Nic Jones and Martin Simpson. Nevertheless, from 1966 until 1969, Carthy formed a duet with fiddler Dave Swarbrick and recorded two of the decade's most important albums, *Byker Hill* and *Prince Heathen*. Although these recordings set new standards for interpretations of traditional music, Swarbrick left to join Fairport Convention. Carthy returned to solo gigs until the trail-blazing electric Steeleye Span recruited his services. Stints in the Albion Band and Brass Monkey went hand in hand with his continued participation in the much-revered *a cappella* quintet, The Watersons. Finally, in 1988, Carthy and Swarbrick more or less picked up where they left off and recorded the album *Life and Limb*. Released in 1990, it made critics lists in such diverse British publications as *Folk Roots*, *The Guardian* and *Q* as one of the best folk releases of the year.

Alexis Korner, on the other hand, parted with skiffle and steeped himself in country blues. In 1961, he formed Blues Incorporated with future Rolling Stone Charlie Watts. This electric band played a pivotal roll in establishing the British blues boom of the mid-sixties and, before it disbanded in 1967, its former members included Long John Baldry, Mick Jagger, Cream's Jack Bruce and Ginger Baker, and Pentangle's Danny Thompson, Terry Cox and John Renbourn. Unlike many of their prestigious peers, Thompson, Cox and Renbourn never succumbed to the temptations of rock. Instead, they formed the mighty, all-acoustic Pentangle with Bert Jansch and Jacqui McShee, and created a distinctive blend of folk, country blues and jazz, accentuated by the brilliant guitar playing of Jansch and Renbourn. Their interaction popularized folk baroque, a fusion of traditional British folk songs and blues originally initiated by Davey Graham. As Renbourn says: "Davey was the one for me, as he was for just about everyone else — I used to follow him around and learn from him."

Davey Graham was the first in Britain to truly expand the boundaries of the folk guitar. His 1961 EP called *3/4 A.D.* — a collaboration with Korner — fused blues, jazz, folk and Indian instrumentals. A public barely into hootenanny had a tough time coping with this bold experiment and largely ignored it. Three years later Graham released a solo album, *Folk, Blues and Beyond*. It includes an Indian instrumental which blends into a spirited version of Leadbelly's *Leavin' Blues*, an intricate bluesy rendition of the British traditional song *Seven Gypsies* (the first example of folk baroque), a Moroccan instrumental, contemporary songs by Bob Dylan and Cyril Tawney, and experiments with jazz pieces written by Bobby Timmons and Charles Mingus. The follow up, *Folk Roots, New Routes*, broke even more ground. This time Graham teamed up with English traditional singer Shirley Collins to record a daring collection of British and American folk songs spiced with the customary blues, jazz and Eastern melodies. While these two albums made little initial impact, over the long term, they inspired such British guitarists as Jansch, Renbourn, John James and Gordon Giltrap. Indeed, no folk guitarist in Britain gained street cred until they mastered Graham's exquisite instrumental *Anji*. Drug addiction, though, hampered his creativity and for the next twenty-odd years he frequently disappeared for extended periods and rarely recorded.

(EFMF)

John Renbourn in 1987 . . . two decades earlier he shunned the temptations of rock in favor of the mighty all-acoustic Pentangle

♪ ♪ ♪

For pure inventiveness nobody matched the Scottish combination of Robin Williamson and Mike Heron, collectively known as the Incredible String Band. Initially a three-man jug band formed in Glasgow in 1965, singer Clive Palmer left shortly after the release of the band's self-titled debut album a year later. That initial album went largely ignored, but their second, *The 5,000 Spirits*, featured Williamson and Heron playing an extraordinary combination of exotic instruments — bowed gimbri, sitar, and tamboura, as well as whistles, harpsichords, flutes, fiddles, mandolins and guitars — and playing them quite splendidly. With these instruments they synthesized melodies from around the globe, which they embellished with mystical yet playful lyrics illustrated by such song titles as *The Hedgehog's Song*, *The Mad Hatter's Song* and *My Name Is Death*.

Embraced by Britain's hippie culture, the Incredible String Band straddled both the folk and rock world with its fresh and exhilarating approach to acoustic music. In one memorable week in 1967, Williamson and Heron shared a bill with Shirley Collins at London's Queen Elizabeth Hall and then opened for Pink Floyd at the Saville Theatre. *The Hangman's Beautiful Daughter*, released in 1968, resounded with their ingenuity, spirituality and humor. As Robin Denselow notes in *The Electric Muse*: "On *The Hangman's Beautiful Daughter*, they managed to combine such oddities as a wailing chant in honor of the powers of water with a Gilbert and Sullivan spoof, *The Minotaur Song.*" Denselow goes on to comment on the songs' "mystical, pantheist involvement in a very live universe." He was particularly taken with "a gently swinging version of the Pindar Family spiritual *Bid You Goodnight*" which "ends with a repeated universal benediction: May the long-time sun shine on you, all love surround you, and the pure light within you guide you all the way on."

Williamson and Heron recorded one more milestone — the double album *Wee Tam And The Big Huge*, released in 1968 — before their creativity began to falter. *Wee Tam* extended into country, calypso and jug band music, with the usual garnish of comical and celestial lyrics. Like its two predecessors, it peaked high on the British album charts. The Incredible String Band toured Europe and America in triumph — indeed, it was the first band booked for Woodstock. But after that, the spark of enthusiasm, excitement and idealism in their work began to diminish. Out went their intriguing acoustic instruments to be replaced by the standard rock line-up of electric guitars, bass and drums. While they struggled on until 1974, they were truly well-spent before they finally called it a day.

But, *Way Back In The 1960s* — to quote a song title from *5,000 Spirits* — nobody took more advantage of the elusive idealism of flower power than Donovan Leitch, "Britain's answer to Bob Dylan." Donovan was born in 1946 in a Glasgow slum but raised in London. After an aborted attempt at art college, he wandered around Britain in 1964, writing songs and performing at the occasional folk club. A demo tape he made impressed a talent scout at the influential BBC Television rock program *Ready Steady Go*. His appearances there led to a contract with Pye Records and his debut single, *Catch The Wind*, made the British Top Ten. Strumming on an acoustic guitar and blowing into a harmonica, comparisons to Dylan were inevitable. A superb cover of Buffy Sainte-Marie's *Universal Soldier*, though, ended Donovan's interest in "protest" folk songs and his writing started to reflect the cultural romanticism of the times. From 1965 to 1969, he recorded a string of immensely successful flower-power anthems — *Sunshine Superman*, *Mellow Yellow*, *A Gift From A Flower To A Garden* — before fading into oblivion in the cynical seventies.

Back in the traditionalist camp, all was not well, either. While Pentangle and the Incredible String Band breathed new life into old songs in concert halls around the world, in the folk clubs of Britain the purists dug in their heels. Traditional songs, after all, were sacred and not to be tampered with — or so they thought. Martin Carthy, in an interview with Ken Hunt for *Folk Roots*, still recalls the negative reaction created by his initial duets with fiddler Dave Swarbrick: "People like Ewan MacColl and Peggy Seeger were very dismissive of him and said he was too jazzy, whatever the hell that meant. To them jazzy was a term of abuse." Swarbrick's contempt for such narrow-mindedness matches Carthy's: "I didn't like seven-eighths of the people involved in the folk club scene. They made it insular; they made their own laws and they were so strict that you couldn't go outside them."

Ultimately, the rigidity of folk clubs discouraged the development of young performers. Elvis

(EFMF)

Long John Baldry, on stage in 1983, played with the pivotal Blues Incorporated before enjoying an influential solo career

Costello's experience at the Crypt in Richmond serves as a prime example. "The very first time I played in public I was a floor singer and Ewan MacColl was the main singer. I got up with my little guitar, and I was fifteen or something, and he sat in the front, head bowed all the way through my set; and I'm sure he just nodded off," he told *Folk Roots* in 1989. "So I had this old bloke falling asleep, or pretending to fall asleep, during my song — as you can imagine, that was pretty crushing." Costello got his revenge years later when he produced The Pogues' second album *Rum, Sodomy And The Lash* and had them "trash" MacColl's *Dirty Old Town*.

♪ ♪ ♪

By the late sixties, traditional folk music needed a creative boost to replenish its vitality and broaden its appeal. Along came Fairport Convention. Formed in 1967 in Muswell Hill, London, the original lineup consisted of Ashley "Tyger" Hutchings (bass), Richard Thompson (guitar), and Simon Nicol (guitar). "I was younger than 15 when Ashley Hutchings contacted me because I was the only kid in Muswell Hill who owned a twelve-string guitar. Ashley was running several bands with different musical policies, and there was an opening for a jangly acoustic noise," Nicol told John Tobler of *Folk Roots*. Hutchings also brought Thompson into the fold on a friend's recommendation. At their first gig in a church hall, Martin Lamble emerged from the audience to offer his services as a drummer. They also added local librarian Judy Dyble, "because we decided we should get someone who could sing."

Initially, this band knew nothing about British traditional music. Hutchings, Thompson and Nicol started out as a jug band and moved towards Bob Dylan, The Byrds and Joni Mitchell as their numbers increased. While this repertoire offered nothing new in terms of the development of folk-rock, it did land them a crucial gig at the UFO, a London underground dance hall where Pink Floyd frequently performed. Joe Boyd, producer for the Incredible String Band, spotted them there and helped them sign to Polydor Records. But before Fairport Convention released its self-titled debut album, it recruited Ian Matthews (then known as Ian MacDonald) from a local pop band to bolster Dyble's shaky vocals. That initial recording deservedly drew little reaction and Dyble left. Over the next twenty-six years, Fairport Convention would make twenty-two changes to its lineup, but possibly none as important as recruiting Sandy Denny.

Denny already enjoyed a considerable reputation around London's folk scene as an exquisite singer with a repertoire of contemporary North American standards as well as traditional English, Irish and Scottish folk songs. Her debut album with Fairport — *What We Did On Our Holidays*, released in 1969 — paid the mandatory compliments to Dylan and Mitchell, but it also featured the traditional *Nottamun Town* (already rejuvenated by Davey Graham and Bert Jansch and its melody used by Bob Dylan for *Masters of War*, which, no doubt, added to its credibility) and *She Moved Through The Fair*. This turned out to be a monumental move, but at the time: "We just asked Sandy to sing some of her favorite songs," says Nicol, "and we tried to follow her." As casually as that, British folk-rock made its modest debut.

What We Did On Our Holidays also featured Richard Thompson's rousing *Meet On The Ledge* (his first recorded solo composition) and Denny's moody *Fotheringay*. Then, midway through recording their next album, *Unhalfbricking*, Matthews left to form Matthews Southern Comfort and promptly recorded a chart-topping version of Joni Mitchell's *Woodstock*. Fairport , however, soldiered on with session fiddler Dave Swarbrick — a veteran of the Ian Campbell Folk Group and partner of Martin Carthy. "Before the session," remembers Carthy, "he was going around saying, 'Joe Boyd's asked me to do this bloody session. I don't know what the fuck I'm going to do! If it was jazz it'd be all right, but it's

(EFMF)

Donovan Leitch (who drew a large crowd in 1986) was hyped as Britain's Dylan but became famous for his flower-power anthems

bleeding rock 'n' roll. I can't stand it.' He came back the following evening and he said, 'I hope you don't take this amiss, but it's great.'"

Oddly enough, the new album included only one traditional song, the superb *A Sailor's Life*. Dylan songs, albeit such rarities as *Million Dollar Bash*, *Percy's Song* and *Si Tu Dois Partir* — a French translation of *If You've Gottta Go, Go Now* — still featured prominently. Yet much to everyone's surprise, *Si Tu Dois Partir* became Fairport's only hit single. Before *Unhalfbricking* was released, drummer Martin Lamble died in a road accident. To cope with the trauma, the survivors added Swarbrick on a permanent basis, replaced Lamble with Dave Mattacks and plunged headlong into recording the landmark *Liege And Lief* — eight extraordinary tracks taken either from the folk music tradition of the British Isles or inspired by it. Epic ballads like *Matty Groves*, *The Deserter* and *Tam Lin* were dusted off and restored with exhilarating vitality. Amid these splendid tales of murder, mayhem and magic, the band added such spirited instrumentals as *Rakish Paddy*, *Toss The Feathers* and *The Lark In The Morning*. Even the hippest laid-back audiences in London danced to these jigs.

Acclaimed as a critical and commercial success, *Liege And Lief* brought traditional British folk music out of the clubs and exposed it to a new, young audience. Even MacColl's former partner A. L. (Bert) Lloyd approved of their efforts. Within months of its release, though, Denny left to pursue a solo career and Hutchings went off to form Steeleye Span. Those that remained recruited bass guitarist Dave Pegg from the Ian Campbell Folk Group. Sandy Denny, they reckoned, was irreplaceable. So Fairport Convention continued as a five-piece and recorded *Full House* in America in 1970. Only half its tracks featured traditional material. Thompson came up with several original gems before he too quit and turned solo. And, to make matters worse, manager Joe Boyd left to work in California. From then until the band prematurely called it a day in 1979, the lineup and consistency of its recordings varied greatly. Brought out of mothballs six years later, Fairport finally stabilized its roster and released a string of credible albums.

♪ ♪ ♪

While Fairport Convention was a rock band that drifted into folk music, Steeleye Span chose "not to be a rock band but traditional musicians working with electric instruments," Robin Denselow wrote. With most of its personnel veterans of the folk club circuit, and an essentially all-traditional repertoire, Steeleye developed into Britain's most successful folk-rock act of the seventies. Like most bands, though, it had its share of teething trouble. The initial lineup of Tim Hart (multi-instrumentalist), Maddy Prior (vocals), Ashley "Tyger" Hutchings (bass) and Gay (vocals) and Terry Woods (multi-instrumentalist) lasted as long as it took to record the stylish *Hark! The Village Wait* album, but never performed live. The Woods left because of artistic differences (Terry now performs with The Pogues). So the band added Martin Carthy on electric guitar and unknown fiddler Peter Knight. This combo recorded two albums — the brilliant *Please To See The King* and the tasteful *Ten Man Mop* before Hutchings left to form the Albion Band and Carthy returned to solo work. Their replacements Rick Kemp (a former bass player with Mike Chapman and King Crimson) and Bob Johnson (a one-time guitarist with Gary Glitter) added a more robust, rockier edge to the band.

With this lineup in place, Steeleye Span scored its first of several British hits in 1973 with an *a cappella* version of *Gaudete*. A year later session' drummer Nigel Pegrum contributed to the album *Parcel Of Rogues* then joined the band on a full time basis for the aptly titled *Now We Are Six*. Produced by Jethro Tull's Ian Anderson, it featured David Bowie on sax on *To Know Him Is To Love Him*.

British folk-rock had come a long way from the first innocent strains of Fairport Convention's *Nottamun Town*. Massive tours of America, Europe and Australia supporting acts like J. Geils and Jethro Tull, sharpened Steeleye's live performances. "If you're trying to reach the back of the L.A. Forum, you learn to perform, because there's 18,000 people there and the furthest ones miles away at the top of this bowl have paid $6 and want to be entertained," Tim Hart told John Tobler of *Folk Roots*. On stage, Steeleye Span dressed in traditional mummers' costumes and sang and danced about the soul's journey from the corpse to purgatory, or allegories about the death of winter and birth of spring. These tales were enhanced with pre-recorded tapes, expensive, subtle lighting and the best P.A. systems money could rent. "We wanted to go out there with the Jethro Tulls and the Sha Na Nas and The Beach Boys and all the other people we were gigging with and actually be on par with those bands. We didn't want to be in this strange folk-rock category that seemed to have a ceiling to it, which I never recognized."

For a while at least, Steeleye Span ran neck and neck with rock's elite. By 1983, though, the band had pretty well run its course. Despite the occasional record and tour, Steeleye today hardly represents the determined, open-minded innovators of the past. As Tim Hart once remarked: "We are the first people to come out of the folk-club scene since Ewan MacColl to actually do something to English folk music." And who could argue with that? Certainly not such brash young upstarts as The Pogues, The Men They Couldn't Hang, and The Foot-Tappers who sat in the wings poised to grab the folk music establishment by the scruff of its elitist neck.

Selected recordings

Ewan McColl: Black and White (Green Linnet 3052)
Lonnie Donegan: The Best Of Lonnie Donegan (Pickwick PWK-076)
Martin Carthy and Dave Swarbrick: Life And Limb (Green Linnet 3052)
Davey Graham: Folk Blues And Beyond (Deram 820988-2)
Pentangle: Cruel Sister (Transatlantic TACD-90058)
Incredible String Band: The Hangman's Beautiful Daughter (Electra 7559-60835-2)
Donovan: Donovan's Greatest Hits (Epic WEK-26439)
Fairport Convention: Liege and Lief (A&M CD-4257)
Steeleye Span: All Around My Hat (Shanachie 79059).

7

Alberta Bound

- After the gold rush ▪ Joni in the Army
and Navy basement
▪ The pre-festivals ▪ Year One at
Goldbar Park ▪ Year Two at Gallagher
▪ k.d. lang blows everybody away ▪

"I've been going to folk festivals since 1965, so I don't say lightly that the 1983 Edmonton (Alberta) Folk Music Festival was one of the two or three finest festivals I've ever attended."
— EMILY FRIEDMAN, EDITOR OF THE VENERABLE AMERICAN FOLK MAGAZINE, COME FOR TO SING.

"THE CAPITAL OF ALBERTA is a city you come from, not a place to visit," Canadian author Mordecai Richler wrote in the *New York Times* in 1984. "On first glance and even third, it seems not so much a city as a jumble of a used-building lot, where the spare office towers and box-shaped apartment buildings and cinder block motels discarded in the construction of real cities have been abandoned to waste away in the cruel Prairie winter."

Since former smuggler Anthony Henday first set foot in the area in 1754, Edmonton has grown erratically, buffeted by periodic boom-to-bust swings in the economy. The Hudson's Bay Company actually built the first Fort Edmonton almost twenty miles east near modern Fort Saskatchewan. But by 1813, Edmonton House sat within the boundaries of the present city and soon became the headquarters of the fur trade for all of the western prairies. Free land brought settlers and the Klondike gold rush brought prosperity. In 1905, Prime Minister Wilfrid Laurier's

Liberals made Edmonton the capital of the new province of Alberta. Calgary, godammit, had voted for the opposition Conservatives in the previous federal election. To add insult to injury, constituency boundaries were then rigged to ensure a Liberal victory in the first provincial election.

The city more or less prospered until the world economy collapsed in 1929 and forced one in seven local families onto relief — a crude forerunner to welfare. It took the Second World War to reverse this calamity. After the Japanese bombed Pearl Harbor, America suspected Alaska was next and jumped to defend it. In one day in 1943, Edmonton's Blatchford Field airport refuelled eight-hundred and sixty planes headed north. The Americans constructed a second airfield at Namao, ten miles from the city centre, and then built the Alaska Highway — 1,523 miles in nine months — from Fairbanks to Edmonton, the gateway to the North.

And its luck held. The oil discovery at nearby Leduc in 1947 turned Edmonton into a major refining and petrochemical centre. Oil created jobs and between 1946 and 1971 the population jumped from just over 100,000 to 400,000, making Edmonton one of the fastest growing cities in North America. As OPEC pushed the price of oil up and up, the value of new building permits rose to $1.7 billion dollars a year until 1981, when the roof caved in. The cost of oil plummeted, sending the local economy into a tailspin from which it had not, by the mid 1990s, fully recovered.

♪   ♪   ♪

Donald Lewis Whalen grew up in Nova Scotia and studied at Dalhousie University in Halifax in the early sixties. During summer breaks, he ran the Halifax Jazz Society and worked with such performers as future vibes giant Gary Burton. "I had no fear of dealing with musicians after that," Whalen said in an interview for this book. "It was a good start for me interacting with people in the music community." He also balanced the lighting and sound at concerts on campus. When Pete Seeger performed at Dalhousie in 1960, Whalen took care of the technical production. "I had never been so enthralled or moved by a person musically up until that point. I was mesmerised totally by Seeger and had a chance to meet with him and talk with him. He came down to our fraternity after the concert and had a couple of drinks with us and we started talking about folk culture in Nova Scotia. And he more or less gave me a nudge and said what have you collected?"

That prod from Seeger inspired Whalen to locate and record traditional Maritime singers. He also collected imported folk albums, which his buddy Denny Doherty — the future Mama and Papa — scoured for material for his band, The Colonials. Whalen bought his vinyl at Bly Records in Halifax. The great ballad singer Finvola Redden worked behind the counter and they became friends. When Redden was invited to perform at the first Mariposa Folk Festival, Whalen too drove to Orillia for the merriment. "I went to the first two, actually. The interest in folk festivals started growing, dwelling in me from there on."

The University of Alberta offered the best scholarships in the country at the time, so Whalen packed his bags and set off for the prairies, hoping to earn a PhD in

(EFMF)

Don Whalen in the spotlight in 1981 . . . without him there would have been no second festival

chemistry. While his academic pursuits demanded much of his time, The Edmonton Folk Music Society met his recreational needs. It ran concerts most weekends in the Yardbird Suite in the basement of the Army and Navy store on Whyte Avenue. Joni Anderson often performed there before she became Joni Mitchell. Various other coffee houses — The Barricade, The Albany, The Forum — also opened and closed around town. Whalen attended these venues as a spectator. He did occasionally handle publicity for local rock promoter Benny Benjamin, who booked the likes of The Who, Jethro Tull and Iron Butterfly into the Edmonton Gardens — a hockey rink and the largest venue in town at the time. "It gave me a chance to see how the concerts were staged, and the planning and the promoting end of it."

Whalen's first serious attempt at promoting folk music began at The Hovel coffee house on the corner of Jasper Avenue and 109 Street. Opened in 1973 by Andy Laskiwsky — a future general manager of the folk festival — The Hovel brought the best of North American folk, blues and bluegrass to Edmonton and quickly became the venue in town to hear live music. Little more than a year after its doors opened, Laskiwsky took off on an extended trip throughout Asia and left Whalen in charge. Science had long lost its allure but his involvement with Benny Benjamin gave him coffee house credibility. So Whalen ran The Hovel full time — often wearing a gas mask because he's allergic to cigarette smoke — until the fall of 1975. By then, his extensive network of contacts allowed him to form his own company, Yardbird Productions, which eventually brought the likes of Arlo Guthrie and John Prine to local concert halls.

♪   ♪   ♪

The local folk scene was also growing on other fronts. The Citizen's Advocacy Society — an Edmonton support group for the disabled — organized a one-day folk festival in August 1976. Five thousand turned up at the Kinsmen Park to hear such headline performers as Bim (Roy Forbes) and Paul Hann. Its success inspired the Universal Folklore Society to stage the three-day Wild Rose Folk Fair at nearby Lake Eden the following year. That festival featured such acts as Valdy, Pied Pear and an unknown singer from the American Midwest by the name of John Hiatt. Society members dug into their own pockets for funding, and 20,000 folk enthusiasts turned up to justify their faith. Gordon MacGregor — another one-time Benny Benjamin associate — produced both of these events and Whalen helped with the booking. In 1978, the fair moved south of the city to the Opalinski Ranch near Ellerslie. Torrential rain, however, turned the site into a swamp and forced MacGregor to reduce all performances to a single day. The Wild Rose Folk Fair never ran again.

Elsewhere in Western Canada, folk festivals were flourishing in 1978. The small, intimate Regina Folk Arts Festival celebrated its eleventh year in existence. The Yukon's Farrago Folk Festival reached five, as did The Winnipeg Folk Festival — now considered the premier event of its kind in North America. Vancouver made an impressive debut and plans were underway for the first Red Deer International Folk Festival and the North Country Fair on the shores of Lesser Slave Lake.

In the fall, Don Whalen and Mitch Podolak approached provincial culture minister Horst Schmid for funding for a festival in Edmonton. Schmid supported the idea as did city alderman Bettie Hewes (now a Liberal MLA for Edmonton-Goldbar). Podolak often drove from Winnipeg to participate in further negotiations with various levels of government throughout the following year. Finally, as Alberta approached its seventy-fifth anniversary in 1980, the provincial government allocated seventy-five million dollars for the celebrations. The Edmonton Folk Music Festival received eighty-nine thousand dollars. As general manager and artistic director, Whalen structured it as a not-for-profit organization with a non-voting membership limited to fifty. He also appointed a board of six directors, with Holger Petersen as

Russ Hewitt (EFMF)

Garnet and Stan Rogers at the Edmonton fest . . . Stan played at first three festivals before his death in an airplane fire

chairman. Petersen owned Stony Plain Records and hosted two blues programs on CKUA Radio.

Now the preparations began in earnest. "My biggest concern was whether we would have the volunteer contingent necessary to do it," says Whalen. "Winnipeg had two or three hundred at the time and it seemed like a pretty big thing to ask from a community that never really had a folk festival before." So he ran advertisements in local newspapers and held a recruitment meeting at Grant MacEwan Community College. He expected a hundred to turn up but twice that many appeared. "From that point, I knew we had it. There was no question. I knew we had what we needed to make it work." Besides, the 75th anniversary committee had hired Mitch Podolak to assemble a troupe of folk singers to tour rural communities from High River to Fort McMurray. With a $120,000 budget, Mitch packed an old school bus with Sylvia Tyson (now separated from Ian and performing with a band, The Great Speckled Bird), John Allan Cameron, Paul Hann, Joan MacIsaac, Stringband, Duck Donald's Bluegrass Band, Jim Post and Stan Rogers. This Travelling Goodtime Alberta Medicine Show provided many of the artists and a significant sound system for the first festival.

For experience, Whalen sent volunteer coordinator Nora Specht to Winnipeg to train under her counterpart, Rosalie Goldstein. Nelson Whalen, Don's brother, went too. He had to learn the ropes as production manager.

EFMF)

Loudon Wainright III offended some in '82, and was quite prepared to do so again in 1983

"From there on it was just a matter of fly by the seat of your pants and work your ass off and try and get everything done." Fortunately, the North American folk festival circuit attracted such rolling stones as J.B. from California, Bush from Minnesota and McGowan from Manitoba, who wandered from one event to the next constructing site after site for free meals. Their considerable experience eased the pressure on rookie Nelson Whalen. "If we didn't have people like Bush, we wouldn't have gotten our stage up. He knew what he was doing right off the bat," recalls Agnes Brennan, then a volunteer and later chairman of the board.

Don Whalen booked fifty-six acts and master of ceremonies Peter Gzowski — now host of CBC Radio's *Morningside* — for the initial lineup. It included such icons as Odetta (an inspiration for both Bob Dylan and Joan Baez), Robin Williamson (of Incredible String Band fame), Doug Dillard (the contemporary bluegrass pioneer) and Sylvia Tyson.

For the most part, the bill remained typical of the times. Singer-songwriters dominated on all fronts. Only the panpipes of Sukay, a South American quartet based in Montreal, really broke the mould. Non-North Americans consisted of Scots Robin Williamson, Hamish Imlach, Cilla Fisher and Artie Trezise. All performers were paid similar rates and acoustic instruments were mandatory — a policy Whalen had mixed feelings about. "It was one of the things that Mitch was really pushy about. I thought, 'Fine,' not to make waves the first year."

The first year ran from August 8 to 10 in Goldbar Park, which lies in the northeast end of the city, between the Imperial Oil refinery and the affluent neighborhood of Goldbar. "You're surrounded by suburbia and the refineries on the other side, and the people's folk festival here. It was so incongruous in a way because there was still a few of the old traditional lefties there . . . surrounded by split-levels and Imperial Oil. That was really funny," recalls Alan Kellogg, a reporter for *The Edmonton Journal* at the time and now its entertainment columnist. Out of the way and difficult to reach, Goldbar Park turned out to be a poor site. Buses dropped fans blocks away from the main gate. From there, they still had a stiff walk. Horses and carts transported some of the more weary to the box office, where a weekend pass cost $23 — $20 if bought in advance.

The first act ever to perform at the Edmonton Folk Music Festival walked out on stage at 7 p.m. on Friday night. Wheatland County took their local brand of bluegrass to the masses. "There weren't that many people there. It was almost a bit of a letdown," says bass player Del Cocks. "We sang well in the situation. We did have friends in the audience and we thought, 'Well, we'll play for them at least'." They impressed Alan Kellogg, who wrote: "Wheatland County kicked things off with a finely honed set of bluegrass standards." Kellogg also praised their "tight, crisp harmonies and considerable knowledge of craft." However, Winnipeg's raucous blues band Houndog created the biggest buzz of the evening before mainstage closed at 10:30.

Overall, the reviews were complimentary. Kellogg figured Debby McClatchy's set of Appalachian ballads dragged. And his *Journal* colleague Graham Hicks reckoned Robin Williamson's lyrics were a pale imitation of Dylan Thomas's, while The Doug Dillard Band was "satisfying, but not exciting. Competent, but lacking any element of surprise." Tom Elsworthy at *The Edmonton Sun* gave the festival his full endorsement. Odetta and Stan Rogers, by all accounts, turned in two of the weekend's strongest performances. As the Sunday night finale loomed, Whalen lined his brawniest security guards along the front of the stage in case fans stormed the barricades. It was time for the traditional last song.

"Everybody was up on stage, you know, all these Americans and the rest of it," Kellogg remembers. "And Stan Rogers just shoots right to the front and instead of doing something everybody knows, he does this new *a cappella* song he'd written, *Barrett's Privateers*. Nobody knows one bloody lyric to it. There's no chorus, essentially. And you see Odetta and Wheatland County stumbling around. It was the perfect embodiment of Stan. On the one hand it was one of the most grotesquely egocentric tricks imaginable; at the same time there was something beautiful about that, you know. What chutzpah! What balls! Notwithstanding the fact that it is a brilliant bloody song."

Finally Odetta brought the weekend's festivies to a close with a moving rendition of *Amazing Grace*. And nobody rioted. "I just remem-

k.d. lang workshops in her debut year, 1984 (EFMF)

ber it as being a very pleasant time, the quintessential folk festival experience," says Hicks, now a columnist with *The Sun*.

♪ ♪ ♪

Close to seven thousand folk music fans trekked through the turnstiles for that first event. It still lost almost $70,000. Creditors would have to wait until after festival Number Two. Whalen hoped for a city grant from SummerFest, the board set up to fund the city's summer arts festivals. He was in for a shock. Out of the $600,000 up for grabs, the folk festival received not one brass button. The bulk of the money went to Northern Light Theatre. Its former chairman, Ken Chapman, now presided over SummerFest's interim committee. Whalen had expected $50,000 and wrote to the mayor and city council in protest. Again, Alderman Bettie Hewes sat in his corner. She advised him to approach Chapman again. Second time around, SummerFest came up with $15,000 in cash and an office. "Don was absolutely dogged in his persistence of having a major folk festival in Edmonton," says Holger Petersen. "Without that persistence, the festival would have stopped there. Had he not called in all of his favors that second year and done a real minimal, cheap festival — the best that could be done under the circumstances — it would have died." Whalen appealed to numerous acts he had worked with in the past to perform for expenses or reduced fees. Many, including Odetta and Stan Rogers agreed.

A second break came Whalen's way when the city proposed that Gallagher Park replace Goldbar as a site for the festival. Named after meat-packing entrepreneur Cornelius Gallagher—mayor of Edmonton in 1896 — it sits in the heart of the river valley on the edge of the prosperous community of Cloverdale, Gallagher Park consists of a flat field surrounded by steep slopes that offer a panoramic view of the city skyline. "I remember the first day I drove over and looked at it from Cloverdale, and thought there is no goddamn way you can hold a folk festival here," recalls Whalen. "But when I drove up to the top of the hill and looked down, it was magic! This was it. 'We can make it happen here'." Easily accessible by bus or bike and close to downtown, the park became the festival's permanent home.

Despite a financial handicap, Whalen put together a stronger and more diverse bill on his second try. This time, he offered thirty-four acts and Peter Gzowski instead of fifty-six. "Gzowski was a wise choice because it gave people somebody they wanted to listen to between acts," notes Tom Elsworthy. Aside from Odetta, the quota of living legends included Woody Guthrie's pals Sonny Terry and Brownie McGhee, and Tom Paley, a founding member of the New Lost City Ramblers. Tom Paxton — a stalwart of the original Greenwich Village coffee house scene and now an international celebrity — turned up. So did the brilliant Louisiana-born songwriter Jesse Winchester. The first Celtic music arrived with Kevin Burke & Michael O'Domhnaill, two former members of Ireland's pioneering Bothy Band. Ferron, arguably the best songwriter in the country at the time, also made her debut. And, on the family stage, Fred Penner entertained children of all ages.

The Empire Strikes Back was running in the cinemas the weekend the festival mounted its own sequel. A local part-time bluegrass combo, the River City Ramblers, opened Friday night. "We were just a garage band that got out of hand," recalls guitarist Bob Remington, now the entertainment editor of *The Edmonton Journal*. "Because we were so inexperienced, non-professional musicians, we went out there and didn't take time for a sound check. I couldn't hear my guitar in the monitors or anything like that. I don't know how we sounded. Probably awful." As for the new site? "It was obviously such a brilliant spot," says bass player Mike Sadava. "What a perfect place for a festival."

Local folk fans certainly thought so. Ten thousand of them turned up to soak up the ambiance and three days of glorious sunshine. Reviews were again overwhelmingly positive, with Jesse Winchester the unanimous highlight. The festival had not only survived but thrived.

♪   ♪   ♪

Funding now became more or less a formality. The federal, provincial, and municipal governments all provided grants for 1982. CBC Radio paid generously to record various performers and Labatt Brewery provided the festival's first major sponsorship. With financial pressures eased somewhat, Whalen could now pay full fees and extend his lineup to fifty-five acts. No Peter Gzowski, though. He had completed two years of research on the Edmonton Oilers for his book, *The Game of Our Lives*, and moved back East. Quebecois culture made its debut, courtesy of Alain Lamontange and Eritage. Electric bluesmen Clarence Gatemouth Brown, Amos Garrett, Tom See and David Wilcox finally ended the all-acoustic policy. And the list of seasoned statesmen grew to include Ramblin' Jack Elliott, Dave Van Ronk, Doc Watson and former New York radio host Oscar Brand, who had provided The Weavers with their first gig in 1949. When the dust had settled on Monday morning, the headline in *The Journal* read, "Festival nearing big league status."

♪   ♪   ♪

Sadly, Stan Rogers' third straight appearance turned out to be his last. The following June he died tragically, trapped in a burning plane after an emergency landing in Cincinnati. He was thirty-three. "I had such a strong admiration for his ability," says Whalen. "There was no question the guy was an icon. After the second year he was here, I said, 'Stan this festival is open to you every year. I want you to phone and tell me if you can play. Yes or No. Just phone me and tell me. The invitation is out and is permanent.' Unfortunately we weren't able to extend it as far as we would have liked." Instead, Whalen invited Stan's wife Ariel to sing the festival's closing song in 1983 — her husband's immortal *Mary Ellen Carter*. "It was my intention that it would be the closing song for the future of Edmonton," says Whalen. "It hasn't worked out that way but it certainly was for 1983, '84 and '85."

In July, Whalen received a second blow. David Bowie announced his Serious Moonlight Tour would play the city's Commonwealth Stadium the same weekend as the 1983 festival. Peter Gabriel and The Tubes opened in serious daylight as 57,000 looked on. In Gallagher Park, Blues legend Willie Dixon, original Byrd Chris Hillman, and the demented genius of Loudon Wainwright III attracted a smaller audience but created more controversy. "Sexist pig! Sexist pig!" chanted a group of feminists as Wainwright sang about turning the frozen body of his dead girlfriend into a surfboard. That didn't seem to bother Emily Friedman,

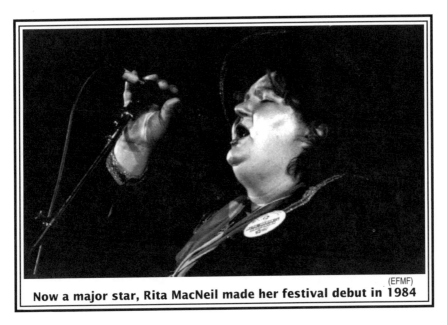

(EFMF)
Now a major star, Rita MacNeil made her festival debut in 1984

editor of the venerable American folk magazine, *Come For To Sing*. Friedman wrote: "I've been going to folk festivals since 1965, so I don't say lightly that the 1983 Edmonton (Alberta) Folk Music Festival was one of the two or three finest festivals I've ever attended." The record weekend crowd of sixteen thousand merely added icing to an already ornate cake.

♪   ♪   ♪

While the festival has presented hundreds of acts over the years, only a handful of performances have passed into local mythology. k.d lang's electrifying Friday night set in 1984 certainly was one. With her debut album, *A Truly Western Experience*, still weeks away, the 22-year-old lang followed Sylvia Tyson on the main stage just as day turned to night. Evening sets normally run for thirty minutes, but the next act, songwriter Peter Rowan and fiddler Mark O'Connor, arrived on site late. Which left lang and her band, The Reclines, with an hour on stage to build up a full head of steam. "I remember the place was struck by a lightning bolt," recalls Peter North, now an entertainment writer with *The Edmonton Sun*. "It was like going from this one plateau to another planet. It was really apparent at that point she was going to go through the roof."

Born in Consort (population 674) in central Alberta, lang had spent the past year in Edmonton developing her cowpunk image — complete with androgynous haircut and cat's-eye glasses with no lenses. She named her band of local musicians The Reclines after country legend

Patsy Cline. k.d. considered herself a reincarnation of Patsy and few doubted her that night. As Stewart McDougall, one of the Reclines recalls: "She was in great voice and knocked everybody dead. That was a big night. That was a lot of fun. It was definitely my most exciting moment on the main stage." McDougall now plays keyboards for the splendid Great Western Orchestra. That night also stands out for veteran festival goer Victor Lehman, who approached k.d. after her performance. "That voice just sort of rolled over the hill and I knew that this was something that was going to go somewhere. I told her that, and she sort of looked at me sheepishly." She didn't seem sure that she'd go much further. Wendy Soley, a Youth Emergency Shelter worker, was also in the audience: "She just blew everybody away. She certainly blew me away."

As it turned out, that night was the most pivotal of lang's career up to that point. Her manager, Larry Wanagas, and Peter North had tried unsuccessfully to get her exposure in Toronto through Richard Flohil, the former publicist with the Mariposa Folk Festival. That year he turned up in Edmonton to hear lang live for the first time. "Flohil went absolutely berserk," says North. "He went back to Toronto and did everything but stand on the street corner with a loud hailer after that performance. He beat the drum for her and booked a bunch of gigs. Once she got there the fanfare was so big that she had full houses — that festival gig really did help launch her down East."

lang's electrifying rock-a-billy-country-swing brought a new sense of aggression and energy to main stage and raised the audience's expectations for the future. No longer would it sit satisfied with songwriter after songwriter. It now needed a faster pace to produce that addictive surge of adrenaline. Country and bluegrass acts such as lang, Asleep At The Wheel, Red Clay Ramblers, Chris Hillman and Bernie Leadon, Peter Rowan and Mark O'Connor, Guy Clark, Dick Damron and Sylvia Tyson (the only veteran in the lineup) dominated in 1984. But Zydeco surfaced for the first time through Queen Ida. And Rita MacNeil, the pride of Big Pond, Cape Breton Island, made her first appearance. The daily headlines provided a credible synopsis: "Folk festival first evening hardly magic." "Stronger lineup on Day 2." "Folk festival deserves our continued support."

♪   ♪   ♪

Don Whalen remembers little about the winter of 1984-85. For the past five years, he had taught adult development courses at Grant MacEwan Community College full time, managed the folk festival, booked its winter concerts and run Yardbird Productions. Making do with very little sleep, "I was slowly starting to feel the impact. It was getting a lot harder to make decisions. It was just a continuous struggle and I was forcing myself to keep going and going." For the first time, he allowed outside influences to sway his artistic decisions. Mayor Laurence Decore, later the leader of the provincial Liberal Party, wanted to expand the festival's multicultural appeal and persuaded Whalen to book high-priced Greek dancer, Vassilios Papachristou. "I went along with it in hopes it was going to work. I saw the preview dance at the Library Theatre and felt my whole being going right down the drain. Like, 'What have I got myself into now? Why did I let this happen?' And then I said, 'I don't give a shit anymore. I've had it and I'm tired.' And I just didn't care."

Severe rain and hail lashed Whalen's sixth and final festival in 1985. Attendance dropped but Spirits were up. Spirit of the West, that is. Equal parts topical and whimsical, this brash, young, part-time trio from Vancouver took the passion of punk and tacked it onto a variety of chaotic Celtic reels and jigs to knock the crowd on its rear end, just as k.d. lang had done a year previously. "It totally changed our lives," says flautist Geoff Kelly. Their just-completed first album outsold every other artist in the festival's record tent, "which totally blew our minds. Through that festival we booked four or five festivals the next year and eventually got going. I doubt there will ever be a weekend like that again." Rogue folk had arrived.

For somebody who didn't care, Whalen still booked an appealing, eclectic lineup. Acts came from everywhere — from Australia (Judy Small) to Zimbabwe (Gwinyai & Sukutai Marimba Ensemble, who were actually based in Seattle) — and varied from the outrageous vaudeville of Al Simmons to the frenzied zydeco of the self-proclaimed prince of the genre, Stanley Dural Jr. And in Jesse Colin Young and the Youngbloods, Whalen had, for the first time, a name act with potential to extend the festival's appeal beyond its traditional audience. The Youngbloods had scored a massive pop hit in the late sixties with the hippie anthem, *Get Together*. However, the lack of incentive to purchase 'early bird' tickets — $30 in advance, $35 at the gate — and the inclement weather, reduced the audience to the diehard faithful. Around a thousand hardcore fans braved Sunday night's downpour to catch such tasteful mainstage acts as bluesman John Hammond Jr. and Buckwheat Zydeco.

Until that weekend, the festival had enjoyed a protracted period of grace with the local media. Now Alan Kellogg described it as "a bloated structure" and the workshop schedule as "ridiculous." He called for an overall reduction in the number of acts but an increase in name attractions. Secretly, he feared for the festival's survival: "I thought this form was pretty moribund. I thought it was heading for the tank. I still have criticisms about the slavish adherence to multiple workshop stages, but the form has shown that it's hardier than I thought it was. It has regenerated to some degree."

Behind the scenes, Whalen's autocratic style of management had begun to wear thin. Several volunteer co-ordinators expressed interest in contributing more to the corporate structure of the festival — a move supported by chairman Holger Petersen. This, after all, was a publicly funded event run, essentially, by volunteers. "Don played things pretty close to the chest so he never followed up on this," recalls Vicki Fannon.

On September 13, 1985, Donald Whalen, 47, pleaded not guilty in provincial court to three counts of gross indecency with three young boys. The festival's whole support network appeared ready to collapse as volunteers and board members grew polarized in their opinions on what to do next. It boiled down to two perspectives: Whalen could stay unless and until proven guilty, or he should go and save the festival from further negative publicity. Seven of the festival's staff of eight quit. Only Agnes Brennan remained. To deal with this crisis, Petersen called several meetings. When the smoke cleared, he reluctantly replaced Whalen as artistic director. Local writer Peggie Graham took over as chairman of a board now expanded to nine members, seven of whom came fresh from the ranks of the volunteers to join previous directors Silvio Dobri and Jan Kozina. The following March, Whalen was sentenced to five months in jail.

Selected recordings

Spirit of the West: Tripping Up The Stairs (Stony Plain SPCD 1098)
La Bottine Souriante: La Traverse De L'Atlantique (Green Linnet 3043)
Loudon Wainwright III: More Love Songs (Rounder CD 3106)
Willie Dixon: Chess Box Set (Chess CHD2-16500)
Tannahill Weavers: Passage (Green Linnet 3031)
Battlefield Band: Anthem For The Common Man (Temple Records COMD 2008)
Ferron: Testimony (Redwood Records LRCD 003)
k.d. lang: Truly Western Experience (WEA CD00086)
     Angel With A Lariat (Warner Bros. 25441)
     Shadowland (Sire CD-25724)
     Ingenue (WEA CD-26840)

From Austin to Addis Ababa

8

Jambalaya

■The singer-songwriters ■Celtic
renaissance ■Waulking in the rain
■Walking to New Orleans ■Tex-Mex
■The Blue Yodeller ■Limitless Austin
■Out of Africa ■Rogue Folk ■

---

*"There's a whole new approach to folk music evolving incited by a bunch of
bands and musicians — some of them even young for Godsake — who have
decided to swing a hefty boot into the crotch of convention. This new breed
are the rogue folk."*
— ENGLISH MUSIC CRITIC COLIN IRWIN

ELEBRATED ROCK CRITIC LESTER BANGS fantasized about
disembowelling James Taylor with the jagged edge of a broken
wine bottle. Rock was in decline and *Time* magazine had just
put Taylor on a March 1970 cover as a sign of growing maturity and
restraint in American pop culture. His album *Sweet Baby James*—a placid
combination of folk and jazz arrangements and intimate, autobiographical confessions of drug addiction and mental illness — dominated the
airwaves in the spring of Tom Wolfe's Me Decade. Taylor "conveyed
almost no sense that there was a big world out there, that there were
social issues and problems bigger than his own private obsessions,"wrote
Ken Tucker in *Rock of Ages.* Yet, his candid revelations of loneliness and
despair created the aura of an artist conquering his personal demons
through his creativity. Emotional disorder has frequently stimulated
great art throughout history, so Taylor was taken seriously. To distinguish his solemn confessions from standard lyricists, the term singer-
songwriter filtered into the lexicon of pop.

The keynote albums of this new genre belonged to Carole King (*Tapestry*), Neil Young (*Harvest*), Don McLean (*American Pie*), Jackson Browne (*Saturate Before Using*) and Joni Mitchell (*Blue*). Arguably, Mitchell expressed her self-absorption in more literate terms than her co-conspirators. Unlike other women who emerged from the coffee houses, she wrote all her own songs. Her lyrics consistently expressed a female point of view, which also made them unique. *Blue* follows Mitchell through a cycle of love songs that starts carefree and optimistic but concludes in despair as she grows disenchanted with her commitment to romanticism. But rather than wallow in self-pity and narcissism, she continually struggles to find meaning in her broken relationships through incisive, conversational lyrics backed with beautifully, complex melodies — maturity that put her on a pedestal.

As these singer-songwriters cornered the album market, the floodgates fell off their hinges. Now, almost anyone with a used copy of Sylvia Plath's *The Bell Jar* and an acoustic guitar could pick up a recording contract. Conceited, tedious, monotone navel-gazing soon became the order of the day and opened the door for such lightweights as Jim Croce, Harry Chapin and John Denver. Folk had by now lost its soul and needed a potent, new thrust to dispel the jeers and derisory cliches. The Celts lit the fuse.

♪   ♪   ♪

The traditional Irish music revival began around the same time as the hootenanny craze got off the ground in North America. In 1959, uillean piper Leo Rowstone recorded *King of the Irish Pipers*, the first Irish-made album of traditional music. The same year Sean O'Riada (1931-1971) released *Mise Eire* (I Am Ireland), an album of orchestral arrangements of traditional airs. O'Riada was assistant director of music for RTE, the national broadcasting organization. RTE made films for television and O'Riada and his band, Ceoltoiri Chualann (the Musicians of Cuala, an old name for south Dublin), arranged the scores. His big breakthrough came in 1962, when he used traditional instruments — an accordion, tin whistles and uileann (elbow) pipes — for the soundtrack of a film adaptation of John Millington Synge's play *The Playboy of The Western World*.

Paddy Moloney, the guiding light behind The Chieftains, played with Ceoltoiri Chualann back then. "The genius was in (O'Riada's) arrangements," Moloney told *Folk Roots*. "His arrangements made me sit up. They made everybody sit up. Thank God he happened. He contributed." Back then, traditional music was considered old fashioned, played by cultchies (a derogatory term for the rural population) for dances, weddings and wakes. For all of its brilliance, it could have remained a functional music. "O'Riada was the watershed," wrote Irish journalist Joe Crane in *Folk Roots*. "After his involvement with Ceoltoiri Chualann, the music was experimented with, its possibilities were recognized, stretched and adapted, and could evolve once more."

Paddy Moloney did his fair share. While still with Sean O'Riada, Moloney and several other members of Ceoltoiri Chualann began experimenting with their own arrangements under the banner of The Chieftains. Formed in 1961, they recorded their debut album four years later. Throughout the next decade, they held day jobs, recorded occasionally and built an impressive list of admirers: Mick Jagger, Paul McCartney, Peter Sellers, Roger Daltry. In 1974, the persuasive British weekly music paper *Melody Maker* nominated The Chieftains band of the year above the likes of The Who, Led Zeppelin and Pink Floyd. In a 1991 article in *Folk Roots*, Colin Irwin recalls interviewing fiddler Martin Fay on the phone in the seventies for Melody Maker. He "was amazed to be put on hold at regular intervals while Fay retired to serve a customer in the post office where he worked."

The soundtrack for *Barry Lyndon* landed The Chieftains an Oscar in 1975, which broke them in North America. Propelled by an immense distaste for complacency, they continued making innovative and appealing albums: *Bonaparte's Retreat* (the first acoustic concept album), *Another Country* (which featured the cream of Nashville's country and bluegrass musicians), *The Chieftains In China* (a live album recorded with various traditional Chinese instrumentalists), and the grandaddy of them all, *Irish Heartbeat* (a collaboration with rock god Van Morrison). Working with Morrison was "an amazing adventure," but it had its ups and downs, says Moloney. "I mean the guy is a genius in his own right. And he's a poet and a good musician. He has tremendous charisma. He's different, let's put it that way. When we met him at first, we spoke for six months about nothing. He was in one of those frames of minds, you know. All of a sudden there was a streak of hilarious laughing that went on. Then we went for a walk around Stephen's Green in Dublin and planned it. I did the shapes as he calls them — the arrangements. And he was delighted. We went into the studio for one week and that was it. Then we went on tour for about six months."

And then there was the other side of the Irish coin: The Clancy Brothers & Tommy Maken and The Dubliners, with their big, bruising, blustery, ballads and rafter-raising rebel songs. The Clancys emigrated to New York in the 1950s and rose out of the Greenwich Village coffee houses via *The Ed Sullivan Show* to conquer America before returning home in triumph. Their Irish repertoire made them unique around the Village. Bob Dylan took their version of *The Leaving of Liverpool* and turned it into *Restless Farewell*. They also performed at the million-dollar bash at Madison Square Garden in 1992 that celebrated Dylan's thirtieth anniversary as a recording artist, featuring the likes of George Harrison, Eric Clapton and Neil Young. "The Clancy Brothers — reunited with Tommy Makem — whose rollicking sea shanty treatment of *When The Ship Comes In* was so saltily vivid you could almost imagine yourself up on the poop deck working your passage," reported *Q* magazine.

With their wild, shaggy hair, mighty beards and broken bottles for voices, The Dubliners were a folk group with attitude. Named after James Joyce's renowned novel, they emerged from the smoke and cigarette ash of O'Donohue's pub, a celebrated watering hole in the nation's capital. "We just wanted to get across the fact the music was still alive," founder Ronnie Drew told *Folk Roots*. "There was a certain amount of fanaticism about it and the thing was regarded as sacred. That attitude divorced a lot of younger people being interested in Irish music. We proved you don't have to be an academic to enjoy Irish music." Indeed, they did. Hit versions of *Seven Drunken Nights* and *Black Velvet Band* would make them household names throughout the British Isles in the sixties.

The inability or reluctance of The Dubliners and The Clancys to evolve their styles and standards eventually limited their popularity. Besides that, the inspiration they provided promising young Irish musicians created an ironic backlash. Now aroused, the new generation arrived armed to the teeth with driving rhythms, more intricate arrangements, and longer hair to make their forerunners look decidedly old-fashioned and technically limited.

Sweeney's Men were first out of the gate with a lineup that consisted of Andy Irvine, Johnny Moynihan, Terry Woods and Henry McCullough. Moynihan introduced the Greek bouzouki to Irish music in 1966. That alone made the Men different. But they also cast aside the simple, bombastic ballads and treated traditional music with a greater degree of reverence on their self-titled debut album released in 1968. A year later they followed that with *Sweeney's Tracks* then scattered to the four winds. Woods eventually co-founded Steeleye Span and ended up in The Pogues; Irvine co-founded Planxty; Moynihan co-founded De Danann; and McCullough joined Joe Cocker's Grease Band before moving on to Paul McCartney's Wings.

In 1972, the strident and charismatic former Dublin bank clerk Christy Moore recorded the album *Prosperous* backed by the likes of Andy Irvine on mandolin, Liam O'Flynn on uileann pipes and Donal Lunny on bouzouki. Up until that point, Moore had covered a lot of comedy songs as well as his fair share of Clancy Brothers and Dubliners covers. *Prosperous*, though, ranged from the beautiful immigrant's lament, *Spancillhill*, to Bob Dylan's eulogy to his hero, *Song To Woody* (listed as a *Tribute To Woody*). While the brothers Finbar and Eddie Furey were the first to combine the uileann pipes with guitar, never had the results sounded more refreshing as they did on such tracks as *Raggle Taggle Gypsy* or *The Cliffs Of Dooneen*.

Prosperous worked out so well that Moore, Irvine, O'Flynn and Lunny formed Planxty to tinker further with traditional tunes. Despite the best intentions of Sweeney's Men, sentimental ballads with dog-eared choruses still propped up the national folk scene. It took the powder-keg of Moore's coercive voice, O'Flynn's marvellous mastery and Irvine and Lunny's furious acoustic rhythms to bring the walls tumbling down. Ha! Perceptions of Irish music changed forever. Their two initial albums — *Planxty* and *The Well Below The Valley* — featured a splendid combination of traditional and contemporary songs and instrumentals played with sublime assurance. And in no time flat Planxty ruled the roost, not only in Ireland, but throughout Britain too.

Donal Lunny left to form the Bothy Band in 1975 and Celtic music took another giant leap forward. This group, with its explosive, free-spirited instrumentals, would prove once and for all that acoustic music could match rock for power, technique and raw emotion. The glorious blaze of sound that was the Bothies in full-flight was ignited by the rough-hewn virtuosity of piper Paddy Keenan and the rampant fiddling of Tommy Peoples. Matt Molloy's flute, Donal Lunny's bouzouki, Micheal Ni Domhnaill's guitar and his sister Triona's harpsichord made them shine like a pair of good Sunday brogues. And through the singing of Triona and Micheal, the Bothy Band became one of the first groups to expose folk audiences to Gaelic songs.

Elsewhere, French harpist Alan Stivell made his presence felt. The son of a Breton teacher, Alan built his own harp in an effort to revive the Celtic music of Northwest France. Next, he immersed himself in Scottish, Welsh and Irish culture and moved to Paris in the late sixties. There he began performing solo in small clubs. Sometimes fellow Breton Dan ar Bras would sit in on guitar. After recording the acoustic album *Chemins De Terre* (Dirt Roads), Stivell and the superb ar Bras assembled the first electric band to perform Celtic music. By 1972, they had built a large enough following to record a live album at Paris' famous Olympia Theatre. *Alan Stivell: En Direct A L'Olympia* made the harpist into a national hero in France and a superstar on par with Steeleye Span and Fairport Convention in Britain.

♪   ♪   ♪

By now, the Scots had started to stir. In 1973, the Edinburgh-based Boys of the Lough made an enormous impression with the release of their self-titled debut album. While half the band — Cathal McConnell (flutes and whistles) and Robin Morton (vocals and bodhran: a hand-held drum) — actually came from came from Northern Ireland, the remainder were local lads Dick Gaughan (guitar) and Aly Bain (fiddle). The exquisite instrumental proficiency of this quartet set the stage for a serious outbreak of talented young bands — Silly Wizard, Tannahill Weavers, Battlefield Band, and Ossian — that began recording in the mid-seventies. And through a process of critical personnel changes, each would develop their own unique sound. Silly Wizard created its compelling rhythms through the fiddle of Johnny Cunningham and the accordion of his brother Phil. The power of The Tannahill Weavers came from the bagpipes of Alan MacLeod. MacLeod later emigrated to Canada and formed a partnership with Alberta bluesman and utility songwriter Bill Bourne. Together they won a Juno award — the Canadian equivalent of a Grammy — for the best roots album (*Dance & Celebrate*) of 1990. The Battlefield Band expanded boundaries with the use of Alan Reid's pedal organ and later synthesizers and electronic drum machines. Ossian initially distinguished themselves through the Gaelic singing of Billy Ross. But by the time they released their third album, *Seal Song*, in 1981, their beautiful acoustic arrangements, propelled by the harp and uileann pipes of Billy Jackson, the cittern, whistle and flute of his brother George, the fiddle of John Martin and the guitar and vocals of Tony Cuffe, put them in the vanguard of Scottish traditional music.

Frank Gasparik (EFMF)

Liam O'Flynn, part of Ireland's legendary Planxty, performing at Gallagher Park in 1993

The best of the Celtic acts arrived in Edmonton on the doorstep of the South Side Folk Club. Founded by a group of expatriate Scots in 1976 to bring the Celtic renaissance to local audiences, the club initially performed in a tiny room on the University of Alberta campus. Within a year, the founding group split up. Now a Roman Catholic from Glasgow operated it out of the Orange Hall in Old Strathcona. There it acted as an informal meeting place for the homesick and the culturally deprived. Jeanette MacLachlan, after all, ran the only venue in town that offered a decent drink and a good sing-a-long. By 1979, the club began to fulfil its primary purpose by booking such bands as The Chieftains, De Dannan, Clannad, Silly Wizard and the Tannahill Weavers. And it also provided a platform for such national talent as Stan Rogers, Barde, Na Caberfiedh (Rare Air), Figgy Duff and Alain Lamontagne.

Back in Europe, the Celtic revival continued unabated, at least for a while. De Danann updated the Irish-American music of the twenties on their album *Star Spangled Molly*. They also did sublime interpretations of Handel's *The Arrival Of The Queen Of Sheba (In Galway)* and *Guilliano's Duo In G*. Then they plundered Lennon & McCartney's catalogue, with an astonishing treatment of *Hey Jude* and *Let It Be*. The independent spirit of Clannad took the impeccable Gaelic singing of Maire Ni Bhraonian and wrapped it in swirling acoustic jazz. Later they coddled themselves in layers of synthesizers and bored the pants off most of their original following. The electric Moving Hearts — another ambitious undertaking pioneered by master Donal Lunny — threw everything but the kitchen sink into their blinding instrumental album, *The Storm*. And the fierce rage and touching tenderness of Scotland's RunRig made Gaelic roots-rock as potent and as stimulating as a twenty-year-old malt whiskey.

For all that, the initial Celtic revival had all but petered out by the mid-eighties. Yet it was only a matter of time before younger musicians picked up the baton. Scotland's Capercaillie were first off the mark. Straight out of Oban high school, they mixed blissful Gaelic waulking songs (chants traditionally used by the women of the Hebredian Islands as they sat around tables and worked the weave of Harris Tweed) with synthesizers, fiddles and accordions. And Altan, Arcady and Four Men And A Dog became the flag-bearers for traditional Irish music. The Four Men actually introduced rap (*Wrap It Up*) on their debut album *Barking Mad*. But all in all these new bands appear determined to uphold the purer values of traditional music against gimmicky compromises that are now generally deemed necessary for any degree of widespread acceptance.

♪   ♪   ♪

The Romans celebrated the arrival of spring with an orgy called Lupercalia. With the arrival of Christianity, such promiscuity required atonement. So the good citizens of Rome had to fast and pray for forgiveness when their hangovers subsided. In New Orleans, Lupercalia became known as Mardi Gras — the day Cajuns and Creoles eat, drink, dance and exercise their naughty parts because, twenty-four hours later, Ash Wednesday signals the start of forty-six days of penance known as Lent. In the past, Louisiana Catholics did not play musical instruments throughout Lent. They did, however, sing *a cappella* songs known as jure. John Lomax first recorded these jure songs in the early thirties, and they provide the first mention of the term zydeco. Supposedly it's named from the expression *les haricots sont pas sales* (the snapbeans aren't salted; a reference to hard times). But as Barry Jean Ancelet noted in *The Makers of Cajun Music:* "The word more likely shares the Afro-Caribbean origins of the music it represents, a gumbo of Cajun, rhythm-and-blues, rock and cayenne."

The historical roots of zydeco start in 1713, when France and Britain signed the Treaty of Utrecht. That document gave the British possession of Acadia, which they renamed Nova Scotia. In 1755, two centuries before ethnic cleansing became a media buzzword, the British deported thousands of French-speaking, Catholic Acadians to Louisiana. More followed in 1763. These white Acadians became known as Cajuns and the indigenous population, Creoles. Later, a Creole came to refer to those of mixed European and African descent who spoke French.

The music of the Cajuns developed from old Acadian fiddle tunes, often played with two fiddlers — one playing lead and the other harmony. Then in the mid-1800s German settlers brought the accordion to Louisiana and because it was louder, it reduced the fiddle to a supporting role. The limited number of notes and keys on the accordion tended to restrict and simplify tunes and musicians adapted old songs and created new ones to feature its sound. Eventually, dance bands added percussion instruments such as washboards, triangles or spoons. Sometimes they included a Spanish box guitar for extra rhythm. And by the early 1900s, Creole musicians Ame de Ardoin and Adam Fontenot began pushing the traditional boundaries by experimenting with the blues which eventually would distinguish zydeco from Cajun music.

From the outset of the twentieth century, outside influences began to influence Creole and Cajun culture. First, the discovery of oil in 1901 brought a flood of Anglo-Americans into the region. Then, in 1916, the state school board banned French from the elementary educational system. The rise of national media networks curbed local programming and forced indigenous culture into the shadows. And improved highways and railways opened up this once-isolated area forever.

These changes, brought new social values to Louisiana. The words "Cajun" and "Creole" became ethnic slurs synonymous with poverty and ignorance. As a result, musicians abandoned their rousing traditional tunes in the mid-thirties and started to imitate the likes of Bob Wills and his Texas Playboys and The Monroe Brothers, Bill and Charlie. Fiddler Harry Choates was the most popular Cajun musician around at the time. Choates often peppered his songs with English lyrics and scored several regional hits with the likes of *Rubber Dolly* and a simplified version of *Jolie Blonde*. But like many of his contemporaries, he moved to East Texas to work in the shipyards and oil refineries during the boom created by the Second World War. This migration brought the Creoles in touch with Texas bluesmen such as Mance Lipscomb and Lightnin' Hopkins, and the real rhythm and blues roots of zydeco started to emerge.

Then in 1954, Clifton Chenier, who preferred the larger piano accordion instead of the smaller button version, began to record at radio station KAOK in Lake Charles with his brother Cleveland on washboard. A year later, Clifton cut such tracks for Specialty Records as *Eh 'Tite Fille* and *Boppin' The Rock* that showed a distinct shift towards rhythm and blues. Chenier did not invent zydeco (Amede Ardoin and Nathan Abshire deserve as much credit as anybody), yet he came to define its sound. Backed by The Red Hot Louisiana Band, which included electric guitars, drums, saxophones and bass, he created an explosive concoction of rock 'n' roll, country, Cajun and New Orleans rhythm 'n' blues that made him a dance hall favorite all along the Gulf Coast. His regional hits would include *Louisiana Blues*, *Black Girl*, *Te Na Ne Na*, *Hungry Man* and *I Am A Hog*. By the mid-sixties he had crowned himself the King of Zydeco. And few could argue, as his feverish four-hour sets vaporized venues throughout North America and Europe.

But just as important, Clifton Chenier provided inspiration and guidance for a new generation of zydeco musicians. His son C.J. Chenier inherited The Red Hot Louisiana Band and continued in his father's footsteps. The flamboyant Alton "Rockin' Dopsie" Rubin also carried the torch for Clifton (Dopsie appears on Paul Simon's award-winning album, *Graceland*). Stanley "Buckwheat" Dural added more soul to his zydeco, Zachary Richard offered politics, and Wayne Toups provided rock 'n' roll showmanship. But no act did as much to popularize zydeco in the 1980s as Queen Ida Guillory. Born in 1929 on a farm near Lake

Charles, she grew up in San Francisco's Bay Area where she raised a family of her own. "When we moved my mum brought her records — her old seventy-eights," she says. "Through her travels back and forth to Louisiana, she brought more albums and later forty-fives. She had Joe Falconz, The Balfa Brothers, and when Clifton Chenier started recording, she brought back zydeco. That's how we kept up with the music ."

On one trip to Lake Charles, her mother returned with an accordion. She wanted her kids to preserve their musical heritage. "All my children were in grade school. So I found myself with spare time on my hands. I was a little lonely, and I picked up the accordion to practise while they were in school." After several years of rehearsal, she felt confident enough to perform at a local Mardi Gras high school fund-raiser. A reporter for the *San Francisco Herald* covered the event and wound up writing a full-page feature on Guillory and her music. It was just the push she needed. Within a decade, she had won a Grammy for best ethnic album: *Queen Ida — On Tour.* And since then, she's added two prestigious W.C. Handy awards (the blues equivalent of the Grammys) as traditional female artist in 1989 and 1990. She still continues to perform around one hundred and fifty-five gigs a year.

The more traditional Cajun revival started with Iry Lejeune. In 1948, Lejeune recorded *La Valse du Pont d'Amour,* in the old raucous, traditional Acadian style — at the time predominantly Americanized and countrified. It created a local sensation and inspired other leading musicians such as Joe Falcon to follow suit. But it took the Balfa Brothers — Dewey (fiddle), Will (fiddle) and Rodney (guitar) — to bring the music out of the bayous and onto the world's stages. In 1964, Alan Lomax used his influence on the board at the Newport Folk Festival to send Ralph Rinzler of the Greenbriar Boys to scout Louisiana for Cajun musicians. He returned with Galdius Thidbodeaux, Vinesse Lejeune (a cousin of Iry) and Dewey Balfa. "I had played in house dances, family gatherings, maybe a dance hall where you might have seen as many as two hundred people at once," recalled Dewey in *The Makers of Cajun Music.* "In fact I doubt that I had ever seen two hundred people at once. And in Newport, there were seventeen thousand. Seventeen thousand who wouldn't let us get off the stage." Such recognition brought a new sense of pride to the French-speaking community in Louisiana.

In 1967, Dewey returned to Newport with his brothers and several friends. And again, knocked the crowd on its rear with their delightfully furious fiddle tunes. From Newport, their fame spread. And they would go on to record numerous gems for Arhoolie Records until the deaths of Will and Rodney in a car accident in 1978. After an extended period of mourning, Dewey returned to performing and went on to collaborate with the likes of Ry Cooder.

Today, accordionist Marc Savoy and fiddler Michael Doucet carry the traditional flame. While they occasionally perform together as The Savoy-Doucet Cajun Band, Michael also fronts the highly successful Beausoleil. Savoy was born in 1940. As a child, he developed a flair for restoring old accordions. By 1965, he began building them on a full-time basis, while performing occasionally with the Balfa Brothers. His accordions soon became the finest in Louisiana and his music store outside Eunice became a clearinghouse for information and instruments. As much a musical curator as an active musician, he and Doucet formed SPECIAL — the Society for the Preservation of Ethnic Culture in Acadian Louisiana — to ensure the survival of Cajun music.

Doucet, on the other hand, spends much of his time on the road with Beausoleil. Born near Lafayette in 1951, he started out on guitar in a folk-rock band per-

(EFMF)

Queen Ida, at the 1984 festival, learned accordion off old zydeco records from Louisiana

forming covers of Bob Dylan, The Byrds and Pete Seeger in the mid-sixties. His great cultural awakening came at Louisiana State University. There he took a course in folklore but found the syllabus had nothing on Acadian music. "The teacher says, 'Oh, that's nothing but English ballads translated into French.' That was the red flag. From that moment I went into this academically," Doucet told *Folk Roots*. An extended stay in France in 1974 with Zachary Richard provided another turning point. By now, an overpowering country influence again subdued Cajun music. It was also a dying art. "I was the only accordion player who wasn't sixty years old. My generation was not interested," says Richard. The French, though, still took great delight in the old-time traditional tunes and their compliments stirred Doucet's resolve. Now he wanted to play Cajun music for a living.

On the way home, he stopped in England and met fiddler Barry Dransfield. "I was scratching on the fiddle at that time. When I heard

Barry play, it completely changed my life. It was how to approach the fiddle. As he said, it's an extension of your arms. It's what you feel. You don't have to play genres, you don't have to play styles. Play what you feel." Back in Louisiana he set out to learn from such legendary Cajun fiddlers as Canray Fontenot, Dewey Balfa and Dennis McGhee. He also formed Beausoleil and eventually began recording for Arhoolie Records. Since then, Doucet and his colleagues have developed into the leading champions of Cajun music — an accomplishment celebrated in the lyrics of Mary Chapin Carpenter's 1990 award-winning hit single *Down At The Twist And Shout.*

♪　♪　♪

Just as they brought the accordion to Louisiana, German settlers also introduced the button accordion to Texas. Patricio Jimenez bought one and learned to play their dance tunes. These he passed on to his son Santiago. In the early thirties, Santiago began to record around San Antonio and added a more dynamic beat to the old German polkas. The rhythm now came from the classic Mexican-American *conjunto* (group) lineup of button accordion, *bajo-sexto* (a low-tuned twelve-string guitar) and string bass. These recordings established Norteno, more commonly known as Tex-Mex. And nobody influenced Norteno more than the Jimenez family.

Like his father before him, Santiago passed his talents on to his sons Leonardo (El Flaco, the skinny one, born in 1939) and Santiago Jr. "Like father like son; the sound came automatically to my ears at an early age," says Flaco. At the age of sixteen, he joined the professional Los Caminantes — a local *conjunto* that performed on San Antonio radio station KEXX and in dance halls as far afield as Houston and Dallas. Two years later, he recorded a single, *Hasta La Vista*, for Tipico Records. "All of a sudden it started selling. More interest came, then I was in the studio every day recording, because Flaco Jimenez was going in steps upward," he told Ian Anderson of *Folk Roots*. Flaco then started to incorporate jazz, blues, country and rock 'n' roll into his playing, and began to build a substantial reputation around Texas.

Meanwhile Santiago, four years Flaco's junior, developed his style along the same traditional lines as his father's. "I think I would play my father's music 'til I die, because that's the way I learned it," Santiago told Dave Peabody of *Folk Roots*. "I could do some arrangements; I could do a little change on the accordion but I would still stick with the old style. Probably one rock 'n' roll on the accordion — I think that's enough. It's not that I don't like it; it's that I'm used to the old style." While a phenomenal accordion player, Santiago's more conservative approach to Norteno meant he would always follow in the shadow of his older brother.

In 1971, Doug Sahm recruited Bob Dylan, Dr. John and Flaco Jimenez to record *The Return Of Doug Saldana*. Sahm had grown up around San Antonio performing rock 'n' roll but moved to California in 1960. Four years later the British invasion got under way, and he renamed his band (which featured Augie Meyer on Vox organ) the Sir Douglas Quintet. Their first single, *She's About A Mover*, featuring a recurring organ line similar to the *conjunto* sound pioneered by the Jimenezes, went into the national Top Twenty. And Sam the Sham and The Pharaohs used the same pattern for *Wooly Bully* — a single that sold three million copies in 1965.

While Doug Sahm exposed Flaco to a wider audience, Ry Cooder made him an international celebrity. "Cooder was touring the San Antonio area and he tuned into some of the Spanish radio stations and one of my records was playing," says Flaco. "So he said, 'What's this? I think I can do something with this type of music.' He tracked me down and said, 'I'm working on a new album and I want you to participate.' And I said, 'Yeah, yeah, why not?' Within a week, I'm on the plane to Warner Brothers' studios in Hollywood." That album turned into Cooder's classic, *Chicken Skin Music* and started a long fruitful association. While they still occasionally record and tour together, Flaco also makes solo albums, fronts his own band, and guests on such hits as Dwight Yoakam's *Streets Of Bakersfield*. And in 1990, he formed the Texas Tornados with Doug Sahm, Augie Meyers and Freddy Fender to play country music, Tex-Mex style.

♪ ♪ ♪

As with most popular music, country developed in the Southern United States — Meridian, Mississippi, to be exact — the birth place of Jimmie Rodgers. Although his recording career spanned a mere seven years from 1927 until his death in 1933, Rodgers established himself as "the father of modern country music." Born in 1897, his mother died of tuberculosis when Jimmie was four. His father worked as a section foreman for the Mobile and Ohio Railroad and brought the boy up with help from various relatives. As a child, Jimmie took a serious interest in show business. He organized local carnivals, sang in amateur talent concerts, and at the age of thirteen, briefly joined a travelling medicine show before going to work with his father. The popular mythology that surrounds Rodgers implies he was first and foremost a railroad man who happened into show business only because he was too ill to work as a brakeman. His biographer Nolan Porterfield clearly disagrees: "Show business was his dream and calling; if hardly a Born Performer, he nevertheless sensed that he was born to perform, and would forever pursue the dream, no matter how brief and dark the reality of it might be."

The M&O provided Rodgers with one of life's great necessities, a pay cheque. It also exposed him to the culture of the Negro laborers who laid and maintained the rails. "During the noon dinner-rests, they taught him to plunk melody from the banjo and guitar. They taught him darkey songs; moaning chants and crooning lullabies," wrote his wife Carrie Rodgers in *My Husband, Jimmie Rodgers*. These melodies he later worked into his own recordings.

Constant illness kept Rodgers unemployed for long stretches but he used this time to perfect his guitar picking and highly personalized, nasal style of singing. The local Meridian newspaper advertised blues records, which Rodgers bought and played repeatedly, drawn by their vitality and uniqueness. Eventually, he made brakeman and travelled around the country. At various stops, he whiled a way the hours with small-time entertainers, singing hobos, and part-time minstrels. In New Orleans, he met a troubadour by the name of Goebel Reeves, who would later record as *The Texas Drifter*. They, and a third musician, Lucien Parks, toured briefly together. According to Reeves, he taught Rodgers how to yodel. This he now added to the blues to create his signature blue yodel.

Railroad work grew increasingly harder to find for a brakeman who often signed off sick. So in 1923, he auditioned for a travelling minstrel show run by entrepreneur Billy Terrell. And in a large tent near Hattiesburg, Mississippi, Jimmie Rodgers performed in front of a paying audience for the first time. "Out came Jimmie, with that big smile on his face," Terrell told Porterfield. "He walked to the centre stage and started whipping that old guitar — then he pulled his train whistle and he had them in his hand." According to Terrell, Rodgers received three encores and a standing ovation when he finally finished.

That gig lasted a month, then he went back on the trains. In the winter of 1924, he made a run to Colorado and returned to Mississippi sicker than usual. He had tuberculosis. After a long convalescence, he formed a dance band with his sister-in-law Elsie McWilliams on piano and a violinist by the name of Slim Rozell. They performed popular melodies. McWilliams would later contribute to many of Jimmie's songs. While he continued to alternate between minstrel shows and the railroads, his TB grew worse. A friend suggested that living at a high altitude in clean mountain air might provide a cure. So in 1927 he moved to Asheville (the town where Pete Seeger discovered the five-string banjo), North Carolina. There he formed a hillbilly band with Claude Grant on tenor banjo, Jack Pierce on guitar and Jack Grant on mandolin. They called themselves The Jimmie Rodgers Entertainers and landed a six-week spot on local radio station WWNC, then toured the southeastern states. In July, an Asheville newspaper ran a story about Ralph Peer of Victor Records looking for "rural talent" to record in Bristol, a town on the Virginia-Tennessee border. The Jimmie Rodgers Entertainers passed the audition. The Carter Family did likewise. They recorded on August 1. Rodgers and his colleagues were booked for August 3, but they fought over whose name went on the label and split up. So Rodgers went solo and between 2 p.m. and 4 p.m., August 4, 1927, cut the old traditional ballad *The Soldier's Sweetheart* and a yodelling lullaby, *Sleep Baby Sleep*.

These songs earned him twenty-seven dollars in royalties and a second session at the Victor studios in Camden, New Jersey, in November. This time, he recorded *Away Out On The Mountain, Ben Dewberry's Final Run* and *Mother Was A Lady*, as well as an original, *T For Texas* (which Ralph Peer released as *Blue Yodel*). "In its structure," wrote Bill Malone in *Country Music USA*, "it resembled the typical blues form, but at the conclusion of the third line, Rodgers raised his voice a higher octave and uttered the blue yodel that made him the most famous hillbilly star in history." It sold a million copies.

By the middle of 1928, he released two more *Blue Yodels* — a series that would eventually include thirteen such titles — and Rodgers became known as the Blue Yodeller. And at the height of the Depression, his records sold by the millions. Such success allowed him to experiment with his music, and he hired jazz bands and Hawaiian steel guitarists for backing. Ravaged by tuberculosis, he entered the studio for one final time in New York City in 1933. Thirty-six hours after cutting *Years Ago*, his lungs hemorrhaged and he lapsed into a coma from which he never regained consciousness. Jimmie Rodgers, Hank Williams and Fred Rose were the first performers inducted into the Country Music Hall Of Fame when it opened in 1961, which is indicative of his importance in the history of country music.

The term "country" initially described the music's rural origins and created a distinction between the more traditional, Anglo-Celtic "mountain music" preserved in isolated communities nestled in the Blue Ridge and Appalachian Mountain Ranges. "Mountain music," wrote Bill Malone, "tended to be more conservative and to rely more on the traditional, songs and instruments, and it was performed in the traditional, high nasal harmony. This type, today represented by bluegrass music, owes many of its essential characteristics to the style produced by the famous Carter Family."

This trio consisted of Alvin Pleasant Delaney Carter, his wife Sara, and his sister-in-law Maybelle. Sara and Maybelle both played guitar, autoharp, and banjo, and A.P. could scrape out the odd tune on a fiddle. A.P., one of nine children, grew up in Maces Spring, Scott County, Virginia, where he initially sang in a church quartet and became a noted collector of local folk songs. His discoveries would include *Will The Circle Be Unbroken*, *Wildwood Flower*, *My Dixie Darling* and *Wabash Cannonball*. "As an arranger he was second to none," wrote John Atkins in *Stars of Country Music*. "It was he who took the songs along for the others to rehearse, and although both Sara and Maybelle would impose their own personality and talent onto each song, it was A.P.'s memory and arrangement that provided the nucleus on almost every occasion."

Aside from their lush harmonies and Sara's deep voice, Maybelle's guitar picking defined the Carter Family sound. Traditionally, country singers used their instruments to fit their voices. The Carter Family made their voices fit Maybelle's guitar. She picked the melody on the bass strings while maintaining the rhythm with chords on the treble strings — a style that Woody Guthrie copied religiously.

Their first recording with Ralph Peer in 1927 produced three 78 r.p.m. singles, all of which sold modestly. The following year, though, they recorded *Wildwood Flower*, and it racked up sales of over a million. It made the Carters as well known on rural radio as Jimmie Rodgers. These two giants actually recorded together in 1931 and country and mountain music finally merged. Domestic disputes, however, began to take their toll on the trio and A.P. and Sara divorced in 1936. While they continued to limp along for several more years, they folded in 1943.

Twenty years later, the folk revival anointed them the patron saints of American traditional. Many of the two hundred and fifty or so songs they recorded wound up in the repertoires of performers as diverse as Joan Baez, Ian and Sylvia and Doc Watson. While A. P. passed away in 1961, Maybelle continued singing and received a phenomenal reception at the 1963 Newport Folk Festival. There, four years later, she and Sara recorded the live album *An Historic Reunion*, their first recording together in twenty-five years. Maybelle also led the singing on the title track of the Nitty Gritty Dirt Band's all-acoustic, trailblazing triple album, *Will The Circle Be Unbroken*. Released in 1973, it brought together the cream of old-time traditional country acts such as Roy Acuff, Merle Travis and Doc Watson with their contemporary successors. Maybelle died in 1978, and Sara a year later.

♪ ♪ ♪

From The Carter Family and Jimmie Rodgers, country music continued to evolve. In the 1930s, cowboy movie star Gene Autry wrote and recorded numerous hit songs with western themes: *Back In The Saddle Again, Tumbling Tumbleweeds, The Last Roundup* (along with seasonal blockbusters *Rudolph The Red Nosed Reindeer* and *Here Comes Santa Claus*). Up until then, country and mountain music were still marketed under the generic title hillbilly music. But through shiftless and illiterate cartoon characters like *Lil' Abner*, hillbilly grew into a derogatory term. To reflect more dignity and respect, Autry's record company began to market his music as country and western and it stuck.

By the end of the thirties, Bob Wills and his eighteen-piece Texas Playboys established western swing — a fusion of string band instrumentals with Dixieland and big band jazz horn arrangements. The forties belonged to Hank Williams — the first Nashville star to firmly bridge the gap be

Frank Gasparik (EFMF)

Flaco Jimenez, shown at the 1989 festival, added jazz, blues, country and rock 'n' roll flavors to Tex-Mex

tween country and pop music. This troubled honky tonk genius offered country music nothing new: "But he did it better, and he did it with a compelling vision. He reached into the darkness within himself and found vivid, haunting images which he delivered with skewering passion," wrote Colin Escott for the biographical notes that accompanied the box set, *Hank Williams: The Original Singles Collection*. Surely, "I'm so lonesome I could cry" must rank as the most achingly beautiful line ever written in any form of popular music.

While highly individual vocal stylists such as George Jones, Patsy Cline, Loretta Lynn and Kitty Wells dominated country throughout the fifties, Charlie and Ira Louvin set new standards for harmony singing. Inevitably, pop crept into country throughout the sixties as the likes of Kenny Rogers and Glen Campbell scored numerous crossover hits. In 1968, Gram Parsons helped launch country-rock through his contributions to The Byrds album *Sweethearts Of The Rodeo*. Even Bob Dylan made a country record, *Nashville Skyline*.

For all that, country held little appeal for a younger generation more concerned with peace, love and understanding. Rednecks with crewcuts played country music — a point highlighted by Merle Haggard's 1970 conservative rant, *Okie From Muskogee*. *Sweethearts Of The Rodeo* was trashed at the time of its release. *Nashville Skyline* too. While such Southern Californian country rock bands as the Flying Burrito Brothers, New Riders Of The Purple Sage, Poco and The Eagles eased preconceptions, the Austin outlaws made the big cultural breakthrough.

As the rock movement and counter-culture took hold, Austin developed a vigorous club scene highlighted by The Armadillo World Headquarters. Opened in August 1970 as a forum for rock bands, the club became a refuge for local hippies. "The Armadillo, however, also featured the occasional country band, and so cowboys and rednecks began to rub shoulders with the long-haired counterculture community," wrote Bill Malone in his revised edition of *Country Music USA*. "Gradually a music culture emerged which enveloped them all, and one which reflected a curious combining of images and symbols: hippie, Texan and, above all, cowboy." And at the head of the table sat such cosmic cowboys as Michael Martin Murphy, Jerry Jeff Walker and Willie Nelson.

Although a successful songwriter, Willie Nelson struggled to find respect in conservative Nashville. In 1972, his home burned down and his marriage disintegrated and he relocated to Austin — a city that always treated him with respect and affection. In the months that followed, he let his hair grow long, grew a beard and began wearing a headband, an earring, jeans and jogging shoes in an attempt to appeal to a younger audience. To draw further attention to himself he started holding his successful picnics every fourth of July. They were really outdoor festivals that often featured such traditional country acts as Roy Acuff, Tex Ritter and Earl Scruggs. Bolstered by his new-found acceptance, Nelson purified his honky tonk, western swing and traditional country music roots and recorded them with a starker, simpler production. Finally, the album *Red Headed Stranger*, with its hit single *Blue Eyes Crying In The Rain*, made him an international star in 1975.

However, the hell-raising, free spirit of Jerry Jeff Walker came to epitomize Austin's new approach to country music. Walker had started out in Greenwich Village as a folk singer. "In the sixties I took off and hitch-hiked on the road for about eight years," he says. "I drank all the time. I smoked a lot, I guess. I'm not endorsing that lifestyle; it just worked out that way." His travels took him to New Orleans, where he wound up in jail for public intoxication. In his cell, he met an old street dancer who inspired his best-known song, *Mr. Bojangles*. Back in New York, he flirted with a psychedelic rock band, Circus Maximus, until *Mr. Bojangles* broke on the radio in 1968. For a brief period, he toured and performed at the Newport Folk Festival with session musician David Bromberg, who recorded with such diverse acts as Bob Dylan and Sha Na Na.

Walker eventually settled in Austin in 1971, attracted by a creative community that let him mix folk, rock, country and anything else that caught his ear. Austin still has an estimated one hundred and fifty clubs. Although not a particularly prolific songwriter, Walker's albums would feature such gems as *L.A. Freeway* and *Desperados Waiting For The Train* mined from Austin songwriter Guy Clark. "I used to sleep on Guy's couch," Walker told John Tobler of *Folk Roots*. "He was a good musician and a craftsman. He was an artist and he built guitars but he never wrote anything. Townes Van Zandt and I used to stay with Guy whenever we came through town and Guy was always looking at us like, 'How hard can it be?' We told him it wasn't very hard, you just pick something you know about and write it down. So one day he wrote five songs." That night, he completed *Desperados Waiting For A Train*.

Jerry Jeff Walker and his Lost Gonzo Band drew such talented country acts as Tom Russell to Texas and inspired the likes of local country misfits Nanci Griffiths, Lyle Lovett, Robert Earl Keen Jr., Jimmie Dale Gilmour and Butch Hancock. "In Austin we try to be different in a way that allows us to go in any direction we want," says Walker. "It's like being an actor not being type cast. The Austin music scene is about all that and maybe having a career that is famous enough to keep you working without dictating to you how you have to be."

♪   ♪   ♪

Economic collapse, famine, civil strife, and foreign intervention motivated many African musicians to migrate to the capitals of Europe in the late seventies. Most arrived in Paris or London. For European record labels, the potential of African music appeared raw material set for exploitation. Several majors tried their hand at recording and selling African music but all fell short when it came to promotions. While Island Records did all right initially with Nigeria's King Sunny Ade, they dropped him when his commercial promise faded. Small, committed, knowledgeable, independent record companies, however, rose to the challenge.

The first of these was Earthworks, run by Mary and Jumbo Van Renen. Jumbo had worked for Virgin Records in London since its formation in 1971, but grew disillusioned by the company's lack of interest in African music. So he wrote to record companies in South Africa and Kenya and offered to license and release their back catalogues. While he started out with two compilations, *Viva Zimbabwe* and *Zulu Jive*, he soon oversaw the British distribution of albums by Ladysmith Black Mambazo, Thomas Mapfumo and Malathini & The Mahotella Queens. Jumbo also put together *The Indestructible Beat of Soweto* — voted one of the top albums of the eighties by *Rolling Stone* magazine. To make these albums available outside of London, Earthworks started a mail-order service. Eventually, Van Renen could bring the various acts on his label to Britain to tour, thus creating an even greater awareness for African music.

However, by 1983, the Mecca in London for "ethnic" music was Stern's African Record Shop. Originally, Stern's sold and repaired electrical appliances but occasionally imported records for West-African students attending nearby London University. In 1983, the store came up for sale and was bought by a trio of young international audiophiles. Their timing was perfect. Island Records released Sunny Ade's successful *Juju Music* and Synchro System and Stern's sold his Nigerian imports by the barrow load. John Peel, the most influential radio disc jockey in Britain, now dropped by the store frequently and played its records on his show broadcast throughout the U.K.

Within two years, Stern's began recording British-based African bands such as Hi-Life International and Segun Adewale, a venture that eventually folded because it was easier to license records from abroad. Now it released the finest albums from Kenya, Tanzania, Gambia and Zaire. But Mali's Salif Keita really put Stern's on the map with the album *Soro* — an extraordinary hi-tech synthesis of traditional rhythms and contemporary rock which he recorded in Paris. It topped most critic's polls as roots album of the year in 1987 and continued the considerable momentum created the year before by Paul Simon's acclaimed *Graceland* — an album dominated by the brilliant harmonies of South Africa's Ladysmith Black Mambazo and the euphoric township jive of The Boyoyo Boys Band, Tao Ea Mateshka and General M.D. Shirinda.

As Earthworks and Stern's distributed their records throughout Britain, ethnic music became known as world music simply as a retailing tool. In 1987, Stern's co-owner Robert Urbanus could report to Chris Stapleton and Chris May — authors of *African All*Stars:* "We feel that a regular market has now established itself. It will develop like jazz or blues or salsa, selling well enough for a company to make a living —

although no one will be riding round in a Rolls." Seven years later the store continues to flourish.

On the festival and concert front, the multi-cultural, British-based non-profit organization WOMAD (World Of Music Arts and Dance), rose to became the leading international promoters. In 1980, Thomas Brooman edited *The Bristol Recorder*, an experimental music magazine that included an album recorded by local bands in each issue. "Being young crafty entrepreneurs, we thought a way of upping sales might be to interview locally based, but famous, popular stars," says Brooman. "During one recording, Peter Gabriel popped in to the studio." The upshot of that chance encounter was that Gabriel agreed to an interview, and to allow some of his music to be included on the record that accompanied one issue of the magazine.

The Recorder's organizational skills impressed Gabriel, who recruited its staff to bring world music to British rock audiences. Within two years, they had formed WOMAD and had run a first festival that featured performers from Burundi, China, Egypt and Indonesia, along with rockers Echo And The Bunnymen and Simple Minds. While it turned into a seminal musical event, it also lost five-hundred thousand dollars for a variety

Frank Gasparik (EFMF)

Ry Cooder's 1992 main stage set held the audience spellbound

of external reasons. Fortunately Genesis, Gabriel's former band, held a reunion benefit concert that paid off the debt.

Bloodied but undaunted, WOMAD carried on, only now, it limited its role to arranging tours for artists while individual promoters took the risk. It did, however, develop a spin-off record company, Real World, to record the acts it worked with. By 1990, Brooman and his staff scheduled regular events in Denmark, Finland, Germany, Spain, Japan and Canada — Toronto's Harbour Front Festival. That year the Edmonton festival's Terry Wickham flew such WOMAD acts from Toronto as Zimbabwe's Four Brothers, Angola's Kafala Brothers and Ireland's Dave Spillane. While Jazz City had brought the likes of The Four Brothers and Senegal's Youssou N'dour to Edmonton in 1988 and South Africa's extraordinary Mahlathini and the Mahotella Queens a year later, this was the folk festival's world music debut. "They've added, not only different types of music but I think they've added a whole spectacle — an exotic feel if you like," Wickham said at the time. It has become a fixture ever since.

♪   ♪   ♪

Late one night in 1982, English music critic Colin Irwin sat down at his typewriter with a bottle of Remy Martin and addressed the current state of folk music for the readers of *Southern Rag* magazine. At the time, Dexy's Midnight Runners sat on top of the pop charts with the single *Come On Eileen* from the album *Too-Rye-Ay*, which featured an assortment of fiddles, accordions, banjos, and tin whistles. XTC had just released *English Settlement*, crammed with folk overtones. And Kate Bush's latest, *The Dreaming*, featured former Bothy Band fiddler Kevin Burke. In more conventional folk circles, Moving Hearts had just put out a *blitzkrieg* of jazz and Celtic folk-rock called *The Storm*. The Oyster Band released *English Rock & Roll — The Early Years 1800-1850*. The title says it all. And Jumpleads made a vicious piece of vinyl called *The Stag Must Die*, which battered and bruised once-sacred traditional ballads with raging rock guitars. "There's a whole new approach to folk music evolving incited by a bunch of bands and musicians — some of them even young for Godsake — who have decided to swing a hefty boot into the crotch of convention," Irwin wrote. "This new breed are the rogue folk." This new catch phrase came to embody a new mood of enterprise, open-mindedness and determination in folk music, much of which came from outside the traditional folk club circuit.

Young musicians disillusioned with punk had started to experiment with folk as an alternative to the hackneyed pop of the day. By 1984, London was crawling with exuberant new bands whacking out their daydreams on accordions, banjos, washboards and guitars. The best of the bunch included The Boothill Foot-tappers, The Men They Couldn't Hang, Poguemahone (Gaelic for kiss my arse), and their kindred spirit, Billy Bragg.

While The Foot-tappers enjoyed minor chart success with the single *Get Your Feet Out Of My Shoes*, The Men took up permanent residence on the indie singles charts with a caustic cover of Eric Bogle's haunting anti-war masterpiece, *No Man's Land* (billed as *Green Fields Of France*). Their debut album, *Night Of A Thousand Candles*, did just as brisk business. Billy Bragg made his first album, *Life's A Riot With Spy Vs Spy*, for three hundred dollars and it sold a quarter-million copies. Bragg had started out in the punk band Riff Raff but left to do solo gigs armed with an electric guitar. Once successful, he continued to tour the country using public transport, sometimes playing three gigs a day. And along the way, he embraced topical folk songs. As he revealed to Colin Irwin: "I'll tell you what finally did it was seeing Leon Rosselson and Roy Bailey at Manchester Free Trade Hall singing *The World Turned Upside Down*. I thought, 'Fucking hell, this is really powerful.' It's like the first time you hear *White Man In Hammersmith Palais* by The Clash or *In The City* by The Jam." Subsequently, Bragg's next recording featured *The World Turned Upside Down* along with Florence Reeves' (a contemporary of Aunt Molly Jackson) *Which Side Are You On?* His own songs — *Between The Wars*, *In Days Like These*, *It Says Here* and *Island Of No Return* — now showed a political and lyrical majesty more attuned to the better folk songwriters.

Poguemahone, on the other hand, grew out of the dainty punk combo, Nipple Erectors. For a lark, lead singer Shane MacGowan and his pals often sang Irish rebel songs in their local pub. Most of them were Irish or of Irish descent. One thing led to another, and soon they had surrounded themselves with a grand melee of acoustic guitar, banjo, whistle, accordion, whistle, bass and drums and released *Dark Streets Of London* as a single with Eric Bogle's *And The Band Played Waltzing Matilda* on the B-side. The BBC subsequently refused to broadcast their name. So arses were kissed and Poguemahone became The Pogues. If anything, they bore the same relationship to Irish music as rockabilly did to country. Their debut album *Red Roses For Me* arrived in the shops in 1984 and featured seven raucous originals with equally tumultuous titles — *Boys From The County Hell* and *Down In The Ground Where The Dead Men Go*, for example. All came from the pen of MacGowan. His compelling, ugly voice coupled with the band's frantic delivery attracted an impressive following, good reviews and minor chart action.

The following year, they recruited Elvis Costello to produce *Rum Sodomy And The Lash*. Above all expectations, MacGowan emerged as compelling and powerful a songwriter as any of his day. While his manic ferocity continued unabated on such adorable tracks as *The Sick Bed Of Cuchulainn*, *Billy's Bones* and *Sally Maclennane*, he also came up with the superb, three-hankie tear jerker *A Pair Of Brown Eyes* and the gloriously sleazy *Old Main Drag*. Besides that, they covered a number of traditional ballads in their usual wanton manner as well as Ewan MacColl's *Dirty Old Town*, which became a highlight of their live sets.

Rum Sodomy And The Lash cracked the U.K. Top Twenty album charts as did the follow up *If I Should Fall From Grace With God*. In 1987, The Pogues joined forces with their soul brothers, The Dubliners, and put the single *The Irish Rover* into the Top Ten. Later that year, The Pogues again topped the charts with MacGowan's sublime *Fairy Tale Of New York*. This time Kirsty MacColl — daughter of Ewan MacColl — shared vocal duties. Here was the offspring of the upright guardian of traditional music mixing it up with the most brazen interlopers to come down the turnpike since Fairport Convention. Oh, sweet irony. Sure, the purists huffed and puffed as always. At the 1985 Cambridge Folk Festival — arguably, the most prestigious in England — The Pogues tore into their delinquent set at 300 miles per hour while artistic director Michael Grosvenor-Myer yawned and read *The Times* of London. But at the end of the day, their turbulent energy and total disregard for convention introduced a whole new generation to folk music and inspired the likes of Canadian bands Spirit Of The West, the Crash Test Dummies and Hardrock Miners. The great roots awakening was now underway. There would be no turning back.

Selected recordings

The Chieftains: IV (Shanachie: 79024)
The Bothy Band: Out Of The Wind Into The Sun (Green Linnet SIFCD-3013)
Planxty: The Well Below The Valley (Shanachie ShCD-79035)
Moving Hearts: The Storm (Island BUACD-892)
Silly Wizard: Caledonia's Hardy Sons (Shanachie SHCD-79015)
De Danann: Song For Ireland (Stony Plain CDSH-01130)
Ossian: Seal Song (Iona IRCD-002)
Clannad: Dulaman (Shanachie 798008)
RunRig: Amazing Things (Chrysalis CDCHR-2000)
Altan: Angel Island (Green Linnet 1137)
The Pogues: Rum Sodomy And The Lash (Stiff 2292-4495-2)
Beausoleil: Cajun Conja (RNA R4 70525)
Queen Ida: Caught In The Act (GNP CRESCNPD-2181)
Jimmie Rodgers: No Hard Times (Rounder CD 1062)
Hank Williams: The Original Singles Collection (Polydor 847 194-2)
Jerry Jeff Walker: Summer Rain (Ryko RCD-10241)
Guy Clark: Old No. 1 (Stony Plain CDSH-01030)

9

Life Is A Carnival

■Holger Petersen and Stony Plain
Records ■A long, dark winter
■The house band ■Into the top ranks
■A special Saturday night ■

"This vehicle pulls up, and there's Ramblin' Jack Elliott. He talks to everyone: 'Man, I've been up all night. I just got back from New York drinking with Dylan and Bobby Neuwirth.' I just couldn't believe that I was in the middle of all this stuff."
— HOLGER PETERSEN HAS HIS FIRST TASTE OF A FOLK FESTIVAL

A CLUSTER OF JUNO AWARDS sit abandoned in a corner like rejected curios on a pawn shop shelf. Gold records cling to the walls as casually as barnacles bond to boats. The colorful collage of musical mementos that cover a large bulletin board offer a hint of intrigue, if not vanity. And amidst this methodical clutter, rests a tasteful photograph of Rodney Crowell, Rosanne Cash and Holger Petersen. The gratitude expressed with the autographs suggests a tale worth a round or two.

From his modest bungalow in the inconspicuous southeast Edmonton neighborhood of Brighton, Petersen runs Stony Plain Records — the most important independent record company licensing roots recordings in the country. It has brought him recognition and reasonable rewards. In his garage, a BMW 633 c.s.i. with a licence plate that reads BLUES4U sits next to a vintage, two-seat Morgan 4-4. His living room is decorated with lithographs signed by John Lennon. Yet Stony Plain had its growing pains, almost folding twice. And then there was the time

Petersen turned down *The Trinity Sessions* album from The Cowboy Junkies. That disc eventually sold almost a million copies worldwide. "Musically it didn't do much for me," he says. "And after their success, I went back to it and it still didn't do anything for me. I guess that's the nature of having a small record label where you're personally involved in everything. . . They probably wouldn't have been successful if I had done something with them." And he laughs. That independent spirit made a significant impact on the development of The Edmonton Folk Music Festival.

Holger Petersen was born in 1949 on the German island of Pellworm in the North Sea near the Danish border. There, his father George worked as a fisherman, trained as a mechanic and dreamed of Canada. In 1954, fantasy became reality and he emigrated to Brandon, Manitoba. The rest of the family including son Holger would follow. Within three years, they had moved again. This time to Edmonton , where Holger grew up and developed an early infatuation with pop and rock music.

His first serious exposure to folk music occurred in the mid-sixties through the CBC television series *Let's Sing Out*, hosted by Oscar Brand. "I remember seeing the Reverend Gary Davis, Sonny Terry and Brownie McGhee, Dave Van Ronk, Doc Watson — really interesting unique people on that show. And then they would have the Kingston Trio with striped shirts and stuff like that, which really wasn't of much interest. But that show opened my eyes to a lot of different kinds of roots music." As he grew older, blues-based British rock bands inherited the earth. And the likes of The Yardbirds and The Zombies took him back to Alexis Korner and Long John Baldry, and through them he discovered the source of the Nile: Muddy Waters, Howlin' Wolf, Robert Johnson, Sun House.

At Bonnie Doon high school, Petersen began playing drums and ended up in local groups such as Hot Cottage and Spiny Norman's Whoopee Band — a quirky combo that wrote "Shitty music; don't come" on its gig posters and released *It's Called Henry Or Harold* as its only single. At the time, his ultimate goal was to produce records — not exactly a profession with a formal apprenticeship. Instead, he enrolled in 1970 in a two-year radio and television arts course at the Northern Alberta Institute of Technology, and before he graduated, started working at the province's CKUA Radio. There, he co-produced the *Acme Sausage Company* — a bi-weekly program that often featured live, touring musicians such as Ry Cooder, Stephane Grappelli and Sonny Terry and Brownie McGhee. Petersen recorded many of his guests live at The Hovel.

This experience gave him the confidence to contact Big Walter "Shakey" Horton, one of the great harmonica soloists of modern blues. In 1972, Horton came to Edmonton and cut a single and later an album backed by Hot Cottage. Next, Petersen recorded and produced blues pianist Roosevelt Sykes, an influence on the likes of Fats Domino, Otis Spann and Pinetop Perkins. Both the Horton and Sykes albums were released through London Records in Canada. Finally, in 1976, Petersen launched his own label, Stony Plain Records, with Paul Hann's album *Another Tumbleweed*. The Stony Plain catalogue now includes more than two hundred titles by acts ranging from Fairport Conven-

Wayne Stiles (EFMF)

Holger Petersen, right, at the site in 1988 . . . former festival manager owns Stony Plain Records.

tion to Ian Tyson and has gold albums for such diverse artists as Robert Cray and Ricky Skaggs. Despite the burden of running a record company, Petersen continued to work at CKUA. He still hosts *Natch'l Blues*, now the longest running blues program in Canada.

In 1975, Mitch Podolak dropped by the station to promote the Winnipeg Folk Music Festival. A friendship developed and Podolak appointed Petersen Winnipeg's regional representative. "It didn't really mean anything, but I got the minutes of the meetings and watched the organization develop." That summer he attended the festival for the first time. "I thought it was the greatest event I had ever been to at that point. I remember waiting for a shuttle bus at the back of the hotel, and this vehicle pulls up, and there's Ramblin' Jack Elliott. He talks to everyone: 'Man, I've been up all night. I just got back from New York drinking with Dylan and Bobby Neuwirth.' I just couldn't believe that I was in the middle of all this stuff. I really felt this was a great way to enjoy people."

Petersen came to know Don Whalen through recording at The Hovel for CKUA. And when Whalen invited him to join the board as chairman, he gladly accepted. Taking over as artistic director was a different matter. Initially, he refused due to his commitments with Stony Plain Records. But the new board then approached him with a second offer:

it would hire a general manager if Petersen handled the artistic duties. "Which absolutely floored me because I had never even considered that a possibility." After consulting with friends, he agreed on a three-year contract on condition he worked out of his office rather than the festival's. "We needed somebody to come in with power to change things. And do it responsibly," recalls Tom Coxworth, then a new member of the board. "We were exceptionally lucky to have Holger around. His presence gave the festival a whole new lease on life. It just opened the doors to a whole lot of new ideas."

Despite his vast knowledge of roots music, Petersen had booked very few acts in the past. In 1971, he co-promoted the Reverend Gary Davis in Dinwoodie Lounge on the University of Alberta campus. "I remember at the time that his asking fee was five hundred dollars plus airfare," recalls Petersen. "The local bands playing the next night were getting more than that. Here was this living legend and this was what he was getting! It was a real eye-opener for me." His next bill involved Jesse Winchester backed by a band that turned into the Amazing Rhythm Aces. In 1975, the Aces' debut album *Stacked Deck* produced the North American hit single *Third Rate Romance*. Other than that, the concerts Petersen promoted were few and far between. Still, he had a game plan and all winter to perfect it.

♪   ♪   ♪

The winter of 1985-86, turned out the most difficult faced by the folk festival to date. "The morale was very low because the festival was on the brink of folding altogether," says Petersen. "It was very tough — I would say probably the toughest position the folk festival's ever been in." For Agnes Brennan, that meant phone calls at three o'clock in the morning — desperate pleas from creditors demanding payment. They figured the festival would collapse without Don Whalen and wanted to salvage their losses while they could. Brennan could offer only sympathy and precarious promises. With the festival's accumulated debts now in excess of fifty thousand dollars, she could do little else: "If everybody we owed money to in the winter of '85 had sued us, we would have been forced to close," says Brennan. She convinced them otherwise.

To raise operating funds, Agnes and her husband Jim Brennan financed and organized concerts. They booked Rita MacNeil in the Provincial Museum Theatre, but were terrified they wouldn't sell enough tickets. Agnes then phoned Jeanette MacLachlan of the Southside Folk Club "to see if anybody owed her a favor." MacLachlan recruited help from Spirit of the West and the show sold out. More money continued to trickle in through benefit bingos. And in the background,

Don Whalen filled out grant applications. Nobody else knew how. The festival also found a permanent, year-round office in the city-owned Ortona Armoury. At a dollar a year, nobody quibbled about the rent. Up until that point, the festival had operated from Whalen's house in the winter and, for the most part, out of the ski lodge in Gallagher Park in the summer.

The following April, the festival board hired Andy Laskiwsky as general manager and Kate Carey as a full-time volunteer co-ordinator. Since leaving The Hovel in 1974, Laskiwsky had spent seven years travelling in Asia, and on his return, completed an MA in communications at the University of Alberta. As a festival volunteer since 1981, he knew its faults and failings. "My interests were to help them market it better, to make it more stable and to help it build," says Laskiwsky. So he charged twenty dollars for an advance pass that cost thirty in 1985, and added a long overdue evening ticket. Subsequently, sales of weekend passes rose from three hundred to two thousand and over the next two years grew to five thousand. This ticket money in the bank before the gates opened offered a financial cushion in case of rain.

Sponsorship had also been a major concern. It never climbed above five thousand dollars. Laskiwsky immediately went after several local radio stations for advertisements to promote the festival. By the time it rolled around, he had generated a total of twenty-five thousand dollars in corporate contributions. His continued efforts would produce donations in excess of ninety-five thousand dollars in 1988.

Kate Carey, a former copy editor with *Maclean's* and *Canadian Business* magazines in Toronto, had volunteered at Mariposa and later worked in Winnipeg for Mitch Podolak. "Winnipeg was pretty intense," she says. "And I was burned out after a couple of years and needed a month's holidays. So I went out to Edmonton and just loved it." So much so, she ended up applying for and accepting the job there as volunteer co-ordinator. Furthermore, Carey's media skills helped with publicity, recalls Peggie Graham. "She had good promotional ideas, which worked really well with Andy. They came up with very imaginative ways to promote the festival." Laskiwsky and Carey added live music to their news conferences and gave free T-shirts to the local media. They had Holger Petersen tour media outlets in Calgary and hired Richard Flohil in Toronto as a publicist to generate national coverage.

Meanwhile, Petersen scrapped the policy of paying a standard rate to all performers. "The way that was being done in Vancouver and Winnipeg was a farce," he says. The CBC subsidized headline acts by paying them a substantial fee for recording privileges. "In theory these other festivals were paying everybody the same. In practice, CBC was paying a lot of their artists."

In 1985, Winnipeg had broken its daily workshop routine with one-hour, main stage concerts on Saturday and Sunday afternoon. Petersen cherished this new format and enlisted Jesse Winchester and Donovan to fill these spots. "Donovan," he concedes, "was not one of the most artistically revered people in the world, but an artist who has sold millions and millions of records." His performance went by the book — hit after hit coupled with frivolous hippie musings. But what was more important, he sold tickets. "I remember somebody from the gate crew saying. 'Look at the lineup.' And it was wrapped all the way around the front — a whole city block. At that point I knew we were probably okay," recalls Kate Carey. The Newport Folk Festival booked recognizable names like The Kingston Trio in 1959 to finance unknown artists like Earl Scruggs. That practice obviously still had merit.

The formation of a "house band" also sat high on Petersen's list of priorities. So he recruited the services of Mitch Podolak's nemesis, Amos Garrett, and Toronto-based musicians Kit Johnson and Bohdan Hluszko, whose session credits stretched from Chris de Burgh to Etta James. They would back blues legend Sunnyland Slim, Texas roots rocker Doug Sahm and ex-Blaster Gene Taylor in Edmonton. "Holger wanted to bring up some blues acts who didn't want to carry a band. And also maybe a country singer or two," says Garrett. "Logistically, it was cheaper for the festival to have a house band to do that." With the exception of their appearance with Solomon Burke in 1990, Garrett and his colleagues start their preparations for the festival in the spring. "We're all pretty ardent musicologists. We're familiar with people's works, and if we aren't, and we need to brush up, we can run out and get some records of what we expect people to play. We usually have time to rehearse the acts when they come into town, and go through the set they're going to do that night. And we're ready. It's one of the most enjoyable and relaxed and organized musical experiences that I go through. "

The blues served as a musical rite of passage for Petersen and now he set about booking such legends as Lowell Fulson, Luther "Guitar Junior" Johnson and Sunnyland Slim, as well as contemporary guitar sensation Robert Cray. These acts, along with country-influenced performers — Guy Clark, Ian Tyson, Prairie Oyster, Townes Van Zandt, Murray McLauchlan and Katy and Hugh Moffatt — provided the backbone of the 1986 lineup.

Swarms of mosquitoes plagued Gallagher Park as the festival blossomed under clear blue skies. John Stewart — a former member of The

Kingston Trio and author of such
hits as *Daydream Believer* and *Gold*
— also created a buzz with his
startling Saturday night set. Robert Cray lived up to his advance
billing, and would go on to become an international celebrity.
Respected Celtic warhorses The
Boys of the Lough brought a sense
of class to various workshops as
did Sunnyland Slim. John Hiatt
made his first appearance at an
Edmonton festival since 1978 and
confirmed his considerable talents
as a songwriter. And a poised Ian
Tyson brought the whole weekend to an agreeable close with
Four Strong Winds. It has ended
every festival since.

The new staff had obviously
done their homework. While they
coped with emergencies — like

Joe Rizzuto (EFMF)

**Lyle Lovett performed at
Gallagher Park in 1988 as a
rising star from Texas**

Sunnyland Slim missing a flight and the toilets running out of paper —
a record-breaking twenty thousand fans turned up to wipe out the
previous year's debt. "The sense was of real relief, because we had a lot
to prove," says Carey. "And it helped us a lot to do that." Aside from the
music, the newly opened beer tent proved a popular addition as the
temperatures soared. And *The Edmonton Journal* gleefully summed up
the whole weekend: "60s vanquished by updated folk." Gulp!

♪   ♪   ♪

With a whole year to prepare and reduced financial pressure, Carey,
Laskiwsky and Petersen approached their second festival with confi-
dence. For the 1987 edition, Petersen booked a number of conspicuous
repeats (including Guy Clark, Doug Sahm and Murray MacLauchlan).
He also added several unsung heroes from the past: Yank Rachell (a
sidekick of Sleepy John Estes), Jethro Burns (best known as the mandolin
virtuoso in the Grand Ole Opry comedy team, Homer & Jethro) and
John D. Loudermilk (author of such classics as *Tobacco Road*, *Abeline*, and
Waterloo). "I wanted to have a full quota of so-called legends," says
Petersen. "People who were getting on and maybe hadn't received their
due. People who had been important in developing certain kinds of
music."

Trailblazers from the sixties included Pentangle's John Renbourn, the Lovin' Spoonful's John Sebastian, and The Band's Rick Danko. Petersen also wanted some new energy and innovation on the bill, and so placed his bets on The Oyster Band (pioneers of the British rogue folk movement), The Shuffle Demons (a hip, quirky jazz-based combo out of Toronto), Eric Bogle (arguably the greatest social songwriter since the young Bob Dylan), and Rodney Crowell and Rosanne Cash (two of the most popular acts in country music at the time).

Crowell and Cash were good friends of Guy Clark, who came to Edmonton in 1986 and gave it his stamp of approval. "The last day, Sunday, I remember standing at the hospitality tent with Guy and he said, 'Holger, what do you think about next year maybe I could bring Rodney Crowell and Rosanne Cash?' I couldn't believe it. I said, 'Well, if you could do that I would be so grateful.' So we set it up and it happened very early in the planning stages of the following year."

Then on July 31, 1987, one week before opening night, a tornado ripped through the city. Twenty-seven people died and hundreds of others were hospitalized or homeless. But as aid poured in for the victims, the festival nervously went ahead. Unlike the seventh festival, temperatures dropped and it rained intermittently throughout number eight. Attendance remained static and the festival went back into the hole for fifty-thousand dollars. Overall, the quality of the performances rose one more big notch.

This time, though, the weekend's highlight occurred at the after-hours volunteer party in the Edmonton Inn, where The Oyster Band, Spirit of West, Rick Danko, Morris Golberg (a key session musician on Paul Simon's *Graceland*) and various other notables, combined forces to deliver the most blistering, life-affirming, shambolic spontaneity ever produced by the festival. "That party has lived on in infamy," recalls volunteer Barry Storeshaw. "I've talked to people all over the place who remember it as the all-time greatest party." *Rolling Stone* reviewer Steve Pond certainly thought so. He would go on to write several features on The Oyster Band on the strength of their performance that night. Throughout the Don Whalen years, musicians usually jammed into the wee hours back at their hotel. It was all informal. The volunteers just wandered around and listened in. "I looked at it as booking another stage and provided professional sound and lighting," says Holger Petersen. "Some of the most magical moments have happened at those parties — just unbelievable things musically."

If The Oyster Band and their assorted colleagues provided the highlight of 1987, John Sebastian performed one of its most embarrassing sets. After the Lovin' Spoonful disbanded in 1968, Sebastian enjoyed brief notoriety as the ultimate tie-dyed, blissed-out, hippie freak at Woodstock and went on to write popular theme tunes for television programs such as *Welcome Back Kotter* and, er, *The Care Bears*. In his Edmonton debut, he mumbled gibberish and sang off-key in a barely audible voice for the best part of forty minutes.

Despite the dreadful Sebastian, Laskiwsky and Carey's publicity attempts began to pay dividends. *Rolling Stone* magazine, which had given the festival a plug earlier in the summer, sent Pond to check it out. *The Globe and Mail* reviewed it as did *The Boston Globe*. Festival highlights "were happily too extensive to fully chronicle," wrote Boston's Susan Wilson. These reviews spread the festival's reputation throughout North America and made it more attractive to musicians. If they are written about from coast to coast, they will come. The festival's generous hospitality and flawless schedules would do the rest, hopefully.

♪ ♪ ♪

By 1988, the operating budget had grown to half a million dollars, up from three hundred thousand in 1986. The volunteer base increased from three hundred to seven hundred and fifty. "They were very exciting years to be involved with the festival," recalls Andy Laskiwsky. And the corporate structure changed from a limited not-for-profit company to a society, which meant it could now have an unlimited membership. Prerequisites for membership included a minimum of two years service as a volunteer and the payment of a nominal fee. The membership now elected the board of directors and they, in turn, hired the staff. Democracy.

Despite last minute cancellations by Cab Calloway and Emmylou Harris, Holger Petersen would outdo himself with his third and final bill. Commitments to his three radio shows, which now included CBC's *Saturday Night Blues*, plus Stony Plain Records, demanded all his time. "Something had to go. It was one of the toughest decisions I have ever made because I truly loved the experience. I felt that I kind of put everything into those three years and it was time to let somebody else do it. The record company was really a going concern at that point, and there was no way I was going to drop that."

Indeed, many of the acts now performing at the festival released albums through Petersen's label, which left him open to criticism. Edmonton, his detractors insinuated, had become the Stony Plain Folk Festival. "I think it's an easy shot to take," he says. "I don't agree. I never felt guilty about that. There was never any motivation to try and do that. I never got a sense from people either that it was a problem."

The 1987 festival is ended with help from k.d. lang . . . Four Strong Winds was by then entrenched as the finale number

Says the *Journal's* Alan Kellogg: "I never completely made up my own mind on it. I heard people say, 'Look, count the number of Stony Plain acts on this list.' And you can't deny it, it was amazing, you know. But by the same token, most of these acts were appropriate acts to play at a folk festival and played other folk festivals." Tom Elsworthy at *The Edmonton Sun* also acknowledges the potential conflict of interest with reservations: "I think that he handled it reasonably well . . . There were a lot of guys that he listened to that he brought into this festival . . . a lot of black musicians who really added an important element to these festivals."

The heart of the 1988 lineup came from Texas. Country-influenced Lyle Lovett, Jimmie Dale Gilmour, Butch Hancock and Marce Lacounture, and Darden Smith stood four-square to Tex-Mex conquistadors Flaco Jimenez, Ponty Bone and Doug Sahm (making his third straight appearance). As for elder statesmen, Petersen scored once again with Bill Monroe and his Bluegrass Boys, Papa John Creach (the former electric violinist with Jefferson Starship and Hot Tuna) and Snooks Eaglin (a stalwart of the New Orleans R&B scene).

The weather forecast called for rain as Friday night rolled by cold but dry. Only Hancock and Lacounture created much of a stir in the early going. But close to midnight, Ian Matthews — the former leader of Matthews Southern Comfort — hauled out his old cover of Joni Mitchell's *Woodstock*. Almost on cue, it started to rain. And it continued through the night and well into the next afternoon. Like the legendary rock festival, Gallagher Park turned into a sea of mud. Amid this upheaval, Terry Wickham arrived at the festival as a guest and marvelled at the morale of the volunteers and organizers as they pulled together to make the event work. "I know there is putting on a brave face, but this went further than that," he said. "It built spirit — not that I like rain — but they were all in this together and got stuck in. And that's what I like about Edmonton: people get stuck in."

The herculean task of performing on the afternoon main stage fell to Jane Siberry. Just as she appeared, the skies really opened up and her fragile, haunting lyrics ended up floundering before the deluge. The weather finally broke in time for Saturday evening, which produced the finest single night of music the festival had yet witnessed. Uncle Bonsai started the ball rolling with their exquisite harmonies and quirky tales of Freudian fixations and beached whales. Through troubadours James Keelaghan and Darden Smith to the rock and rhythm and blues of Papa John Creach, the intensity and energy on stage poured down like silver. The exquisite bluegrass picking of Hot Rize paved the way for a Tex-Mex joyride with the wonderful accordionist Flaco Jimenez and the effervescent Doug Sahm on guitar. Bobby King and Terry Evans — the soulful rhythm and blues vocal muscle behind Ry Cooder — delivered the most exhilarating set seen in Gallagher Park since k.d. lang's in 1984. It earned the first encore of the night.

The Grim Reaper in blue suede shoes followed. Since leaving Fairport Convention, Richard Thompson developed into the most prominent folk-roots songwriter in Britain. A masterful guitarist too, he had fine-tuned his talents and produced his customary raw, dazzling performance. Like Robert Cray, Lyle Lovett was on the verge of international acclaim when he made his Edmonton debut. Poised, acerbic, ludicrous and utterly splendid, his cool idiosyncrasies made instant converts out of much of the masses. Which left The Band's mighty Garth Hudson and Rick Danko to send a tired and emotional audience home with classics like *Stagefright* and *Life Is A Carnival*. This night was the ultimate legacy of Holger Petersen.

Selected recordings

Richard Thompson: Hand of Kindness (Hannibal/Ryko HNCD 1313)

Townes Van Zandt: Rain On A Conga Drum (Mausoleum 269575-2)

Lyle Lovett: Pontiac (MCA MCAMD-42028)

Robert Cray: False Accusations (WEA HCD-8005)

Tom Russell: Road To Bayamon (Stony Plain CDPH 01116)

James Keelaghan: Small Rebellion (Tranquilla Music TMCD002)

Bobby King and Terry Evans: Live And Let Live (Stony Plain SPCD-02089)

Ian Tyson: Cowboyography (Stony Plain SPCD-1102)

Jane Siberry: The Speckless Sky (Duke Street DSMD-31019)

The Oyster Band: Deserters (Rykodisk RCD 10237)

The Great Western Orchestra: Wind In The Wire (Center Fire Records CFA002)

10

We Are The World

■From Ireland to Alberta
■A promoter is born ■World Beat
comes to Edmonton ■Sunny days,
rain-drenched nights■

---

*"No one was coming on stage and it was an hour after the show was
supposed to start. And I wander backstage and start asking people, 'Who is
supposed to be playing? Where is the artistic director?' Nothing had been
organized for the show. Musicians were in complete confusion. And they
were all pointing at me and saying, 'But you are the artistic director.'"*
— TERRY WICKHAM'S RECURRING NIGHTMARE

THE ARCHBISHOP OF DUBLIN ONCE THREATENED to excommuni-
cate Catholics who attended Trinity College — the exclusive
domain of the Protestant Anglo-Irish aristocracy. By the time
Terry Wickham studied economics there in 1972, it was no longer a
mortal sin. "I remember asking my dad when I was young, 'If the
country's poor, why doesn't it print more money?' So I just had a
fascination with money."

His interest in folk music came from his older brother Kevin, who was
fascinated with flamenco guitarists Sabicas, Carlos Montoya and Paco
Pena, but also listened to John Renbourn, Bert Jansch and Robert
Johnson. "Kevin was the main person who brought music into the house.
He certainly nurtured my love of music." Concerts came next — Jethro
Tull, Blodwyn Pig, Pentangle — followed by clubs and pubs. For ten
Irish pence (twenty cents Canadian), the Universal Folk Club offered
shows by such local performers as members of The Chieftains. Slattery's
on Capel Street booked the likes of Barry Moore, now known as Luka

Brent Kirby (EFMF)

Terry Wickham, left, chats with Bill Bourne

Bloom. And The Meeting Place on Dorset Street did the same. "I didn't drink until I was nineteen, but seeing Planxty just as they were forming — playing in two-hundred-seat pubs — and paying a couple of pounds to get in was very exciting. Planxty was my introduction to Irish music, which I had never taken seriously before, or never really enjoyed. That was a revelation — it opened up such a wide field of other folk music."

Kevin emigrated to London, Ontario, in 1971 and Terry spent the next three summers there, supplementing his student income working odd jobs. In 1975, the two brothers hitch-hiked to Calgary and were captivated by the beauty and friendliness of Western Canada. So much so that Terry found a job at a local branch of the Bank of Montreal and emigrated in 1976. Wickham revelled in the vitality and uniqueness of boomtime Alberta. For a year, he stuck the nine-to-five routine of a banker. "But to use a pun, I lost interest. I just felt it was time to take a year or two to myself." So he quit and spent the next three years dedicated to the pursuit of pleasure — playing soccer for the Calgary Mustangs of the Canadian Soccer League. For spending money, he drove a cab.

By 1979, he and Kevin shared a house. And one day in the fall, Kevin popped into Buckdancer's Choice Music — an instrument and record store owned by J.P. Huang, who occasionally promoted folk concerts. "I'd been in there and I had talked to him a few times about records," says Kevin, "and I asked him if there was any music coming up that I'd be interested in. He just mentioned to me that he'd been offered a contract to do Clannad but wasn't interested." The quintet from Donegal sang in Gaelic, not in English. "I just said, 'What would a person need in order to do it?' And he said, 'You just need to pay the band and get a hall.' So I said, 'I'd like to do it if I could; I'd like to try it.' So he said, 'Here take this with you.' It was the contract and it had a phone number for Nicky Ryan." Ryan was Clannad's manager and now produces Enya's albums. The band wanted five-hundred dollars U.S. and to play in a concert hall. "We didn't have to pay any money up front — that was the big thing. That mattered a lot to me."

So Kevin booked a five-hundred-seat theatre at the University of Calgary for November 2, 1979, and filled it at five dollars a ticket. "It just turned out to be such a magical event. Terry got the bug from that because he had a lot of fun." Says Terry: "I got to thinking afterwards — 'I've been looking for something to do and I love music, and I understand finances' — and then I decided to really turn my attention to this business."

Kevin left for university in the East and his younger brother talked to journalists, ticket agents and lawyers, then booked The Chieftains into the Calgary Jubilee Auditorium. Another success. Alan Stivell, John Renbourn, and the Battlefield Band followed but audiences and venues grew smaller and smaller until a nightmare show with the Scottish duo Gaberlunzie brought his new career to a temporary halt. Everything that could go possibly wrong with that gig did. He put the wrong address on the tickets. Even his car broke down on the way home. "I decided I wasn't doing any more concerts until I had a financial backer — that was very important." So he found the sympathetic ear of Jerry Libin. Libin's family made its money in real estate, but Jerry formed Sounds of the World — a company that earned its first break promoting the Irish Rovers across North America. Most of his tours dealt with the likes of magician David Copperfield or the Vienna Boys Choir. "He would unashamedly say, 'I'm not into this to sponsor it, I'm not an artist. This has to make money or it's not going to work.' So it was that pressure." Together they promoted acts as varied as Andre Phillipe Gagnon and Billy Bragg with moderate success and the odd failure.

Then in 1985, the Calgary Centre for Performing Arts opened and hired Terry Wickham to co-ordinate its programming. It booked fifty shows a year that ranged from Russian symphonies to Mexican folk dancers. As his experience increased, so too did his work load. The Centre doubled its concert schedule and organized tours in Western Canada for the likes of country singers Crystal Gale and Emmylou Harris. His folk-roots promotions put him in touch with people like Holger Petersen in Edmonton. Robert Cray performed at the Edmonton folk festival in 1986 and Wickham booked him in Calgary on the same weekend. Two dates back to back made it more feasible for Cray to tour Alberta.

Still, the bureaucratic manner in which the Centre operated began to stifle Wickham's creativity and he quit in the fall of 1987 to return to his partnership with Jerry Libin. A year later, Petersen invited Wickham to apply for the position of artistic director with the Edmonton Folk Music Festival. At first, he declined. Now married to Alberta poet Lorie

Frank Gasparik (EFMF)

Emmylou Harris's perfor-mance in 1990 set a new stan-dard for the festival's after-noon shows

Miseck, and with a young daughter and a new home, he didn't want the upheaval of moving to Edmonton. Besides, all his business connections were in Calgary. "Talking to Kevin changed my mind," says Terry. "He said, 'You're a fool. That's the best show in Alberta. It would be a great place to work and it would be good for you.' " So he applied in January of 1989 and made an instant impression. It didn't hurt to have Holger Petersen in his corner. "I had some communications with Terry over a couple of years. I found him very professional to deal with," says Petersen. "I recommended that he be my successor and it worked out real well."

Wickham walked into a pressure cooker in February. The festival was again almost fifty thousand dollars in debt. Kate Carey had left to raise a family. Andy Laskiwsky had spent several months at the helm but left due to stress and was replaced in January by Loro Carmen, a former organizer for the provincial New Democrats. They depended on charity bingos to pay staff wages. Obviously, the festival needed a serious financial plan. First Carmen paid all the creditors a visit and spoke to them frankly. "They were told in the two previous years, 'No problem, give us credit and we'll make it right with you before the year end.' I wanted to let them know exactly what the situation was and not to paint any rosy pictures." Those owed money were offered a tax-deductible charitable receipt that changed their debts into donations. Some agreed. Some couldn't afford to. Those in dire straits received post-dated cheques. " She really worked hard to get the deficit down, cut really good deals and brought a real business perspective to the festival that I have been able to carry on," says Terry Wickham. Adds Carmen: "What I remember most is coming to work very early and going home very late and there were times that I did not sleep."

With or without sleep, Carmen still charmed sponsors into contributing a phenomenal ninety-one thousand additional dollars in 1989.

Frank Gasparik (EFMF)

Nashville quartet Women in the Round, who were second up on Friday night in 1990, included future country star Pam Tillis (in hat)

Volunteers pitched in and handled most of the clerical duties while she supervised the site construction in Gallagher Park. They also managed much of the marketing, hanging hundreds of advertising signs around the city and setting up information and ticket booths in various malls.

As artistic director, Terry Wickham had little to do with the financial restructuring. "But I couldn't help sticking my nose into it with my background in economics. I found that the ticket price was too low. It was still twenty-five dollars for a weekend when I came. Most good concerts were twenty-five dollars to see, you know, John Prine and Arlo Guthrie." So an 'early bird' weekend pass rose to thirty dollars. The average fan could afford a minimal increase — a 1988 festival survey found out that almost forty-five percent of the audience were university graduates between the age of thirty and thirty-nine earning more than thirty-eight thousand dollars per year. As it turned out, the festival sold a record number of advance tickets for 1989. For their thirty dollars, fans received a bill obviously influenced by Holger Petersen — the return of Doug Sahm for the fourth straight year was one example. Yet, Wickham also provided a platform for such young, inventive performers as

Timbuk 3 (ex-buskers Pat MacDonald and Barbara K., known for their hit *The Future's So Bright I Got To Wear Shades*), Michael Hedges (the flamboyant, new-age, Windham Hill guitarist), T Bone Burnett (the quirky Texas songwriter who has collaborated with the likes of U2, Elvis Costello and Bob Dylan), and Capercaillie (Scotland's leading contemporary Gaelic chanters). On the home front, Wickham booked the strongest contingent of Canadian talent seen at the festival since the early years. Sarah McLachlan, Bill Bourne and Alan MacLeod, James Keelaghan, Garnet Rogers, Spirit of the West, The Great Western Orchestra, Connie Kaldor, and Jane Siberry were all scheduled for the main stage.

Still, opening night preyed on Wickham's unconscious. "I used to have a recurring nightmare," he says. "I was standing out in the audience and no one was coming on stage and it was an hour after the show was supposed to start. And I wander backstage and start asking people, 'Who is supposed to be playing? Where is the artistic director?' Nothing had been organized for the show. Musicians were in complete confusion. And they were all pointing at me and saying, 'But you are the artistic director.' That was a basic insecurity right there. I still get these dreams now and then."

Environment Canada predicted a seventy percent chance of showers for all three days of the 1989 festival, but the sun shone for the whole weekend and brought out record crowds. As for the music, Friday night retained its reputation for mediocrity. Only Capercaillie rose above the humdrum. Roger McGuinn — the founder and driving force behind The Byrds — came up flat on his Saturday afternoon main stage set. The evening belonged to the guitar pyrotechnics of Michael Hedges, the dobro mastery of Nashville's Jerry Douglas and the irrational ingenuity of Timbuk 3. Sunday appeared more promising from the moment former New York City street urchin Steve Forbert began a powerful afternoon main stage set. Forbert's delightful, asthmatic whispers, interrupted by the odd snarl of a harmonica, lit up his bohemian vignettes of romance and social concerns. Night rolled in and Loudon Wainwright III returned after being cast as a "sexist pig" in 1984. This time he came prepared to "offend everyone" with *Colors* — an ode to dog excrement. No offence taken; the set was a triumph. The charming debauchery of Austin country outlaw Jerry Jeff Walker followed. And Jane Siberry held her own until the exquisite Jerry Douglas joined the literary T Bone Burnett for what turned out to be the most exhilarating set of the weekend.

As *Four Strong Winds* faded into the river valley, Carmen and Wickham had pulled off a minor miracle. For the first time, the combined three-day audience rose above thirty thousand. Paid attendance not only wiped out the deficit, but also produced an extra fifty-five thousand dollars surplus. "A lot of people were really thankful," says Wickham. "I think they figured we saved the festival. I don't think that is right. The festival saved itself and got lucky."

♪ ♪ ♪

With money in the bank, the board of directors could now buy computers and hire more staff. Roberta Magnusson signed on in November, 1989, and Richard Davis the following April. Magnusson had supervised rural circulation representatives for the *Edmonton Journal*. Davis came straight from the University of Alberta with a BA in History. Both had worked in the festival office the previous summer under Loro Carmen, so preparations for 1990 ran smoothly — for a while at least. Then, less than two weeks from show time, a disgruntled former member of the board of

Brent Kirby (EFMF)

Crash Test Dummies (that's Brad Roberts in the foreground) in 1990 . . . too original to amount to anything?

directors sued the festival, alleging financial mismanagement and claiming it owed him one hundred and sixty thousand dollars for services he had provided. As a result, the festival's bank account and ticket revenue were frozen, which brought the festival to the brink of bankruptcy. "Just days before you're ready to open, you need that cash flow" to pay performers and run the festival, Loro Carmen explains. And then there was the prospect of turning away thousands of people who'd already bought tickets. "It was pretty damn scary," says Carmen.

With only two days before the gates opened, festival lawyer Percy Odynak managed to get crucial operating funds freed up. The show could go on. The claim against the festival was eventually dismissed entirely, and by fall all of its funds were released. "What this did do was force the festival to become even more professional," says Odynak.

Joe Rizzuto (EFMF)

Fatala's exuberant singing and dancing earned a standing ovation in 1990

"There had been an instance when filing cabinets were gone through and an envelope was found with six hundred U.S. cash in it." Not anymore. Now, its books receive an annual audit by chartered accountants.

The big event — possibly the finest festival to date — got underway on August 10, with nothing but blue skies as far as the eye could see. Wickham added twenty-one hours of workshops and cut back main stage by three acts. Pioneering British guitarist Davey Graham and blues belter Koko Taylor accounted for the annual contingent of veterans. While world beat awareness had begun in Europe in the early eighties, only now did it make its presence felt in Gallagher Park with arrival of The Kafala Brothers (Angola), Fatala (Guinea) and The Four Brothers (Zimbabwe). Papa Wemba (Zaire) cancelled at the last minute. Appropriately, Juba, a local act, opened the festival with a set of South African freedom songs. And for once, Friday night crackled with a variety of fresh, exhilarating new bands led by the unknown Crash Test Dummies

("Stars of the future? Don't be silly; they're too original," one Rod Campbell wrote in the next morning's *Edmonton Journal*.)

Future celebrities were not limited to the Dummies that night. Women In The Round followed Juba. This Nashville-based quartet included Pam Tillis, who has since recorded numerous country hits. And Ontario harpist Loreena McKennitt has made the odd gold album since following Dutch country blues guitarist Hans Theessink and his tuba-wielding partner John Sass late that hot August night.

Anita Maloney (EFMF)

Saffire, the Uppity Blues Women, performed a hilarious set of sassy, feminist humor in 1991

Although a good idea, afternoon main stage showcases now resembled an elephant's graveyard, where relics of yesteryear paused briefly before passing into oblivion — Steve Forbert being a notable exception. All that changed with the arrival of country diva Emmylou Harris on Saturday. Here was an artist in her prime, dishing out such gems as Rodney Crowell's *Leaving Louisiana In The Broad Daylight* and Hank William's *Jambalaya* from a twenty-year-old treasure chest, easily earning her a standing ovation. On Sunday, Fatala's joyful costumes and exuberant singing and dancing produced the same response.

And yet, 1990 will mostly be remembered for the phenomenal set from Solomon Burke, who rolled into town Saturday afternoon with several of his twenty-two children instead of eleven musicians. His band had crashed in Montana and were stranded. Now it was up to Amos Garrett and the house band. "Terry was as pale as a ghost. He came over to the hotel; he was just about to have a cardiac arrest," says Garrett. "I was sweating bullets too." Still, they recruited a horn section from the Edmonton Jazz Ensemble and called a rehearsal hours before headlining that night. "We all tuned up, and he sat down. He was tired and he picked up his microphone and just sang a phrase to test it. The hair went up on the back of my neck, and we all looked around at each other and we knew right then. It was electric."

Frank Gasparik (EFMF)

Violent Femmes in 1991 . . . thousands flocked to hear their sonnets of murder and mayhem

Burke arrived at Gallagher Park in his white Cadillac dressed in a large ermine robe. Folk music had changed considerably since Woody Guthrie and Pete Seeger hopped freight trains between gigs. As Burke arrived, media co-ordinator Doug Ianson sat backstage with his nine-year-old son: "My son yelled out, loud enough for everyone to hear, 'Hey dad, look, it's a wrestler'!" After shaking hands with the stage crew, the one-time king of Rock 'n' Soul returned from exile. Two of his sons stood poker-faced on stage by his side in tuxedos, wiped his brow and arranged his clothing as he opened with a medley of his brilliant early sixties hits — *If You Need Me, Tonight's The Night, Just Out Of Reach, I Can't Stop Loving You.* That glorious, gigantic, warm and endearing voice of his had lost little in the meantime, as the magnificent house band roared along behind him more than equal to the task. "When we walked off stage that night — it's the first time I think, and only time, I might have levitated," recalls Amos Garrett. "I remember for a few seconds where I couldn't feel the soles of my shoes touching the plywood backstage."

♪   ♪   ♪

By the end of 1990, the festival had a hundred and thirty thousand dollars in its war chest, but no general manager. Loro Carmen had quit. "I guess I could have had the patience and maybe a little bit more staying power, but I was low on energy at the time and I didn't feel as comfortable. Looking at the toll it had taken on me personally, emotionally and physically, I thought, 'Can I really produce another festival that's quality, that's bang on, and put up with the political shit too?' I didn't think I could. So I resigned." Terry Wickham now took over her portfolio and hired Don Snider — a former colleague at the Calgary Centre for Performing Arts — to handle production duties.

Aside from the last-minute cancellations of South Africa's premier *a cappella* singers, Ladysmith Black Mambazo, and Mali's kora master, Toumani Diabate, preparations for 1991 passed without a crisis. For once. The previous year, Wickham had booked such world beat performers as The Kafala Brothers, The Four Brothers and Davey Spillane. This year, the international presence included Mari Boine Persen (Norway), Rossy (Madagascar), Toto La Momposina y sus Tambores (Colombia), Guo Yue (China), Joji Hirota (Japan) and Pol Brennan (Ireland). This great global awakening also included the Mexican-American band Los Lobos, the Gaelic speaking Scots, Capercaillie and Mouth Music, Cajun zydeco accordionist Zachary Richard, and Jamaica's Inner Circle.

The temperature hovered around a hundred degrees Fahrenheit as local country warbler Jane Hawley and her Cranky Brats kick-started the revelry. Two nights later Los Lobos brought it all to a close buffeted by a monsoon. Still, close to forty-thousand trekked through the turnstiles over the three days. Capercaillie earned the only encore Friday. Tight and superbly confident, their manic jigs and reels and celestial songs of love and fishermen were undeniably top drawer. A wonderful Chicago trio, Saffire — The Uppity Blues Women, also sparkled through a hilarious set of sassy, feminist humor. Saturday afternoon, Milwaukee's Violent Femmes held court on main stage with their terminally beautiful sonnets about murder and mayhem, sex and suicide, faith and flamingos. Having just released *Why Do Birds Sing?*, their most acclaimed album in almost a decade, the Femmes produced the biggest single-day walk up audience in festival history. A predominantly youthful crowd — vital for the future health of the festival — bought over a thousand tickets to witness the apocalyptic urgency of the three brilliant Femmes. It took another eight hours for the Oyster band to replenish the same ferocious intensity with their magnificently delinquent combination of traditional English country dance tunes and rock 'n' roll. Sunday afternoon, Inner Circle took over and the crowd danced like demons. Brooklyn cowboy Tom Russell and Ferron stole the heart of Sunday night before Los Lobos dazzled in the downpour to bring the main event to a close for another year.

♪   ♪   ♪

The local music community mourned the passing of Clarence "Big" Miller as the festival approached its thirteenth anniversary. Throughout his long and colorful career as a jazz trombonist and singer, he performed with the likes of the Lionel Hampton and Jay McShann orchestras. Miller also became a regular fixture at gospel workshops in Gallagher Park, highlighted by his superb Sunday morning set with Solomon Burke in 1990. The Rankin Family provided the musical backdrop as the festival announced its 1992 lineup in the tiny Cloverdale

Frank Gasparik (EFMF)

Angelique Kidjo, in 1993, was in the lineup for the festival's first Thursday night

community hall. Within a year, the Rankins would fill the twenty-seven-hundred-seat Jubilee Auditorium in Edmonton.

Not only did Wickham reveal his bill, but also unveiled a new site layout. In the past, sound often bled from one workshop stage into another. To eliminate the problem, he spread these stages west by several blocks. A mixed bag of international, high-energy, dance bands dominated the latest schedule: Edward II (Great Britain), Thomas Mapfumo & The Blacks Unlimited (Zimbabwe), The Bhundu Boys (Zimbabwe), Toots and The Maytals (Jamaica) and Alias Ron Kavana (Ireland). For headliners, Wickham produced the exquisite roots aficionado Ry Cooder and Montreal's Kate and Anna McGarrigle. Links to the past increased for the first time in several years and included bluesman Robert Jr. Lockwood (the adopted son of the peerless Robert Johnson, hence Robert Jr.), Charlie Louvin (one of the all-time great country harmonizers) and Peggy Seeger (the British folk club stalwart and partner of the late Ewan MacColl).

Ry Cooder made his only Canadian appearance in 1992 accompanied by his thirteen-year-old percussionist son Joachin and multi-talented, multi-instrumentalist David Lindley. Highly anticipated, Cooder and his colleagues seized the day with a sublime set that rode on a slipstream as broad as zydeco (*Les Bon Temps Roulez*) and gospel (*Jesus On The Mainline*). All the same, Ron Kavana may have proved himself the man of the hour. His Saturday night Cajun ceilidh raised such a response, that he returned to fill in for the missing Toots and The Maytals on Sunday night. Only this time around, Kavana brought along Amos Garrett and his colleagues, Arcady (the fine Irish traditional band) and David Lindley for a ruthlessly spirited and spontaneous finale.

"Folk music fest joins big leagues," reported The *Edmonton Journal* ten years after it suggested "Festival nearing big league status." God and copy editors work in mysterious ways.

♪   ♪   ♪

Almost forty-five thousand men, women and children attended the 1992 festival. To date, that remains an attendance record even though Wickham added an extra evening in 1993. His initial plan was to book a recognizable performer such as Van Morrison to perform on Thursday night — someone to lure the uninitiated into Gallagher Park. Instead, he ended up with the relatively unknown but intoxicating West African blend of Baaba Maal (Senegal), Ishmael Lo (Senegal) and Angelique Kidjo (Benin) along with the sullen charm of American J.J. Cale. As it turned out, these four acts drew a modest audience of around three-and-a-half thousand, but still broke even.

The mythical Planxty first exposed Terry Wickham in the sixties to traditional Irish music. And although that quartet broke up in 1976, he now brought three of the original members — Andy Irvine, Liam O'Flynn and Donal Lunny — to perform individually in Edmonton. For more Celtic flavor, he added Paddy Glackin and Triona Ni Dhomhnaill (both ex-Bothy Band), her sister Maighreda Ni Dhomhnaill, Johnny Cunningham (ex-Silly Wizard) and Mary Coughlan (although Coughlan is more of a torch singer). Wickham also booked English traditional instrumentalists Chris Wood and Andy Cutting along with the more contemporary accordionist Keith Hancock to ensure a decent measure of reels and jigs, polkas and hornpipes.

Once again, the weather played havoc with main stage performances as it poured continuously throughout most of Friday and Saturday night. Daytime, though, remained glorious. As a result, the workshops, for once, surpassed the nightly concerts for quality and consistency. While the Celts made the sparks fly so did the lucid, lively and literate song and dance man Rory McLeod. The fabulous Fairfield Four gospel singers provoked earnest elation as did Robert Earl Keen Jr.'s captivating tales of redemption, remorse and barbecues.

Aside from Randy Newman's hilariously caustic Saturday afternoon set, this weekend produced the most unconventional show-stoppers yet: the Tuva Ensemble. Looking like extras from Bernardo Bertolucci's movie *The Last Emperor*, their honest-to-god out-of-this-world-voices left the assembled wide-eyed and breathless. Each singer in this group from the steppes of the former Soviet Union can somehow produce two harmonies simultaneously — a low, guttural humming and a rustic whistling. Throat singers they get tagged. It would, after all, be bloody difficult to sing without one.

"What we will have now is now is four nights of good music instead of three," says Terry Wickham. "I think that is to be celebrated. That was the beauty of 1993."

Selected recordings

Capercaillie: Sidewaulk (Green Linnet 1094)
Garnet Rogers: Small Victories (Snow Goose Songs SGS1117)
Joe Louis Walker: The Gift (Hightone 801Z)
Lucinda Williams: Sweet Old World (Chamelion/WEA 61351-2)
Steve Forbert: Alive on Arrival (Nemperor 35538)
Grievous Angels: One Job Town (Stony Plain SPCD-1162)
Hans Theessink: Johnny And The Devil (Stony Plain Records CDFF-70545)
Emmylou Harris With The Nash Ramblers: At The Ryman (WEA CD-26664)
Solomon Burke: A Change Is Gonna Come (Rounder 2053)
Angelique Kidjo: Logozo (Mango CCD-9918)
Thomas Mapfumo: Chamunorwa (Mango CCD-9900)
Fatala: Fatala (WOMAD WOMCD-11)

A year in the life of a festival

11

All together now

■Summer in January ■Putting together
the bill ■The volunteer army ■People
of the hill ■Dancing with with Long
John ■Showtime! ■

---

*"He didn't know who I was, but he'd look at me and he'd always say, 'Hi,
honeychild. You want your favorite?' I'd say, 'Yep.' And he'd do it, St. Louis
Blues."*
— FESTIVAL VOLUNTEER NOREEN TATE REMEMBERS BIG MILLER'S SUNDAY
WORKSHOPS

A SPIRITLESS JANUARY SUN creeps through the windows of
the Ortona Armory. The temperature outside hovers around
minus twenty-five degrees Celsius as the city digs itself out after
weeks of continuous snow. Inside the modest world headquarters of the
Edmonton Folk Music Festival at the foot of Bellamy Hill, a large color
photograph of Emmylou Harris spreads an elusive warmth throughout
the main office. Above the rattle and hum of ancient radiators, the joyful
rhythms of Abana Ba Nasery (Nursery Boys Go Ahead) — the guitar and
bottle kings of Kenya — resound, carefree and compelling.

Oblivious to this informal cacophony, Terry Wickham phones an
agent in Washington, D.C., who books tours for South Africa's premier
mbaqanga act, Mahlathini and The Mahotella Queens. Wickham wants
them for the 1994 festival but their summer tour of North America ends
before Edmonton's August dates. Undaunted, he dials Edinburgh,
Scotland. The manager of The Proclaimers answers. Twins Craig and
Charlie Reid conquered the airwaves on both sides of the Atlantic in
1988 with the single *I'm Gonna Be (500 Miles)* and Wickham wants them

Frank Gasparik (EFMF)

Solomon Burke and the late Big Miller give a gospel workshop in 1990

for their youth appeal. Again, tour dates do not coincide. The Proclaimers will, however, perform an indoor concert for the festival during their swing through Alberta later that summer.

And so the horse trading continues. Serious negotiations with Van Morrison started in earnest in 1993, when Mary Coughlan brought saxophonist Richie Buckley to Edmonton. Buckley also plays and records with Morrison and passed on a good word. To make this gig even more attractive, Wickham booked Solomon Burke, one of Morrison's heroes. That approach worked in the past when David Lindley's presence tickled Ry Cooder's fancy. And if it doesn't, Terry Wickham is a persistent lad and there's always another year.

Wickham will make hundreds of these calls throughout the year in his efforts to construct a balanced bill. Years of experience have taught him how to dicker for a fair fee. Given a choice, he prefers to approach singers or musicians directly rather than go through their agents or managers — more for artistic reasons than financial. For instance, Irish piper Liam O'Flynn readily accepted his offer in 1993 once he knew his friends and fellow countrymen Donal Lunny and Paddy Glackin were on the same bill. Agents, of course, want as much for their acts as they figure a promoter can afford. Their asking price can get preposterous: $100,000 for a performer Wickham valued at $30,000. Fees paid to artists have ranged from $750 Cdn to $17,500 US. On top of that, they receive accommodation and transportation to and from Edmonton. On average, each act costs about $5,000, which comes out of an artistic budget set in 1993 at $270,000.

The formation of each year's lineup starts with two or three return engagements. Then throughout the winter, Wickham will sift through more than five hundred biographies, cassette tapes and compact discs sent to the office annually by various acts hoping for a booking. This process will produce one, maybe two more contracts. Additional acts are added as touring schedules become more apparent. Most of the remaining program, however, crystallizes after discussions with various personal contacts that range from international folk-roots celebrities to local media. Which just leaves his wish list of high-profile performers who he tries for every year — Van Morrison, Christy Moore, Sweet Honey In The Rock, Billy Bragg and Joni Mitchell, whom he finally collared in 1994. "Our obligation is to open as many minds to folk music as we can. If we can book a major name that brings in the kids — The Proclaimers, Bonnie Raitt or a Van Morrison — I can almost guarantee we'll keep them," says Wickham. "They'll see it's a cool place to hang out and they'll have a good time."

Generally, Wickham prefers to have all contracts signed by the end of May in time for the press conference held to publicize each year's event. Still, there are always last-minute no-shows. Those absent without leave in the past include Cab Calloway, Toots and The Maytals, Nanci Griffith and Ladysmith Black Mambazo. Reasons for cancellations vary. Steel guitarist Leon McAuliff (a former member of Bob Wills' pioneering Texas Playboys) and blues belter Eddie Cleanhead Vincent both died shortly before their dates in Edmonton. Most of the others bowed out because of illness. Inevitably, it means Wickham searches for replacements up to the last minute. And the more prestigious the cancellation, the more vulnerable he becomes. When an agent senses desperation fees rise. "Pass!" One act will not make or break the whole weekend, Wickham reckons.

Once an agreement in principle is reached, his assistant handles the paperwork. Richard ("I guess I'm really just a computer geek at heart") Davis will develop a file on every performer booked to appear at the festival. Besides a complete weekend itinerary that starts and ends with transport to and from Edmonton, each listing outlines the various special needs of individuals. These can range from an extra strong bed for a three-hundred-pound-plus performer like Solomon Burke to a comfortable first-class flight for six-foot, seven-inch tuba bluesman John Sass. The technical requirements for sound and lighting are also recorded. Furthermore, Davis takes care of work permits and tax waivers for international artists. Those from the U.S. can earn $15,000 in Canada before paying taxes. Overseas performers can make $5,000. Few exceed their limit in Edmonton but the festival must still file a T-4 on their behalf.

As show time approaches, Davis passes his information on to the appropriate volunteers. The airport crew meets flights and shuttles performers to their hotel, where the hospitality crew awaits to escort them to their rooms. Transportation to and from Gallagher Park departs every fifteen minutes and once on site all of an artist's needs are taken care of. Day and night a guard watches over their instruments. Golf carts will carry them to various workshops. Masseurs are available to knead aching muscles. The kitchen caters for every diet imaginable, while the Green Room provides sustenance for the nervous and neighborly.

For Wickham, the last serious artistic task involves arranging the nightly main stage lineup and the daily workshop and mini-concert schedules. Held on seven small stages scattered throughout the site, Wickham's workshops bring together diverse acts to sing or play around common themes. An insightful example in 1993 fell under the heading Sing Out!, which featured the Fairfield Four (a gospel quintet from Nashville), the Tuva Ensemble (a trio of throat singers from the steppes of Russia) and Moxy Fruvous (an *a cappella* pop quartet from Toronto). Depending on the chemistry on stage, this process can produce either wonderful interaction between performers or it can simply turn into a disjointed free for all. It takes experience and a great deal of intuitiveness to find the right blend. Self-critical, Wickham reckons he may finally have the hang of it after an inconsistent start.

♪ ♪ ♪

Despite all of the excitement and prestige of the actual event, Wickham and his full-time staff — Davis and administrator Roberta Magnusson — spend considerably more winter hours on mundane office business. Budgets need preparation, reports need deliberation, meetings need co-ordination, staff need vacations. While Magnusson handles most of the year-round clerical duties and accounting, selecting a new logo for publicity material requires a team endeavor. The difference between a good graphic (1993) and a bad (1992) on souvenir clothing can mean the loss of $10,000 in weekend sales.

The intrepid trio also combines efforts to apply for various government funding. Grants can amount to $160,000. Seventy-five thousand dollars, by far the largest contribution, comes from the City of Edmonton. The federal government, however, provided little support until 1992. In

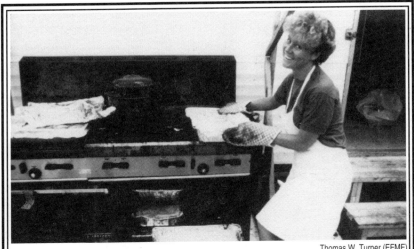

Thomas W. Turner (EFMF)
Kitchen crew volunteer from 1986 . . . feeding hundreds of performers and volunteers is no small task

1993, the Department of Communications handed over $20,000, while Canada Council gave $750. "In my view, council support of folk music is tokenism at its worst," says Wickham. "As a blatant example, in 1993, the Calgary Philharmonic Orchestra, with a budget of $4 million to $5 million, receives $750,000 from the Canada Council. The Edmonton Folk Music Festival, which has a budget of $1.15 million, receives $750." He considers the council elitist — "If it's not classical music, it doesn't count!" — and wants more help to develop promising new talent.

Considerably more assistance comes from local sponsors. In the past, individual benefactors have donated up to $50,000 annually, mainly in goods in kind. These contributions can vary from carpentry nails to advertising and added up to almost $300,000 in 1993. In return, major sponsors receive advertising on all of the festival's publicity material, which raises their public profile and strengthens their relationship with the community. All donations, of course, are tax deductible.

By the end of March, Wickham, Davis and Magnusson have completed most of their tedious winter duties. "Pressure starts to build in May for the June news conference, then begins again closer to the festival," says Magnusson. Once the lineup is more or less finalized, press packages with biographical sketches need to be written and publicity posters and pamphlets prepared. Three hundred thousand color brochures are distributed throughout the country. These provide provincial tourist boards with details on everything from the beer sold on site to the cost of Park 'n' Ride. The festival rents city buses to ferry fans to Gallagher Park. Local media outlets receive an extensive information package along with a cassette that features the various acts. It's hoped the publicity will boost "early bird" ticket sales. An adult weekend pass bought in June 1993 cost $44. Individual tickets bought in August added up to $100. "Ninety-six percent of the box office is in the bank when the gates open," says Davis. All this increased activity requires extra staff. Contract employees such as production manager Don Snider and co-ordinator of volunteers Vicki Fannon return to the fold in April and additional summer students are hired in May. They will manage the festival's box office at the Ortona Armory, while volunteers set up booths in shopping malls around the city. Throughout the winter, Snider spends his time looking after the technical needs of such touring country kingpins as Hank Williams Jr. and George Strait. Come spring, this young man's fancy turns to . . . semitrailers. It will take twenty loads to carry all the festival equipment from the warehouse to Gallagher Park and Snider must find some generous sponsor to donate a suitable vehicle plus a crane, a tractor and several trucks to raise and raze the complete site.

His prayers also mention rain a lot. Due to potential damage, heavy vehicles do not cross Gallagher Park when it's wet. Construction, then, slows down. Considering he has little more than two weeks to put the whole site together, delays can create serious complications. But assuming there is a god in heaven, he will unload the first semitrailer at the park with one task in mind: to install a field kitchen. With full stomachs, his volunteer crew will then assemble seven kilometres of fence around a site five-and-a-half city blocks by two. Once this area is secure, construction begins in earnest. Forty-seven makeshift structures, mostly tents, need erecting. They include a huge main stage and a second kitchen — a sixty-two-hundred square foot facility, that creates fifteen hundred hot meals twice a day for all the volunteers, staff, performers and guests.

Finally, the production crew will provide the labor to install the thirty thousand watt main stage sound system (an average home stereo belts out fifty watts). "Testing! Testing! One, two!"

♪   ♪   ♪

While Don Snider supervises his crew, Vicki Fannon oversees the other thirty-seven crews — thirteen hundred individuals in all and a waiting list of another two hundred. "I believe we have the strongest volunteer corps of all the major folk festivals in Canada ," says Wickham. "In Edmonton, the volunteers carry a lot more responsibility. They do more tasks, which keeps our staff low, which keeps our prices down."

Like her colleagues Magnusson and Davis, Fannon started out as a volunteer. From 1983 to 1991, she greeted performers at the airport and still laughs about the surprise expressed by several American acts after discovering hotels and paved roads in Edmonton. In all that time, though, she never once saw the festival. She simply enjoyed helping people she admired — performers such as former Pentangle guitarist John Renbourn and country outlaw Jerry Jeff Walker.

Each volunteer must log at least forty hours prior to the festival or sixteen during it, mainly in four, four-hour shifts. In return, they receive a T-shirt, all their meals, free access to the extraordinary nightly parties and very little public recognition. "What you get out of it is more than the time and effort you put in," says thirteen-year veteran Connie Banigan, who heard all of half a song one particularly busy weekend. While each crew has its own co-ordinator, Fannon meets with each unit before the fun begins in earnest. Newcomers and veterans alike receive updated orientation and shift details. Volunteers who fail to show up for their shifts can have their privileges revoked and in rare cases find themselves banned from the site.

Once the gates open, the staff hand over the festival to the volunteers to run. Only Roberta Magnusson remains busy tallying the daily revenue. The rest critique and take care of last minute glitches. For instance in 1993, Senegal's Ishmael Lo went missing prior to his main stage performance, forcing Wickham to juggle his lineup. The same year, Richard Davis spent most of his Saturday morning searching for a Russian translator for the Tuva Ensemble and a bottle of oxygen for English songwriter Roy Harper. Minor details.

There is no such thing as a typical volunteer, says Fannon. Their backgrounds are as diverse as the tasks they perform. Here the functional illiterate and research scientist work side by side with the casual laborer and doctor. Their motivation also varies greatly. Take Bruce Bischoff who tunes the festival's three pianos, for instance: "The folk festival is a place to let your alter ego hang out. I'm a frustrated composer. This way I get to work on the best pianos on stage in front of thousands of people." Dressed in a white lab coat cut like a tuxedo with tails, no less.

As for stage crew co-ordinator Dave Charette: "Everybody's got their cause and this is mine." Others such as Glenn Jenkins and Jennifer McGregor inherited their enthusiasm from their parents. Glenn first volunteered at the age of ten and Jennifer at thirteen. Seven years later she still revels in the camaraderie: "It's like a family after you've volunteered for a couple of years." Brad and Sue Hare will attest to that. They fell in love and married after working on the site crew in 1988.

Thomas W. Turner (EFMF)

Children under 12 go to the festival for free, and get their own entertainment like Major Conrad Flapps in 1993

Other couples such as Brian and Toni Nickurak travel from Jasper each summer to make their contributions, while Calgary's Vic Bell has done the same for more than ten years. Bell, incidentally, wrote *Snap The Line Tight*, which James Keelaghan recorded on his debut album, *Timelines*.

Volunteering can also have its drawbacks. Ken McGregor worked on the stage crew in 1980. "Stan Rogers was at an early workshop on a Sunday morning, and that's a tough thing to do after partying all night. He wasn't particularly happy and there weren't that many people there." His microphone did not work properly and McGregor went to fix it. Rogers snapped, "If you touch that mike I'll break your head." They settled their differences amiably after his set. Omer Saucier worked on the stage crew in 1993 and cringes at the memory of the Women of Reggae — Judy Mowatt, Sister Carol and Sister Breeze. "They were a horrible, horrible band to deal with. Their manager, everyone, was running around smoking pot, because it's part of their religion." After numerous delays, this talented trio ended up singing just two songs in an hour. "People in the audience just were looking at us (the stage crew) like, 'Kill, kill.' "

For Alan Toft one of the most unpleasant tasks was pulling drunk performers out of the parties to ferry them to the airport. "I had to get Townes Van Zandt. He was just out of it. I had to stop him from putting his half-empty gin bottle back in his case. It was just like taking a child. But I got him through customs and on to the plane."

Despite their frailties, these same performers provide endearing moments, too. "The one thing I always loved was Sunday when Big Miller did his workshops," says kitchen co-ordinator Noreen Tate. "He didn't know who I was, but he'd look at me and he'd always say , 'Hi, honeychild. You want your favorite?' I'd say, 'Yep.' And he'd do it, *St. Louis Blues.*" Her colleague Brendi Walls recalls sitting at a party listening to a group of musicians playing one of her favorite waltzes. "Without a partner, my feet started to move, because I love to dance. I looked up and there was this man standing there. He said, 'You can dance. Dance with me.'" It was Long John Baldry.

One of the greatest moments for utility volunteer Andy Donnelly occurred in the acoustic room at the performers' hotel in 1992. Seated around a table jamming were some of the high kings of Celtic music: Dick Gaughan, Ron Kavana and Arcady. "They were all sitting there playing and there was one wee boy who was a volunteer from Edmonton with his guitar. Kavana turned to him and says, 'Come on , give us a tune lad.' The boy was dead nervous and reluctant to do it and Kavana says, 'Ah, come on.' And this wee volunteer started playing and they all played with him and it was just tremendous. That to me was really something."

As co-ordinator of performer hospitality, Louise McKay deals more with the various musicians and singers than most. Star-struck volunteers do not make her crew. "We get to see a different side of the performers. You never know with some of these people what they're going to be like." Demanding, drunk, temperamental, rude, polite, placid, sober or con- tent: it takes all kinds to fill a bill. While inflated egos can make McKay's job difficult, the more courteous often seek her out to offer their gratitude. That, she concedes, makes it all worth while. "The thing with performers is that a lot of times these guys have been in a different city every day of the summer. They're lucky if they remember their names, so it's not surprising if they're a little crabby. We just try to make them happy again."

♪ ♪ ♪

Fans line up around four o'clock on Friday afternoon for the gates to open at five. At the appointed hour, hundreds stampede across the grounds to stake prime positions in front of the main stage — the area turns instantly into a gigantic patchwork quilt of nylon tarps and blankets. "You have to be in good physical condition to get a decent spot," says long-time fan Ian Perry. "We've been using thirteen or fourteen-year-old boys. If you don't have one of those in your group, you're out of luck." Once settled, the hungry can find nourishment at numerous concession stands. All stall owners must submit menus to the festival office prior to the event in order to ensure a variety of quality food for a reasonable price. The opening act — a sacrificial lamb for the most part — appears at five-thirty. The stature of the artists will increase as the program advances. As dark descends, thousands of candles fill the arena with a serene sense of occasion. "Sitting on the hill at night, it's a pretty peaceful atmosphere," says Gerry McFadyen, a seasoned campaigner.

Traditionally, the most boisterous acts arrive on stage around ten o'clock and perform to closing time. Terry Wickham wants fans dancing out the gate. If they leave contented, he figures, they are more likely to return the following day. The revelry returns at eleven the next morning. Saturday's first six hours feature a combination of over forty workshops and mini-concerts, as well as a mid-afternoon main stage, headline performance — a serious challenge even for fit fourteen-year-olds.

Children have their own stage and craft area around the park's regular playground. Kids under twelve enjoy free admittance to the festival. Here, hundreds of painted faces turn waste material into art destined for the fridge door. In a feces-free sand pit, budding paleontologists hunt for fossils, while dozens of would-be Tarzans and Janes swarm over the jungle-gym. A hot day will turn the paddling pool into a cauldron of little bare bums and saturated parents offering mock threats of retribution. Then there are the wandering jugglers and clowns who compete for attention with actors, storytellers, magicians, puppets and pets. Menageries of rats and cats and elephants, eensy weensy spiders and even frogs that went a-courting are indispensable for all singalong specialists.

For those past puberty, few vantage points compete with the beer gardens. Its patrons can drink up to 200 kegs of beer on a good weekend and dance to the most animated acts on offer. Stacey McCue, a relatively recent festival convert, recalls one particular rave there in 1991. "It was Saturday afternoon and about thirty-seven degrees. I was in there with a couple of beers. Then Zachary Richard came on the stage nearby and started playing *Jambalaya On The Bayou*. It was so good: that hot, hot summer day, the Louisiana Cajun music, which I like anyway, and the beer. The atmosphere, that to me was the folk festival."

Few festivals though, come and go without the odd downpour. Rain can affect the box office by as much as $120,000, Wickham estimates. It can also ruin more pensive performances such as Jane Siberry's in 1988. In the trenches, the fans can adjust or leave. The more resilient include John Wilson and his young son Gregory. Disabled and legally blind, Gregory spends most of the weekend in his wheelchair lulled by the lure of hidden voices. "That kid will listen to the music and not go to the bathroom for fourteen hours straight," says John. "He knows it's an inconvenience for someone to take him. And he doesn't pee himself either. He doesn't want to leave." The festival prints schedules in Braille and those in wheelchairs can listen and watch the nightly concerts from an accessible area close to the main stage. The workshops require more mobility which inclement weather makes more challenging.

"It was a Saturday morning," recalls John. "I'm with Gregory. It's pouring. I'm pushing the wheelchair and there's six inches of mud on the wheels. We're going to take in a harmonica workshop." Slip sliding away, they finally reach their destination. "We're all sort of huddled around, twenty or thirty of us. In comes Long John Baldry, all six-feet, whatever there is of him and he's solid white — white shoes, white pants, white hat, everything. He's like a god. He starts to back his harmonica player for two songs. Then it's just a free-for-all jam. I'll never forget that."

Sunday's schedule follows along the same lines as Saturday's, only with more gospel workshops. Also, the main stage ends earlier with a tribute to the volunteers and the singing of the festival anthem, *Four Strong Winds*. Terry Wickham

Frank Gasparik (EFMF)
Ron Kavana made one young volunteer's day in 1992

rounds up as many performers as possible to participate in this ritual. Many are backstage in the hospitality Green Room feeling no pain by this point. Alan MacLeod enjoys the odd beer. In 1992, he stood at the bar long enough to lodge his belt buckle on the counter. As Andy Donnelly recalls: "It was just before the finale and Bill Bourne says to him, 'Come on, we've got to go.' And MacLeod says, 'My legs don't seem to be working.' His wife tried to grab him and somebody else did and just about pulled the whole bar over. There were three people hauling him away and another three holding on to the bar." MacLeod eventually answered the call to perform *Amazing Grace* on his bagpipes.

♪   ♪   ♪

As the last notes fade over Gallagher Park, the dismantling of the site begins. The sound and lighting systems come down first to prevent possible rain damage. It takes a minimum of twenty-five volunteers to return Gallagher Park to its natural state within the allotted time. After three late nights of partying, not everyone meets the bell the next morning. "Everybody gets burnt out. It's the biggest volunteer problem we have actually," says Terry Wickham. Incentives for punctuality include draws for free return flights to Toronto and one-way bungee jumps.

The tear-down occurs in reverse order from construction, with the field kitchen left standing until most of the other equipment is stacked on pallets and returned to the festival's warehouse — a 5,500-square-foot facility that costs $10,000 a year to rent. Finally, officials from Parks and Recreation inspect the site for damage. The festival must meet all reparations, which normally amount to grass repairs. Bluegrass they can handle. Seed and sod too, as it turns out.

Meanwhile, back at the Ortona Armory, Roberta Magnusson balances the books. All the revenue generated at the festival's various concession stands and box offices is initially dumped into one account. Now she must determine where it all came from and pay outstanding bills. The hotel tab alone totals more than $33,000. Miscellaneous costs — such as the $20 spent on Polident for senior blues pianist Charles Brown in 1993— also need recording. While some performers demand payment in cash, others more familiar with Edmonton know their cheques won't bounce. All fees must correlate with receipts. With her audit complete, it's time once again to apply for new grants and file reports.

Selected recordings

Mahlathini and the Mahotella Queens: Thokozile (Virgin CDEWV-6)
Zachary Richard: Women In The Room (A&M 75021-5302-2)
John Renbourn: Black Balloon (Shanachie SHCD-97009)
Ron Kavana: Coming Days (Chiswick CDWIKD 94)
Dick Gaughan: A Different Kind Of Love Song (Festival CMCD-17)
Billy Bragg: Brewing Up With (Polygram POLM42005)
Townes Van Zandt: Townes Van Zandt (Tomato Tom-222)
Van Morrison: Astral Weeks (Warner CD-01768)
The Proclaimers: Sunshine on Leith (Chrysalis VKW-41668)

And where are they now?

12

One More Time

- The major festivals today
- Numero uno • Visions fulfilled
- Why they do it •

"Edmonton right now is a lot closer to what Mariposa was in the old days. It's a real surprise how much it feels like that."
— MITCH PODOLAK ASSESSES THE FESTS

LIKE LAZARUS, THE NEWPORT Folk Festival rose from the dead. Its demise passed without a whimper in 1969. Sixteen years later, though , a ghost of the original howled throughout the Rhode Island seaport town. Newport 1985 offered a limited series of seated concerts with no workshops. The heart of that lineup included Joan Baez, Judy Collins, Dave Van Ronk, Tom Paxton, Ramblin' Jack Elliott, and Mimi Farina — time bandits living off the distant past. Committed to this new format, it has since booked such vital and powerful performers as Billy Bragg, Michelle Shocked, Suzanne Vega and Nanci Griffith. And although its audience now falls considerably short of the eighty-thousand that attended in 1965, Newport appears to be healthy, if not quite the North American folk flagship of yesteryear.

Mariposa, too, remains a shadow of its former self. Although cancelled in 1981, it then limped from one location to another around Toronto before returning to Olympic Island in 1993. There the festival ran throughout the day but moved into various clubs around the city at night. A committee of four booked that lineup of sixty-nine acts. Of these, forty-two came from Ontario and only six from outside of the country. "It still has lots and lots of acts. The problem is they haven't got lots and lots of adventurous acts," says Richard Flohil, now a music industry publicist. Audiences remain sparse and finances fickle. "Until it finds somebody who can bankroll, or can put together the sort of program that's needed, it just ain't going to happen."

Estelle Klein left her post at Mariposa in 1980 due to health problems, and now attends only sporadically. This festival, she says, must offer a program distinct from local venues. Toronto, unlike Edmonton, attracts the elite of the folk-roots community throughout the year. "There is a lot of competition for the buck," says Klein. "You have to carve out a niche in that market that fulfils a need. If you repeat what other people are doing, if you are not any different, if you're not offering interesting workshops, or something to see, why should they come?"

Out West, Winnipeg continues to prevail despite several years of chronic financial difficulties. Rain fell on every festival from 1983 to 1986 and created debts of one-hundred-and-sixty-thousand dollars. Now in the black, it runs Thursday night and all day Friday, Saturday and Sunday on its original site, Birds Hill Park. It features epic bills of around seventy acts and takes few chances artistically. While this festival relies heavily on obscure North American performers, it does occasionally book such celebrated international acts as South Africa's Malathini And The Mahotella Queens and Madagascar's Tarika Sammy. And its audience remains fairly consistent. At its peak in 1977, Winnipeg attracted a paid three-day weekend attendance of twenty-seven thousand. With an extra night and by charging admission to children over the age of five, it broke that record by three hundred in 1993.

While Mitch Podolak retired as artistic director in 1986, he still remains on the festival's advisory board. After organizing twenty festivals around the country in thirteen years he needed a rest. "My brain could no longer do it," he says. "I was just tired and burnt out and fed up." Not for long, though. A year later, he helped found the city's Westend Cultural Centre — a non-profit venue established to develop Manitoba's musicians, poets and theatre groups. He still works there.

Irrepressible as ever, Podolak still has grand plans. He now hopes to establish The World Next Door — a broad community-based festival that will include everything from Scrabble tournaments to grunge rock — in four different locations around North America. In his spare time, he continues to attend various folk festivals across Canada. "Edmonton right now," he says, "is a lot closer to what Mariposa was in the old days. It's a real surprise how much it feels like that. Everybody wants to be numero uno, whether they say that or not. Edmonton is numero uno at the moment."

♪　♪　♪

With very few exceptions, the format for North American folk festivals remains virtually unchanged since Albert Grossman and George Wein put together the first bill at Newport in 1959. The music, of course, evolved naturally. Gradually, the eternal optimism of Pete Seeger's *We Shall Overcome* gave way to the pragmatic pessimism of Bruce Cockburn's *If I Had A Rocket Launcher*. And as the music changed, the attitudes of folk festival staff had to follow in order for such events to remain vibrant. "The artistic director is the vision," says Podolak, "the one who achieves the balance; the one who will reach into areas they don't necessarily like." The artistic director of the Cambridge Folk Festival may have yawned as The Pogues tore into a *Gentleman Soldier* in 1985, but he still had the fortitude to book them in the first place. And the very same year, Don Whalen embraced the equally brash Spirit Of The West as they ripped into *Drowsey Maggie*. Not only that, he also had the foresight and the courage to feature the bril-

Frank Gasparik (EFMF)

Ani DiFranco in Edmonton in 1993 . . . the music evolves and the best festivals keep up with it

liant, eccentric but relatively unknown k.d. lang in one of the most prominent spots in 1984.

Without the single-minded determination of Don Whalen, it's doubtful the Edmonton Folk Music Festival would exist today. Yet it took the alchemist Holger Petersen to develop its international profile. First he strengthened the festival's inner ambience. "We really emphasized performer hospitality," says Petersen. "We absolutely bent over backwards. If the performer was happy, everybody would be happy." So he stocked a bar back stage and provided fabulous food and generous accommodation. Then he went out of his way to book acts — mainly country, blues and bluegrass — that respected and complemented each other on the workshop stages. As often as not the sparks flew. And the likes of Guy Clark sat up and took notice and returned with prestigious friends, Rodney Crowell and Rosanne Cash. And so the word spread.

Finally, Petersen created more enjoyment for the festival's volunteers. Their unprecedented after-hours parties not only provided just reward for hours of valuable drudgery, but also installed a greater sense of worth and camaraderie.

Andy Laskiwsky first marketed the festival with a professional attitude. Loro Carmen upped the ante. And by the time Terry Wickham added the general manager's duties to his portfolio in 1990, the festival enjoyed a healthy surplus, which he and his current staff have maintained through rain and a recurring recession. As finances stabilized for the first time, the artistic budget increased. "I felt that the audience had gone up and we could take more of a chance," says Wickham. "We had to spend a little money on dreams rather than just looking at each market and saying, 'Well, let's get this person and that.'" So he focused on world music, Celtic, gospel, rabble-rousing rogues, and name acts with more flair and vitality. "I think the audience is a big part of that. I think the audience reacts very well to hard rock and rootsy bands here — The Oyster Band, Ron Kavana, k.d. lang, Bobby King and Terry Evans. You need that kind of buzz going." Whatever the focus, the audience has grown every year except 1985 and 1993, which surely dispels any speculation that the festival's audience favors one genre of music.

But just as important, Terry Wickham granted volunteers almost complete autonomy. Now their considerable experience allows the festival to flow as gracefully as good poetry. "You know what is really obvious to me," says Mitch Podolak, "is when you get to Edmonton and the way some of the volunteers operate. They are motivated. I overheard a conversation in the shuttlebus between one of the drivers and one of the stage managers describing their jobs to each other, what their responsibilities were to the festival, and why they were doing it. And they were right on the number. It used to be like that in Winnipeg. It's not like that anymore. And in Vancouver, I don't know — I can't find any passion there. But you find that passion in the volunteers in Edmonton. It's a wonderful thing to encounter. 'Why am I here? I'm here to have a good time.'"

And so the Edmonton Folk Music Festival approaches its fifteenth anniversary — barely past puberty, and already a role model. Extraordinary.

Selected recordings
(Author's wish list: artists I'd love to see at Gallagher Park)

Geoffrey Oryema: Exile (Realworld: CDRW-14)
Ali Farka Toure: River (Mango: WCD-17)
Paul Brady: Hard Station (WEA: K58312)
Nanci Griffith: One Fair Summer Evening (MCA: MCA-42255)
John Martyn: Sappire (Island: IMCD-164)
Black Umfolosi: Unity (World Circuit: WCD 020)
Boubacar Traore: Kar Kar (Stern's Africa: STCD1037)
The Levellers: Levelling The Land (Electra: 61325-2)
RunRig: Amazing Things (Chrysalis: CDCHR-2000)
Brendan Croker &The 5 O'Clock Shadows: Brendan Croker
 & The 5 O'Clock Shadows (Silvertone: ORECD - 505)

BIBLIOGRAPHY

Alaton, Salem. "Protest lost in the Newport shuffle." *Toronto Globe And Mail*. Monday, August 10, 1987.

Ancelet, Barry Jean, and Elemore Morgan Jr. *The Makers of Cajun Music*. Austin, University of Texas Press, 1984.

Anderson, Ian. "Billsville: Billy Bragg Tells Tales Of The Lumpenfolk And The Earthed Audience." *Folk Roots*. July 1991, No 97.

— "A World Music Meeting." *Folk Roots*. July 1986, No. 37.

— "San Antonio Sound: As Tex-Mex takes off in Britain, we talk with the King." *Folk Roots*. August 1985, No. 26.

Baez, Joan. *And A Voice To Sing To With: A Memoir*. Scarborough, Plume, 1985.

Barker, Gerry. "Mariposa Folk Festival behaves in Toronto the Good." *Toronto Daily Star*, Saturday, August 8, 1964.

Brand, Oscar. *The Ballad Mongers*. Westport, Connecticut, Greenwood Press, 1962.

Brown, Peter, and Steven Gaines. *The Love You Make: An Insider's Story of The Beatles*. Toronto, McGraw-Hill, 1983.

Campbell, Rod. "Northern Delights: Rod Campbell Collects Up Some Of The Current Canadian Cookies." *Folk Roots*. January/February 1993, Nos. 115/116.

— "Jerry Jeff Walker: Still a hellraiser." *Calgary Herald*, July 12, 1992.

— "Chieftains have no time for complacency: Ireland's Celtic kings put best foot forward." *Red Deer Advocate*, November 27, 1991.

— "Thumping the worldbeat drum: WOMAD seeks exposure for all the songs of the planet." *Edmonton Journal*, August 9, 1991.

— "Cajun flair edged with caution: Zachary Richard sings for minority rights." *Edmonton Journal*, August 8, 1991.

— "Delta Blues Singer Endures." *Edmonton Journal*, May 8, 1991.

— "Queen of zydeco leads Mardi Gras revelry." *Edmonton Journal*, February 28, 1991.

— "Their own brand of feverish folk has Spirit moving." *Edmonton Journal*, March 18, 1990.

— "Lightfoot: Canada's Musical Icon Returns." *Edmonton Journal*, November 26, 1989.

— "Onetime outlaw remains defiant: Jerry Jeff hits straight, narrow." *Edmonton Journal*. August 13, 1989.

— "Flaco Jimenez: king of the accordion." *Edmonton Journal*, August 11, 1988.

— "Pearls of wisdom from an Oyster." *Gateway*, Tuesday, November 10, 1987.

Charters, Samuel. *The Blues Makers*. New York, Da Capo Press, 1991.
— *The Country Blues*. New York, Da Capo Press, 1975.

Clifford, Mike, editor. *The Harmony Illustrated Encyclopedia of Rock*. New York, Harmony, 1992.

Coleman, Ray. *Brian Epstein: The Man Who Made The Beatles*. London, Viking, 1989.

Coxson, Sarah. "A Stern Look." *Folk Roots*. March 1989, No. 69.
— "The Carthy Era: Sarah Coxson finds the Great Man in great form." *Folk Roots*. November 1987, No. 53.

Crane, Joe. "Start Of The Gael: Joe Crane Looks Back On The Gael Linn Progress." *Folk Roots*. December 1993, No. 126.
— "The Flawless Piper: Joe Crane's Admiration For Liam O'Flynn Knows No Bounds." *Folk Roots*. June 1993, No. 120.

Crosby, John. "Mighty Earthworks." *Folk Roots*. March 1986, No. 23.

Dafoe, Chris. "Write 'Em Cowboy." *Globe And Mail*. Saturday, February 5, 1994.
— "Head and shoulders above the competition." *Globe And Mail*. Tuesday, August 10, 1993.

Davies, Hunter. *The Beatles*. New York, McGraw-Hill, 1978.

Denselow, Robin. *When The Music's Over: The Story Of Political Pop*. London, Faber and Faber, 1990.

Deevoy, Adrian. "Million Dollar Bash." *Q*, December 1992.

Dunaway, David King. *How Can I Keep From Singing: Pete Seeger*. New York, McGraw-Hill, 1981.

Du Noyer, Paul. "The Quality Controller." *Q*. March 1989.

Elsworthy, Tom. "First Folk Festival: Music flows 'n' glows." *Edmonton Sun*, August 11, 1980.

Fong-Torres, Ben. *Hickory Wind: The Life and Times of Gram Parsons*. New York, Pocket Books, 1991.

Friedman, Emily. "Edmonton Folk Music Festival Review." *Come For To Sing*. Vol. 9, #4 Autumn, 1983.

Gillett, Charlie. *The Sound Of The City: The Rise Of Rock 'n' Roll*. London, Souvenir Press, 1984.

Gomez, Adekunle. "Irish Vinyl: Adekunle Gomez looks at Dublin's Claddagh Records." *Folk Roots*. November 1989, No. 77.

Graham, Ronnie. *The Da Capo Guide To Contemporary African Music*. New York, Da Capo Press, 1988.

Gudgeon, Chris. *An Unfinished Conversation: The Life And Music of Stan Rogers*. Toronto, Viking, 1993.

Guralnick, Peter. *Searching For Robert Johnson.* New York, E.P Dutton, 1989.

— *Feel Like Going Home: Portraits in Blues and Rock 'n' Roll.* New York, Harper & Row, 1989.

— *Sweet Soul Music.* New York, Harper & Row, 1986.

— *Lost Highway. New York*, Harper & Row, 1979.

Guthrie, Woody. *Pastures Of Plenty: A Self-Portrait.* eds. Dave Marsh and Harold Leventhal, New York, Harper Collins, 1990.

— *Bound For Glory.* London, Picador, 1974.

Hardwick, Chris. "Loosely Irvine: Chris Hardwick encounters a Patrick Streetperson." *Folk Roots.* April 1987, No. 46.

Harper, Colin. "The Book Of Bert." *Folk Roots.* March 1994, No. 129.

Heilbut, Anthony. *The Gospel Sound: Good News and Bad Times.* New York, Limelight Editions, 1985.

Hicks, Graham. "10 really good sets out of 12 make first folk festival a success." *Edmonton Journal*, August 11, 1980.

Holland, Maggie. "Roots of Renbourn: Maggie Holland Unfolds The John Renbourn Story And The Tale Of Pentangle's Progress." *Folk Roots.* April 1993, No. 118.

Hopkins, Jerry, Jim Marshall and Baron Wolman. *Festival!* Toronto, Macmillan, 1970.

Humphries, Patrick. "Fairport Continuation: The show that never stops — a Patrick Humphries update." *Folk Roots.* August 1985, No. 26.

— "The Brothers Clancy: Greenwich Village Days With Guthrie, Dylan, Farina." *The Southern Rag.* Issue #23, Vol., 5 No.3, Jan. 1 to Mar. 31, 1985.

Hunt, Ken. "African Decade: Sterns Are 10. Ken Hunt Shares The Jelly & Trifle." *Folk Roots.* August 1991, No.122.

— "Duo-Tones." *Folk Roots.* April, 1991, No. 94.

Irish Press. "Even the skyscrapers are nice in Edmonton, says Mary." Wednesday, September 1, 1993.

Irwin, Colin. "Dub Version: The Bearded Ones Recently Celebrated 30 Years On The Road. 'We're just starting,' The Dubliners tell Colin Irwin." *Folk Roots.* March 1992, No. 117.

— "July Jigging: The Chieftains Are About To Take The Stage With The Pogues, Among Others! Colin Irwin Boggles." *Folk Roots.* July 1991, No. 97.

— "Floor Singer's Revenge: In case you hadn't guessed, Elvis Costello knows his folk music. Colin Irwin hears all about it." *Folk Roots.* July 1989, No. 73.

— "Folk's Willie Nelson: Colin Irwin hears Ashley Hutchings' ambitions." *Folk Roots*. March 1989, No. 69.

— "Street Cred: Colin Irwin sinks a few with Patrick Street persons." *Folk Roots*. December 1988, No. 66.

— "Heart Of The Hearts: Colin Irwin just resists kissing Donal Lunny's feet." *Folk Roots*. October 1987, No. 52.

— "Pogueology: Colin Irwin cracks a bottle or six with Shane and Terry." *Folk Roots*. August 1987, No. 50.

— "Extraordinary Man: Colin Irwin whiles away an afternoon with Christy Moore." *Folk Roots*. January 1987, No 43.

— "When Worlds Collide." *Folk Roots*. December 1985, No.30.

— "A Sudden Bragg." *The Southern Rag*. Issue #24, Vol. 6 No. 4, April 1 to June 30, 1985.

— "A Parcel Of Rogues: Colin Irwin celebrates the rogue folk movement." *The Southern Rag*. Issue # 14, Vol. 4, No 2, Oct. 1 - Dec. 31, 1982

Johnson, Terry, Jonathan Cote and Lori Cohen. "The folk festivals rebound: Musical eclecticism rebuilds the West's showcase reputation." *Alberta Report*. August 17, 1987.

Jones, Simon. "Prior Engagement." *Folk Roots*. July 1988, No. 61.

Kellogg, Alan. "Diehard fans braved folk fest downpour." *Edmonton Journal*, Monday August 12, 1985.

— "Weekend full of great moments: Magic close to gala folk-fest." *Edmonton Journal*, August 11, 1980.

— "Prairie treasures shine in folk festival opener." *Edmonton Journal*, August 9, 1980.

Klein, Joe. *Woody Guthrie: A Life*. New York, Ballantine Books, 1986.

Kolko, Gabriel. *Confronting The Third World: United States Foreign Policy* 1945-1980. New York, Pantheon, 1988.

Kroetsch, Robert. *Alberta*. Toronto, Macmillan, 1968.

Ladd, Chris. "Try it, You'll Like It." *Winnipeg Free Press*. Saturday, August 10, 1974.

Laing, David, et al. *The Electric Muse: The Story of Folk into Rock*. London, Methuen, 1975.

Lloyd, A.L. *Folk Song In England*. St Albans, Paladin, 1975.

Lomax, Alan. Liner notes: *Woody Guthrie: Library of Congress Recordings*, Rounder Records, CD 104/2/3.

Malone, Bill. *Country Music USA: Revised Edition*. Austin, University of Texas, 1985.

— and Judith McCulloh, editors. *Stars of Country Music*. Chicago, University of Illinois Press, 1975.

— *Country Music USA: A Fifty-Year History*. Austin, University of Texas Press, 1968.

MacGregor, James. *A History of Alberta: Revised Edition*. Edmonton, Hurtig Publishers, 1981.

McKeon, Ed. "Charter Accounts: Ed McKeon meets the couple who have recorded and photographed decades of American roots music." *Folk Roots*. May 1989, No. 71.

Oakley, Giles. *The Devil's Music: A History Of The Blues*. London, Ariel Books, 1983.

O'Brien, Peter. "The Ian Tyson Show: The Great Canadian Tour." *Omaha Rainbow*. #25, Autumn, 1980.

Oliver, Paul. *Blues Off The Record*. New York, Da Capo, 1984.

Palmer, Howard, and Tamara Palmer. *Alberta: A New History*. Edmonton, Hurtig Publishers, 1990.

Palmer, Robert. *Deep Blues*. Markham, Ontario, Penguin, 1981.

Pareless, John, and Patricia Romanowski. *The Rolling Stone Encyclopedia of Rock 'n' Roll*. New York, Rolling Stone Press, 1983.

Peabody, Dave. "In Father's Footsteps: Santiago Jimenez keeps to the family squeezebox tradition." *Folk Roots*. February 1989, No. 68.

— "The Bow of Beausoleil." *Folk Roots*. March 1988, No.57.

Richler, Mordecai. "Wayne Gretzky: King of the new Canada." *Edmonton Journal*, October 6, 1985. Reprinted from *The New York Times*.

Rogers, Stan. "On Festivals." *The Calgary Folk Festival Program*. 1981.

— Liner notes: *Stan Rogers, Fogarty's Cove*, Fogarty's Cove Music Records, FCM 1001.

Rosenberg, Neil. *Bluegrass: A History*. Chicago, University of Illinois Press, 1985.

Rosselson, Leon. "A Cristall Ball." *Folk Roots*, July 1988, No 61.

Rosson, Gloria. "Edmonton Folk Music Festival." *Dirty Linen*, Issue #49, December/January, '93-'94.

Sandberg, Larry, and Dick Weissman. *The Folk Music Sourcebook*. New York, Knopf, 1976.

Savage, Jon. *England's Dreaming: Sex Pistols and Punk Rock*. London, Faber and Faber, 1991.

Scaduto, Anthony. *Bob Dylan*. New York, Signet, 1973.

Schiff, Marvin. "Three Harried Days at Stadium Maturing for Mariposa Festival." *Globe And Mail*, August 10, 1964.

Shelton, Robert. *No Direction Home: The Life And Music of Bob Dylan*. Bury St. Edmunds, New English Library, 1986.

— "Folk Music Fills Newport Coffers." *New York Times*, July 26, 1965.

— "Bob Dylan: A Distinctive Folk-Song Stylist." *New York Times*, September 29, 1961.

— "Folk Joins Jazz At Newport." *New York Times*, July 1, 1959.

Snow, Mat. "The Minstrel's Tale." *Q*. December 1988.

Spitz, Bob. *Dylan: A Biography*. New York, W.W. Norton, 1989.

Stambler, Irwin, and Grelun Landon. *The Encyclopedia of Folk, Country & Western Music*. New York, St. Martin's Press, 1983.

— *The Encylopedia of Folk, Country & Western Music*. New York, St Martin's Press, 1969.

Stapleton, Chris, and Chris May. *African All*Stars: The Pop Music Of A Continent*. London, Paladin, 1989.

Sutcliffe, Phil. "Organised Chaos." *Q*. May 1989. *New York Times*. "Programs Of The Week." March 3, 1940.

Tobler, John. "Class of '67." *Folk Roots*. August 1992, No.110.

— "Open Hart: Tim Hart spills the beans to John Tobler about early Steeleye, '60s folk clubs, folkie accents and the glinting audience." *Folk Roots*. May 1991, No. 95.

Tyson, Ian. Interview album recorded for radio, Columbia Records CDN-123.

Usher, Bill, and Linda Page-Harpa eds. *For What Time I Am In This World: Stories From Mariposa*. Toronto, P. Martin Associates, 1977.

Ward, Ed, Geoffrey Stokes and Ken Tucker. *Rock of Ages: The Rolling Stone History of Rock & Roll*. New York, Rolling Stone Press, 1986.

Welding, Pete. Liner notes: Ian and Sylvia, *Four Strong Winds*, Vanguard, VRS-9133.

Wickham, Terry. "A View From The Hill." *Edmonton Folk Music Festival Program*. 1993.

Wilson, Susan. "In Edmonton, a time for celebration." *Boston Globe*. August 10, 1987.

Winter, Eric. "The Big Ewan: Eric Winter looks back at the great, but often controversial, career of Ewan MacColl." *Folk Roots*. January-February 1990, Nos. 79/80.

Wolfe, Charles, and Kip Lornell. *The Life & Legend of Leadbelly*. New York, Harper Collins, 1992.

Woods, Fred. *Folk Revival: The Rediscovery of a National Music*. Poole, Blandford Press, 1979.

Yurchenko, Henrietta, assisted by Marjorie Guthrie. *A Mighty Hard Road: The Woody Guthrie Story*. New York, McGraw-Hill, 1970.

INDEX

AUGUST 8, 1980

7 to 10:30 p.m. Main Stage
Wheatland County, Shari Ulrich, Bob Carpenter, Margaret Christl, Houndog, Valdy, Sylvia Tyson and the Great Speckled Bird

AUGUST 9, 1980

Stage 1
10:30 a.m. **Good Morning Singaround**
Bob Carpenter, Tom Jackson, Al Lamonica, Diamond Joe White, Cilla Fisher & Artie Trezise
11:30 a.m. Richard White
12:00 p.m. Karen Bryce
12:30 p.m. **Women Writing Songs For and About Women**
Connie Kaldor, Shari Ulrich, Joan MacIsaac, Beverly Ross, Sylvia Tyson
1:30 p.m. David Sereda
2:00 p.m. **Some New Tunes By the Girls From Home**
Connie Kaldor, Karen Bryce, Joan MacIsaac, Mairi MacLean, Beverly Ross
3:00 p.m. Joan MacIsaac
3:30 p.m. Caitlin Hanford & Linda Morrison
4:00 p.m. **Hot Licks and Finger Picks**
Paul Hann, Billy Constable, Darcie Deaville, Bill Garrett, Danny Greenspoon,
Stage 2
10:30 a.m. **Contemporary Song Jam**
 Bill Garrett, Oliver Krol, Joan MacIsaac, Sylvia Tyson, Valdy
11:30 a.m. Fat Chants
12:00 p.m. Frank Gay, Nick Van Der Meent, Holly Wright
12:30 p.m. **Bluegrass Special**
Doug Dillard Band, Duck Donald Band, Wheatland County
1:30 p.m. Hamish Imlach
2:00 p.m. **Salute to Nashville**
Ken Bloom, Bim, Saul Broudy, Duck Donald Band, Caitlin Hanford & Linda Morrison
3:00 p.m. Saul Broudy
3:30 p.m. Marie-Lynn Hammond
4:00 p.m. **Fiddle Faddle**
Ross Campbell, Chris Crilly, Zeke Mazurek, Ted Smith, Shari Ulrich
Stage 3
10:30 a.m. **Banjo Songs & Music** Debby McClatchy, Ken Bloom, Doug Dillard, Mitch Podolak, Jim Walker
11:30 a.m. **Seventy-fifth Anniversary Historical Review**
The McDade Family Band
12:30 p.m. **No Nukes is Good Nukes**
 Rick Scott, Joe Mock, Jim Post, Stringband, Valdy
1:30 p.m. Randy Raine-Reusch
2:00 p.m. **Fiddle Tunes for Other Instruments**
Robin Williamson, Bryan Bowers, John Allan Cameron, Billy Constable, Doug Dillard
3:00 p.m. **Living in the Country**
Valdy, Oliver Krol, Denise Larson, Pied Pear, Diamond Joe White
4:00 p.m. **The Out of Ordinary**
Ken Bloom, Ma Fletcher, Randy Raine-Reusch, Sukay, Frank Gay
Stage 4

10:30 a.m. **Old Time Fiddle Tunes From Both Sides of the Ocean**
John Allan Cameron, Ted Smith, Chris Crilly, Bill Bourne, Robin Williamson
11:30 a.m. Danny Greenspoon
12:00 p.m. Sweetgrass
12:30 p.m. **The Art of Backup**
Clare Lawrence, Ken Bloom, Saul Broudy, Chris Crilly, Dave Woodhead
1:30 p.m. Mose Scarlett
2:00 p.m. **Contemporary Canadian Singaround**
Bob Bossin, Bob Carpenter, Tom Jackson, Mose Scarlett, Sylvia Tyson
3:00 p.m. **Ballads**
Margaret Christl, Cilla Fisher & Artie Trezise, Stan Rogers, Peter Paul Van Camp, Richard White
4:00 p.m. **Rowdy and Raunchy**
Debby McClatchy, Margaret Christl, Hamish Imlach, Connie Kaldor, Pamela Morgan
Stage 5 & Children's Area
10:30 a.m. Building Workshop
12:00 p.m. **Singing & Clowning Around**
Fender
1:00 p.m. **Punch and Judy Show**
Manitoba Puppet Theatre
1:30 p.m. Supervised Games
2:00 p.m. The McDade Family Band
3:00 p.m. Paul Hann
3:45 p.m. Al Simmons & Barbara Freundl
4:30 p.m. Manitoba Puppet Theatre

5:30 to 10:30 p.m. **Main Stage**
Denise Larson & Friends, Bryan Bowers, Diamond Joe White
Doug Dillard Band, Connie Kaldor, Stan Rogers, Robin Williamson, Pied Pear, Paul Hann, Sukay

AUGUST 10, 1980

Stage 1
10:30 a.m. **Contemporary a cappella**
Stan Rogers, Bryan Bowers, Denise Larson, Jim Post, Shari Ulrich
11:15 a.m. Beverly Ross
11:45 a.m. **Different Traditions Singaround**
Marie-Lynn Hammond, Sukay, Hamish Imlach, Tom Jackson, Caitlin Hanford & Linda Morrison
12:45 p.m. Valdy
1:30 p.m. Chris Crilly
2:00 p.m. **Songs to Change the World**
David Sereda, Bim, Bob Bossin, Pied Pear, Stan Rogers
3:00 p.m. **Nostalgia Concert**
The Pied Pumpkin String Ensemble
3:45 p.m. **Ragtime Swingtime Anytime**
Houndog, Ken Bloom, Fat Chants, Mose Scarlett, Frank Gay & Nick Van Der Meent
Stage 2
10:30 a.m. **Squeezzzables**
Ken Bloom, Bob Bossin, Geoff Butler, Robin Williamson
11:15 a.m. Figgy Duff
11:45 a.m. **Swing Guitar**

Allan Stein, Ken Bloom, Frank Gay, Thomas Handy,
Brent Parkin
12:45 p.m. Doug Dillard Band
1:30 p.m. **Gospel**
Cilla Fisher, Doug Dillard Band, Jim Post, Connie Kaldor, Debby
McClatchy, Artie Trezise
2:30 p.m. Curly Boy Stubbs
3:00 p.m. **Homegrown Songs**
Ma Fletcher, Karen Bryce, Joan MacIsaac, David Sereda,
Richard White
3:45 p.m. **Country Influences**
Paul Hann, Bim, Denise Larson, Sweetgrass,
Sylvia Tyson, Diamond Joe White
Stage 3
10:30 a.m. **For Musicians Only: How I Play the Dulcimer**
Rick Scott, Debby McClatchy, Randy Raine-Reusch
11:15 a.m. Holly Wright
11:45 a.m. **Love Songs: Sweet & Sour**
Sylvia Tyson, Bob Carpenter, Joan MacIsaac, Paul Hann,
Stan Rogers
12:45 p.m. Bryan Bowers
1:30 p.m. **Music of the Andes**
Sukay
2:00 p.m. **Mandolin Magic**
Duck Donald Band, Frank Bartl, Dave Little, Dave Panting,
Daniel Sheppard
3:00 p.m. **New Dimensions for Old Instruments**
Bryan Bowers, Ken Bloom, Randy Raine-Reusch
3:45 p.m. **Celt Melt**
Hamish Imlach, Margaret Christl, Figgy Duff, Robin Williamson,
Cilla Fisher & Artie Trezise
Stage 4
10:30 a.m. **Good Morning Gospel**
Saul Broudy, Margaret Christl, Duck Donald Band, Sweetgrass
11:15 a.m. Oliver Krol
11:45 a.m. **The Art of the Harmonica**
Saul Broudy, K.C. Cramer, Gord Kidder, Rob Storeshaw,
Nick Van Der Meent
12:45 p.m. Odetta
1:30 p.m. Bill Garrett, Curly Boy Stubbs
2:00 p.m. **Blues: Town & Country**
Rob Storeshaw, Houndog, Mose Scarlett, Mark Dowding,
Caitlin Hanford & Linda Morrison
3:15 p.m. **Take Me Out to the Ballgame**
Peter Paul Van Camp, Bob Bossin, John Allen Cameron
4:00 p.m. **Contemporary Guitar Styles**
Joe Mock, Bill Garrett, Curly Boy Stubbs, Harris Von Berkel,
Holly Wright
Stage 5 & Children's Area
10:30 a.m. Building Workshop
12:00 p.m. Fender
12:30 p.m. Supervised Games
1:00 p.m. Manitoba Puppet Theatre
1:30 p.m. Supervised Games
2:00 p.m. John Allen Cameron
2:30 p.m. Supervised Games
3:00 p.m. Al Simmons & Barbara Freundl
3:45 p.m. Supervised Games
4:30 p.m. Manitoba Puppet Theatre

5:30 to 10:30 p.m. **Main Stage**
Duck Donald Band, Odetta, Tom Jackson, Ken Bloom,
Cilla Fisher & Artie Trezise, Jim Post, Bim, Stringband,
Debby McClatchy, John Allan Cameron

AUGUST 7, 1981

7 TO 10:30 p.m. **Main Stage**
River City Ramblers, Don Freed, Connie Kaldor, Bim,
Pied Pear, Odetta

AUGUST 8, 1981
Stage 1
11:30 a.m. **Mixed Bag**
Su Chong Lim, Lost in the Colonies, Lyall Steel
12:15 p.m. **I'm New Here Myself**
Tom See, Don Freed
1:00 p.m. Lyall Steel
1:30 p.m. Big Dave McLean
2:00 p.m. **Guitar Styles**
Ma Fletcher, Ken Bloom, Brownie McGhee, Michael O'Domhnaill,
Lyall Steel
3:00 p.m. **Banjo Go-Round**
Tom Paley, Michael Calihoo, Beverly Cotten, Craig Korth, Cathy
Murphy, Luke Wilson
4:00 p.m. **Danceable Tunes**
Pied Pear, Muddy York, Lost in the Colonies, Pattie B. MacDonald,
Kevin Burke & Michael O'Domhnaill
Stage 2
11:30 a.m. **Take Good Care of Yourself**
Peter Alsop, Joan MacIsaac, Pied Pear, Jim Post
12:15 p.m. **Songs for Philosophers and Other Dreamers**
Bim, Ferron, Pied Pear, Stan Rogers
1:00 p.m. **The Women's Dilemma**
Heather Bishop, Peter Alsop, Margaret Christl, Ferron, Connie
Kaldor
2:00 p.m. **Odes to Mother Nature**
Vera Johnson, Peter Alsop, Don Freed, Pied Pear, Jim Post
3:00 p.m. **Careless Love**
Stan Rogers, Heather Bishop, Don Freed, Joan MacIsaac,
Diamond Joe White
4:00 p.m. **Songs I Wouldn't Sing to My Mother**
Paul Hann, Margaret Christl, Vera Johnson, Connie Kaldor, Tom
Paley
Stage 3
11:30 a.m. **Songs of the West Old and New**
Fred Penner, Ken Bloom, Connie Kaldor, Diamond Joe White
12:15 p.m. **Hear the Wind Blow: Instruments Using Air**
Ken Bloom, Maggie McKaig, Randy Raine-Reusch, Scott Sheerin
1:00 p.m. **Old Timey Tunes**
Tom Paley, Beverly Cotten, Muddy York, River City Ramblers
2:00 p.m. **Country Tunes**
Bim, Beverly Cotten, Paul Hann
2:45 p.m. **Keep On the Sunny Side - Carter Family Songs**
The Romaniuk Family
3:15 p.m. **Squeeze Me Pleez**
Ian Bell, Merv Bell, Ken Bloom, Calvin Cairns
4:00 p.m. **Blues Mixer**

Rob Storeshaw, Dave McLean, Sonny Terry & Brownie McGhee,
Tom See
Under the Tent
12:30 p.m. **Folk Guitar for Beginners**
Ma Fletcher
1:30 p.m. **Let's Write a Song Together**
Stan Rogers
2:30 p.m. **Blues Harp Technique**
Sonny Terry
3:30 p.m. **So You Want to Play Bluegrass: a Short History of**
     Bluegrass Techniques, River City Ramblers
Stage 4 Children
11:30 a.m. Supervised Activities
12:15 p.m. Ian Johnstone
1:30 p.m. Paul Hann
1:50 p.m. Supervised Activities
2:30 p.m. Shamrock Players
3:15 p.m. Fred Penner
4:00 p.m. Cirque Alexandre

5:30 to 10:30 p.m. **Main Stage**
Lost in the Colonies, Ferron, Vera Johnsone, Brownie McGhee,
Paul Hann, Kevin Burke & Michael O'Domhnaill

AUGUST 9, 1981
Stage 1
11:30 a.m. **Diff'rent Strokes**
Dave McLean, Ron Casat, Lyall Steel, Nathan Tinkham
12:15 p.m. **String-Things**
Cathy Murphy, Ken Bloom, Andrej Hornjatkevyc, Randy Raine-
Reusch
1:00 p.m. Ma Fletcher
1:30 p.m. Randy Raine-Reusch
2:00 p.m. Heather Bishop
2:30 p.m. **My Favorite Songwriters**
Mike Sadava, Su Chong Lim, River City Ramblers, The Romaniuk
Family
3:15 p.m. **For Voice Alone**
Margaret Christl, Ken Bloom, Connie Kaldor, Stan Rogers Jesse
Winchester
4:00 p.m. **Come Dance With Us**
Beverly Cotten, Muddy York
Stage 2
11:30 a.m. **There Ain't No Justus in This Here World**
Ferron, Peter Alsop, Heather Bishop, Vera Johnson, Su Chong Lim
12:30 p.m. **Women in Love**
Connie Kaldor, Heather Bishop, Margaret Christl, Joan MacIsaac,
Ferron
1:30 p.m. **Thinking of You: Songs of Love From the Man in the**
House, Jim Post, Bim, Stan Rogers, Diamond Joe White, Jesse
Winchester
2:30 p.m. **What About the Workers**
Peter Alsop, Don Freed, Vera Johnson, Stan Rogers
3:15 p.m. **Wittie Ditties**
Fred Penner, Peter Alsop, Joan MacIsaac, Pied Pear, Jim Post
4:15 p.m. **Songs of Youth and Home**
Jesse Winchester, Bim, Don Freed, Connie Kaldor
Stage 3
11:30 a.m. **Songs of Faith**

Diamond Joe White, Jim Post, River City Ramblers, The Romaniuk
Family
12:30 p.m. **Such is Life in the Colonies**
Luke Wilson, Lost in the Colonies, Kevin Burke & Michael
O'Domhnaill
1:00 p.m. Su Chong Lim
1:30 p.m. Tom Paley
2:00 p.m. Andrej Hornjatkevyc
2:30 p.m. **Fiddle-Dee-Dee**
Tom Paley, Kevin Burke, Calvin Cairns, Anne Lederman
3:15 p.m. **Slip-Slidin' Away (Slide Guitar Styles)**
Tom See, Bim, Dave McLean, Luke Wilson
4:00 p.m. **Traditions**
Kevin Burke, Andrej Hornjatkevyc, Pattie B. MacDonald, Michael
O'Domhnaill, Randy Raine-Reusch, Tom See
Under the Tent
11:30 a.m. **What You Always Wanted To Know About Fiddle**
     Playing But Were Afraid to Ask, Kevin Burke
12:30 p.m. **Basic Dulcimer Playing**
Rick Scott
1:30 p.m. **Mandolin Basics**
Luke Wilson
2:30 p.m. **Basic Blues Guitar**
Ma Fletcher
3:30 p.m. **Banjo Techniques Basic and Beyond**
Tom Paley
Stage 4 Children
11:30 a.m. Supervised Activities
12:30 p.m. Shamrock Players
1:00 p.m. Peter Alsop
1:30 p.m. Supervised Activities
2:00 p.m. Ian Johnstone
3:00 p.m. **Aardvark Presents**
Doc Myles Snow Travellin' Show
4:00 p.m. Supervised Activities
4:30 p.m. Fred Penner

5:30 to 10:30 p.m. **Main Stage**
Muddy York, Diamond Joe White, Joan MacIsaac, Tom See, Peter
Alsop, Beverly Cotten, Jesse Winchester, Ken Bloom, Stan Rogers

AUGUST 6, 1982
6 TO 10:30 p.m. **Main Stage**
Hotfoot Quintet, Tom See, Don Freed, Pied Pear, David Sereda,
John McEuen, Dolores Keane & Reel Union, Connie Kaldor, Amos
Garrett & David Burgin

AUGUST 7, 1982
Stage 1
11:00 a.m. **Ramblin' Round**
Jeff Cahill, Steve Cormier, Utah Phillips, Jon Sirkis, Dave Van
Ronk
12:00 p.m. **The 5-String Banjo**
Mitch Podolak, Beverly Cotten, Doug Dillard, John McEuen, Luke
Wilson
1:00 p.m. Jeff Cahill
1:30 p.m. **Vocal Chords (a cappella)**

Jim Post and David Sereda, Dolores Keane, Su Chong Lim, Betsy Rose & Kathy Winter

2:30 p.m. Steve Cormier

3:00 p.m. Mike Absalom

3:30 p.m. **Clog-In**
Beverly Cotten, Benoit Bourque

4:00 p.m. **Feets Massage**
John Malone, Beverly Cotten, Muddy York

Stage 2

11:00 . **Stories and Story Songs**
Betsy Rose, Kathy Winter, Ramblin' Jack Elliott, The Folktellers, Don Freed

12:00 p.m. **Free to be You and Me**
David Sereda, Peter Alsop, Heather Bishop & Laurie Conger, Betsy Rose & Kathy Winter

1:00 p.m. McDade Family Band

1:30 p.m. **I Like to Play With Myself (Self Accompaniment)**
Holly Arntzen, Peter Alsop, Don Freed, Tom See, Will Millar

2:30 p.m. Muddy York

3:00 p.m. Betsy Rose & Kathy Winter

3:30 p.m. **Blues Blast**
Dave Van Ronk, Ken Hamm & Luke Wilson, Houndog, Dave McLean, Tom See, Holly Arntzen

Stage 3

11:00 . **CISN Country Swing**
Dakota Dave Hull & Sean Blackburn, The Dillards, Hotfoot Quintet

12:00 p.m.**Dulcimers**
Rick Scott, Holly Arntzen, Grindl Kuchirka, Kate Murphy

1:00 p.m. Lyall Steel

1:30 p.m. **Once in a While I Write a Song Just for the Hell of It!**
Mike Absalom, Joan MacIsaac, Utah Phillips, Jon Sirkis

2:30 p.m. John Malone

3:00 p.m. Joan MacIsaac

3:30 p.m. **You Don't Have to be Crazy to Get Through This Old World-But It Sure Helps,** Ramblin' Jack Elliott, Mike Absalom, Su Chong Lim, Utah Phillips, Jim Post, David Wilcox

Stage 4

11:00 . **Celtic Transplants**
Dolores Keane & Reel Union, Na Cabarfeidh

12:00 p.m. **Hot Harmonicas**
David Burgin, Gord Kidder, Alain Lamontagne, Raymond Philippe, Rob Storeshaw

1:00 p.m. Brandy Wine

1:30 p.m. **Back Porch Bluegrass**
John McEuen, Dennis Bailey, Bill Constable, Doug Dillard, Rodney Dillard, Dean Webb

2:30 p.m. Ken Hamm & Luke Wilson

3:00 p.m. Dave McLean

3:30 p.m. **Six String Seduction (Guitar Styles)**
Dakota Dave Hull, Sean Blackburn, Billy Constable, Bob Frank, Amos Garrett, Joe Mock, Lyall Steel

The Tent

12:00 p.m. **Slide Guitar Instruction**
Dave McLean

1:00 p.m. **Tin Whistle and Recorder Techniques**
Mark Roberts

2:00 p.m. **The Art of Storytelling**
The Folktellers

3:00 p.m. **Let's Write a Song Together**

Will Millar

4:00 p.m. **Mandolin Technique**
Dean Webb

Children's Stage

11:00 . Supervised Play Activities

12:00 p.m. Brandy Wine

12:30 p.m. Bob Schneider

1:00 p.m. Ronnie Burkett

1:30 p.m. Heather Bishop

2:00 p.m. McDade Family Band

2:30 p.m. Merry Time Clown & Puppet Company

3:00 p.m. Peter Alsop

3:30 p.m. **Little Red Riding Hood**
Steve Hansen

4:00 p.m. Barry Louis Polisar

4:30 p.m. Playtime

5:30 to 10:30 p.m. **Main Stage**
Doug Dillard Band, Peter Alsop, Alain Lamontagne, Beverly Cotten, Ramblin' Jack Elliott, Tom Paxton, David Wilcox, John Bayley, Heather Bishop & Laurie Conger

AUGUST 8, 1982

Stage 1

11:00 . **Singing for a Purpose**
Peter Alsop, Oscar Brand, Ramblin' Jack Elliott, Tom Paxton, Dave Van Ronk

12:00 p.m. **Disgusting Dialogue & Terrible Tunes**
Oscar Brand, Jeff Cahill, Steve Cormier, Su Chong Lim

1:00 p.m. **Mighty Mandolins**
Dean Webb, Roland Kausen, Claudine Langille, Anne Lederman, Ian McLeod

2:00 p.m. **Fiddlin' Around**
John Faulkner, Vincent Ouellet, Stephen Slottow

2:30 p.m. Jon Sirkis

3:00 p.m. The Folktellers

3:30 p.m. **A Continent Usque Ad Continent**
Will Millar, Alain Lamontagne, Muddy York, Na Cabarfeidh, Dolores Keane & Reel Union

Stage 2

11:00 a.m. **Ballads and Blues**
Holly Arntzen, Joan MacIsaac, Heather Bishop & Laurie Conger, Dave McLean

12:00 p.m. **Tea For Two (Duo Dynamics)**
Ken Hamm & Luke Wilson, Pied Pear, Betsy Rose & Kathy Winter, Dakota Dave Hull & Sean Blackburn

1:00 p.m. **Spontaneous Combustion The Art of Back-up**
Heather Bishop, Roger Brant, David Burgin, Laurie Conger, Amos Garrett, Linsey Umrysh, Luke Wilson

2:00 p.m. **The Art of Satire**
Oscar Brand, Mike Absalom

2:30 p.m. Houndog

3:00 p.m. Holly Arntzen

3:30 p.m. **A Mare Usque Ad Mare**
Pied Pear, Heather Bishop & Laurie Conger, 'Eritage, Ken Hamm & Luke Wilson, Merry Time, Anne Mortifee & Robbie King

Stage 3

11:00 . **Songs to Stir the Soul**

John Bayley, Doug Dillard Band, Hotfoot Quintet, Jim Post
12:00 p.m. **Tales Short n' Tall**
Utah Phillips, The Folktellers, Ramblin' Jack Elliott
1:00 p.m.**I Got Rhythm**
John Bayley, Benoit Bourque, Trevor Ferrier, Alain Lamontagne, Dave Van Ronk
2:00 p.m. **Working Together**
Joan MacIsaac, Lyall Steel
2:30 p.m. Su Chong Lim
3:00 p.m. Dakota Dave Hull & Sean Blackburn
3:30 p.m. Doc & Merle Watson
4:00 p.m. **Country Grass**
Rodney Dillard, The Dillards, Doug Dillard Band, Hotfoot Quintet
Stage 4
11:00 .**Story Songs**
Jeff Cahill, Brandy Wine, Steve Cormier, McDade Family Band
12:00 p.m. **Songs That Leave An Impression**
Don Freed, Tom Paxton, David Sereda, Jon Sirkis
1:00 p.m. **Please Me — Squeeze Me**
Ian Bell, Calvin Cairns, John Malone, Martin O'Connor, Raynald Ouelette
2:00 p.m. **Sharing The Stage**
Tom See David Wilcox
2:30 p.m. Jim Post
3:00 p.m. Utah Phillips
3:30 p.m. **Rock n' Roll is in My Soul**
Amos Garrett, Roger Brant, David Burgin, Gord Kidder, Dave McLean, Jim Post, Brent Parkin, Tom See, Linsey Umrysh
The Tent
12:00 p.m. **Bluegrass Banjo**
Doug Dillard
1:00 p.m. **Basic Guitar**
Jon Sirkis
2:00 p.m. **Turning Bad Situations Into Good Songs**
Peter Alsop, Don Freed, Tom Paxton
3:00 p.m. **Tuning Your Vocal Chords**
David Sereda
4:00 p.m. **Advanced Guitar Technique**
Lyall Steel
Children's Stage
11:00 . Supervised Play Activities
12:00 p.m. Mike Absalom
12:30 p.m. Brandy Wine and the McDade Family Band
1:00 p.m. Bob Schneider
1:30 p.m. Pied Pear
2:00 p.m. Will Millar
2:30 p.m. Merry Time Clown & Puppet Company
3:00 p.m. Barry Louis Polisar
3:30 p.m. Ronnie Burkett
4:00 p.m. **Punch n' Judy**
John Styles
4:30 p.m. The Folktellers

5:30 to 10:30 p.m. **Main Stage**
The Dillards, Oscar Brand, Na Cabarfeidh, Will Millar, Dave Van Ronk, 'Eritage, Stan Rogers, Anne Mortifee, Clarence Gatemouth Brown with Houndog, Doc Watson

AUGUST 5, 1983

6 to 10:30 p.m. **Main Stage**
Whiskeyjack, David Essig, Reilly & Maloney, Holly Arntzen, Tom Jackson, Eclectricity, Diamond Joe White, Mike Cross, John Bayley

AUGUST 6, 1983

Stage 1
11:00 a.m. **Songs Of and For Working People**
Utah Phillips, Rodney Brown, Margaret Christl, Paul Hann, Tim Harrison
12:00 p.m. Paddy Tutty
12:30 p.m. **Prairie Schooner**
Tom Jackson, Crooked Creek, Paul Finkleman, Sid Marty, Winston Wuttunee
1:30 p.m. Crooked Creek
2:00 p.m. **Voice Instruments**
Margaret Christl, Robin Flower Band, Walt Michael & Co., Paddy Tutty
3:00 p.m. Rodney Brown
3:30 p.m. Sweet Tweet
Randy Raine-Reusch, Alpaka, Brahan Seer
4:15 p.m. **Homegrown Songs**
Bev Ross, Todd Butler
Stage 2
11:00 a.m. **CBC Special Cross-Country Checkup**
Tom Jackson, La Bottine Souriante, Stringband, Paddy Tutty, Winston Wuttunee
12:00 p.m. Bev Ross
12:30 p.m. **Country Swing**
David Maloney, The Banfields, Eclectricity, Robin Flower Band, Reilly & Maloney
1:30 p.m. Tom Paley
2:00 p.m. **String Band Selections**
Bob Bossin, Crooked Creek, J.P. Nystroms, Stringband
3:00 p.m. Bob Carpenter, Ken Dalgleish
3:30 p.m. **All in the Family**
Holly Arntzen, Lloyd Arntzen, The Banfields, Christy & Fred Cook
4:15 p.m. **Country Dance**
Gilbert Parent, La Bottine Souriante
Stage 3
11:00 a.m. **With My Banjo on My Knee**
Tony Trischka, Duncan Fremlin, John Hickman, Bob Lucas, Tom Paley
12:00 p.m. Tod Butler
12:30 p.m. **Country Songs**
Bim, Dave Essig, Paul Hann, Diamond Joe White
1:30 p.m. Pied Pear
2:00 p.m. **It's So Lonesome in the Saddle Since My Horse Died**
Mike Cross, Riders in the Sky, Gamble Rogers, Jon Sirkis
3:00 p.m. Tim Harrison
3:30 p.m. **Songs We Used To Sing and Still Do**
Rick Scott, Bim, Pied Pear, Riders in the Sky, Chris Hillman & Al Perkins
4:30 p.m. Bob Schneider
Stage 4
11:00 a.m. **American Fiddle Styles**

Byron Berline, Mike Cross, John Kirk, Tony Michael, Crystal Reeves
12:00 p.m. Paul Finkleman
12:30 p.m. **Songs of People, Places, and Things**
Bob Carpenter, Lee & Sandy Paley, Bob Schneider, Jon Sirkis
1:30 p.m. John Bayley
2:00 p.m. **I Like My Grass..."Blue"**
Tony Trischka, The Banfields, Skyline, Whiskeyjack, The Mason Williams Ensemble
3:00 p.m. Paul Hann
3:30 p.m. **Fingerstyle Guitar**
Tom Paley, Robin Flower, Marty Marxer, Gamble Rogers
4:15 p.m. **Jet Age Guitar**
David Essig, John Hammond, Leo Kottke, Danny Weiss
The Tent
11:00 a.m. **So...You Want to be a Professional Songwriter**
Bim, Diamond Joe White
12:00 p.m. **Tuning and Playing the Hammered Dulcimer**
Christy Cook, Fred Cook, Walt Michael
1:00 p.m. **The Fine Art of Spinning Yarns**
Gamble Rogers, Utah Phillips
2:00 p.m. **Basic Fingerstyle Guitar**
Ma Fletcher
3:00 p.m. **Body Awareness and Movement**
O.J. Anderson, Gumboot Lollipop
4:00 p.m. 5-String Banjo Skills Bluegrass and Beyond
Tony Trischka
Children's Stage
11:00 a.m. Playtime
12:00 p.m. Gumboot Lollipop
12:30 p.m. Gilbert Parent
1:00 p.m. Incredible Isreal
1:30 p.m. Puppet Mongers Powell
2:00 p.m. Paul Hann
2:30 p.m. Pied Pear
3:00 p.m. Bob Schneider and Friends
3:30 p.m. Lee & Sandy Paley
4:00 p.m. Tiv the Clown
4:30 p.m. **Good Time Songs**
Whiskeyjack

5:30 to 10:30 p.m. **Main Stage**
Robin Flower Band, La Bottine Souriante, Walt Michael & Co., John Hammond, Gamble Rogers, Chris Hillman & Al Perkins, O.J. Anderson, Bim, Leo Kottke, Riders in the Sky

AUGUST 7, 1983
Stage 1
11:00 a.m. **There's a World of Purty Girls Out There: Songs to and For Women,** Bob Carpenter, Rodney Brown, Tod Butler, Paul Finkleman, Tim Harrison
12:00 p.m. Sid Marty
12:30 p.m. **CHED Firequacker Special Yuks & Yarns**
Bryan Bowers, Utah Phillips, Gamble Rogers, Mason Williams
1:30 p.m. Artis
2:00 p.m. **Women in Song: Songs For and By Women**
Margaret Christl, Robin Flower Band, Marie-Lynn Hammond, Bev Ross, Paddy Tutty
3:00 p.m. Randy Raine-Reusch

3:30 p.m. **Tunes We Dance to in the Old Country**
J.P. Nystrom, Tom Paley
4:30 p.m. **Open Stage**
Stage 2
11:00 a.m. **Gimme That Old Time Religion**
Bob Lucas, Bryan Bowers, Lee & Sandy Paley, Diamond Joe White, Chris Hillman with Al Perkins
12:00 p.m. Barb & Howie Banfield
12:30 p.m. **European Influences**
Walt Michael, La Bottine Souriante, Brahan Seer, Walt Michael & Co.
1:30 p.m. Winston Wuttunee
2:00 p.m. **We Choose the Blues**
Long John Baldry, Holly Arntzen, John Hammond
3:00 p.m. Jon Sirkis
3:30 p.m. **New Grass**
Robin Flower, Robin Flower Band, Tony Trischka & Skyline, Mason Williams and His Friends
4:30 p.m. **Open Stage**
Stage 3
11:00 a.m. **Mandolin Manoeuverin'**
Dave Essig, Robin Flower, John Hoffman, Jerry Mills, Barry Mitterhoff
12:00 p.m. Christy & Fred Cook
12:30 p.m. **International Interaction**
Bill Schwarz, Alpaka, Eclectricity, J.P. Nystroms
1:30 p.m. Alpaka
2:00 p.m. **New Songs**
Bim, Murray McLauchlan, Jon Sirkis, Loundon Wainwright
3:00 p.m. Utah Phillips
3:30 p.m. **Beyond Words**
O.J. Anderson, Gumboot Lollipop
The Incredible Isreal, Tiv the Clown
4:30 p.m. **Open Stage**
Stage 4
11:00 a.m. **Fiddle Tunes From Around the World**
Tom Paley, Gilles Losier, J.P.Nystroms, Lisa Ornstein, Miriam Sturm
12:00 p.m. Margaret Christl
12:30 p.m. **Harmonizing Together in Song**
Tom Jackson, Crooked Creek, Reilly & Maloney, Riders in the Sky
1:30 p.m. Rick Cunha
2:00 p.m. **Against the Stream: Action Songs**
Bob Bossin, Sid Marty, Pied Pear, Rodney Brown, Winston Wuttunee
3:00 p.m. Gene & Tony Michael
3:30 p.m. **Rock Around the Clock**
Bim, Tod Butler, Tim Harrison, John Hammond, Kim Cramer, Ron Casat, Linsey Umrysh
4:30 p.m. **Open Stage**
The Tent
11:00 a.m. **Join Us in a Rhythm Jam**
Artis, Bill Schwarz, Gilbert Parent, Randy Raine-Reusch
12:00 p.m. **Everything You Ever Wanted To Know About The Fiddle But Were Afraid to Ask**
Byron Berline
1:00 p.m. **Tips on Playing The Dulcimer**
Randy Raine-Reusch, Holly Arntzen
2:00 p.m. **Care and Feeding of the Autoharp**

Bryan Bowers
3:00 p.m. **What Say We Write a Song Together?**
David Essig
4:00 p.m. **Working With a Partner**
Reilly & Maloney Children's Stage
11:00 a.m. Fun and Games
12:00 p.m. Paul Hann
12:30 p.m. Artis
1:00 p.m. Gilbert Parent
1:30 p.m. The Fun Clown
Gumboot Lollipop
2:00 p.m. It's Magic Time
The Incredible Isreal
2:30 p.m. O.J. Anderson
3:00 p.m. Paul Finkleman
3:30 p.m. Sing Along
Bob Schneider & Friends
4:00 p.m. The Maraberries
4:30 p.m. Absolutely Everybody Loves
Lee & Sandy Paley

5:30 to 10:30 p.m. **Main Stage**
Tony Trischka & Skyline, Bryan Bowers, Stringband, Long John
Baldry, J.P. Nystroms, Mason Williams & Friends, Murray
McLauchlan, Willie Dixon & The Chicago Blues, Loudon
Wainwright III, Allstars, Brahan Seer, Finale

AUGUST 10, 1984

6 to 10:30 p.m. Main Stage
Blue Flame Stringband, Paul Hann, Alley Scatz, Dick
Damron, Ken Hamm, 'Eritage, Peter Rowan & Mark
O'Connor, Sylvia Tyson, k.d. lang, Dr. John & Maria Muldaur

AUGUST 11, 1984

Stage 1
11:00 a.m. **Edmonton City Limits**
Paul Wood, Gaye Delorme, Shawn Easley, k.d. lang, Joan
MacIsaac, Doug Johnson
12:00 p.m. Danny Greenspoon
12:30 p.m. **In The Juggler Vein**
Moshe Le Nuage
1:00 p.m. **Fiddle Sticks**
Mark O'Connor, Vassar Clements, Darcie Deaville, Sandra
Layman, Crystal Reeves, Peter Rowan
2:00 p.m. David Essig
2:30 p.m. Joan MacIsaac
3:00 p.m. **Roberta and the Bus**
Sylvia Tyson, Darcie Deaville, Danny Greenspoon, Marie-Lynn
Hammond, Paul Hann, Joan MacIsaac, Jim Post, Garnet
Rogers
4:00 p.m. **Putting a Band Together**
Gaye Delorme, Vassar Clements, Morris Goldberg, Al
Kates, Marilyn Lerner, Martha Jean Stubb, Sylvia Tyson ,Linsey
Umrysh
Stage 2
11:00 a.m. **Guitar Stylings**
Colin Linden, Kimbal Dykes, Beth Marlis, Al Perkins, Roger

Wade
12:00 p.m. Denise Larson
12:30 p.m. Bob Brozman
1:00 p.m. **Stomach Steinways**
Marty Reynard, Gaby Haas, John Malone, Raynald
Ouelette, Queen Ida
2:00 p.m. Si Kahn
2:30 p.m. Colin Linden
3:00 p.m. **If This Was the Grand Old Opry, This is What I'd Sing**
Peter Rowan, Guy Clark, Dick Damron, Gary Fjellgaard,
Denise Larson
4:00 p.m. **Vaudeville Showtime**
Peter Paul Van Camp, Brian Glow, Avner the Eccentric, Major
Conrad Flapps, Hamish Imlach, Moshe Le Nuage
Stage 3
11:00 a.m. **Balladeers & Balladesses**
Ginni Clemmens, Hamish Imlach, Lisa Martin, Peter Rowan
12:00 p.m. Shawn Easley
12:30 p.m. Stevie Beck
1:00 p.m. **Around the World in 60 Minutes**
Quentin Badoux, Tony Bird & Morris Goldberg, Kin Lalat, Patric
Mark Ensemble, Sukay
2:00 p.m. Marie-Lynn Hammond
2:30 p.m. Peter Alsop
3:00 p.m. **I Came From Alabama**
Cathy Fink, Roy Gullane, Jud Hepburn, Bernie Leadon, Steve
Lehner
4:00 p.m. **Songs That Begged to be Written About Things That
Needed to be Said**
Peter Alsop, Tony Bird, Ginni Clemmens, Si Kahn, Jim Post
Stage 4
11:00 a.m. **Oh Give Me a Home: Songs of the West Old & New**
Peter Paul Van Camp, Paul Hann, Blue Flame Stringband, Cathy
Fink, Steve Lehner & Maureen May
12:00 p.m. Kin Lalat
12:30 p.m. Darcie Deaville
1:00 p.m. **Blues Mixer**
Bob Brozman, David Burgin & the Nightshades, Ginni
Clemmens, Ken Hamm, k.d. lang
2:00 p.m. David Burgin & the Nightshades
2:30 p.m. **Swing Your Pardner**
Maurice Bellamy, The Gaby Haas Band
3:15 p.m. **Cajun-Zydeco**
Alan Senauke, Queen Ida & Band, Blue Flame Stringband,
4:00 p.m. **Swingin' on a Star**
Bob Brozman, Alley Scatz, Blue Flame Stringband, Soupe du Jour
Tent I
12:00 p.m. **A Long Story About the Short History of Bluegrass**
David Essig, Chris Hillman-Bernie Leadon Band
1:00 p.m. **The Cimbalom** Alexander Eppler
2:00 p.m. **The Music of India**
Patric Marks, Dr. Margaret Otto, Ranchhod Pandya
3:00 p.m. **Traditional Music of French Canada** 'Eritage
4:00 p.m. **The Music of the Andes**
Sukay
Tent II
12:00 p.m. **The Harsh Realities of the Music Business**
Richard Flohil, Emily Friedman, Mo Marshall, Holger Petersen
1:00 p.m. **Basic Classical Guitar Technique**

D'arcy Greaves
2:00 p.m. **Autoharp Instructional Workshop**
Steve Beck
3:00 p.m. **Mandolin Manoeuvres**
David Essig
4:00 p.m. **So You Want to Learn to Juggle!**
Jeff Jenkins
For the Children
12:00 p.m. Major Conrad Flapps
12:30 p.m. Peter Alsop
1:00 p.m. Jeff Jenkins
1:30 p.m. Cathy Fink
2:00 p.m. Paul Hann
2:30 p.m. Brian Glow
3:00 p.m. Si Kahn
3:30 p.m. One Yellow Rabbit
4:00 p.m. Isreal's Balloons
4:30 p.m. 'Eritage

5:30 to 10:30 p.m. **Main Stage**
Robin Flower Band, Tannahill Weavers, Soupe du Jour, Four Guitars, Sukay, Chris Hillman-Bernie Leadon Band, Tony Bird, Avner the Eccentric, Rita McNeil, Valdy, Queen Ida and the Bon Temps Zydeco Band

AUGUST 12, 1984

Stage 1
11:00 a.m. **Places I've Been and People I've Seen**
Valdy, Guy Clark, Joan MacIsaac, Rita McNeil, Peter Rowan
12:00 p.m. Gaye Delorme
12:30 p.m. Paul Wood & Doug Johnson
1:00 p.m. **Ever Heard a Song About This Before?**
Marie-Lynn Hammond, Ginni Clemmens, Shawn Easley, Rita McNeil, Garnet Rogers
2:00 p.m. Ginni Clemmens
2:30 p.m. **The French Connection**
Marie-Lynn Hammond, 'Eritage, Folle Avoine, Soupe du Jour
3:30 p.m. Peter Paul Van Camp
4:00 p.m. **Evolution of a Stringband**
Emily Friedman, 'Eritage, Red Clay Ramblers
4:45 p.m. Open Stage
Stage 2
11:00 a.m. **Six Days on the Road**
David Essig, Dick Damron, Gary Fjellgaard, Paul Hann, Denise Larson
12:00 p.m. Garnet Rogers
12:30 p.m. Hamish Imlach
1:00 p.m. **There are Many Ways to Tell a Story**
Peter Paul Van Camp, Tony Bird & Morris Goldberg, Hamish Imlach, One Yellow Rabbit, Peter Rowan
2:00 p.m. Patric Marks Ensemble
2:30 p.m. **New Directions in Acoustic Music**
Robin Flower Band, Vassar Clements, Mark O'Connor, Chris Hillman-Bernie Leadon Band, Stockton's Wing
3:30 p.m. Mark O'Connor
4:00 p.m. **Big Hands Small Neck**
David Essig, Gaston Bernard, Chris Hillman, Steve Lehner
4:45 p.m. Open Stage

Stage 3
11:00 a.m. **Duos With a Difference**
Ken Hamm, Bruce Everett, Darcie Deaville, Lisa Martin, Steve Lehner, Maureen May, Paul Wood, Doug Johnson
12:00 p.m. Joella Foulds
12:30 p.m. Gary Fjellgaard
1:00 p.m. **Meetin' at the Building**
Chris Hillman, Stevie Beck, Bernie Leadon, Lee & Sandy Paley, Red Clay Ramblers
2:00 p.m. Original Balkan Jam
2:30 p.m. **We Play You Dance**
Don Buskirk, Blue Flame, String Band, Kin Lalat, Original Balkan Jam,Sukay
3:30 p.m. Steve Lehner & Maureen May
4:00 p.m. **Wimmen' Jammin'**
Cathy Fink, Darcie Deaville, Robin Flower Band, Lisa Martin
4:45 p.m. Open Stage
Stage 4
11:00 a.m. **Continental Musicale**
Gaby Haas Band, Alexander Eppler Group, Original Balkan Jam, Tannahill Weavers
12:00 p.m. Sweetgrass
12:30 p.m. Cathy Fink
1:00 p.m. **Celidh**
Margaret Christl, Stockton's Wing, Tannahill Weavers, Wild Colonial Boys
2:00 p.m. Jim Post
2:30 p.m. **Rockin' Rollers**
Jim Post, Tony Bird, David Burgin, Roger Brant, Gaye Delorme, Morris Goldberg, k.d. lang, Stewart McDougall, Linsey Umrysh
3:30 p.m. Margaret Christl
4:00 p.m. **Nashville Cats**
Peter Rowan, Vassar Clements, Mark O'Connor & Bill Bryson, Guy Clark
4:45 p.m. Open Stage
Tent I
12:00 p.m. **Labour Songs in Action**
Si Kahn
1:00 p.m. **Vocal Chords**
Sue Spirk, Alley Scatz, Folle Avoine, Steve Lehner, Maureen May, Soupe du Jour
2:00 p.m. **Old Timey Banjo Techniques**
Cathy Fink, Tommy Thompson
3:00 p.m. **Using Songs to Support Social Change**
Ginni Clemmens, Si Kahn
4:00 p.m. **Let's Create a New Song**
Valdy
Tent II
12:00 p.m. **Stage Craft**
Bob Brozman
1:00 p.m. **Tips for Fiddlers**
Vassar Clements, Mark O'Connor
2:00 p.m. **On Accompanying One's Self & Others on Guitar**
Colin Linden
3:00 p.m. **The Use of Humor in Dealing With Sensitive Issues**
Peter Alsop
4:00 p.m. **Care and Feeding of the Guitar**
Stevie Beck

Tent for Children
12:00 p.m. Doc Myles Snow
12:30 p.m. Valdy
1:00 p.m. Brian Glow
1:30 p.m. Peter Alsop
2:00 p.m. Avner the Eccentric
2:30 p.m. Lee & Sandy Paley
3:00 p.m. Paul Hann
3:30 p.m. One Yellow Rabbit
4:00 p.m. The Wild Colonial Boys
4:30 p.m. Major Conrad Flapps

5:30 to 10:30 p.m. **Main Stage**
The Wild Colonial Boys, Alexander Eppler Group, Red Clay Ramblers, Folle Avoine, Vassar Clements, Guy Clark, Asleep At the Wheel, Stockton's Wing, Joan MacIsaac & Margaret Christl, Finale

AUGUST 9, 1985

6 to 10:30 p.m. **Main Stage**
McDade Family Band, Vera Johnson, Bob Brozman, Leon Rosselson & Frankie Armstrong, La Bottine Souriante, Al Simmons, Spirit of the West, Gryphon Quintet, Queen Ida and the Bon Temps Zydeco Band

AUGUST 10, 1985

Stage 1
11:00 a.m. **Me and My Mandolin**
Jack Tuttle, Jeff Rose & Mark Schrock, Mitch Le Page, John Hoffman, Bev Futtrell
12:00 p.m. **Story Songs & Stories**
Paddy Tutty, Winston Wuttunee, Paula Jardine, Ian Johnstone, Laughing Moon Theatre
1:00 p.m. Ma Fletcher
1:30 p.m. Moshe Le Nuage
2:00 p.m. **Looney Toones & Merry Maladies**
Ginni Clemmens, Fun Country, Girls Who Wear Glasses, Vera Johnson, Laughing Moon Theatre
3:00 p.m. **Songs to Right the Wrongs**
Frankie Armstrong & Leon Rosselson, Vera Johnson, Faith Petric, Shingoose, Judy Small
4:00 p.m. **My Favorite Songwriters**
Leon Rosselson, k.d. lang, Judy Small, Jesse Colin Young, Chris Whiteley & Caitlin Hanford
5:00 p.m. Open Stage
Stage 2
11:00 a.m. **Piano Stylings**
David Amram, Ron Casat, Linda Morrison, David Raffenaud
12:00 p.m. **Slip-Slidin' Away**
Bob Brozman, Al Kates, John Hammond, Carol McComb
1:00 p.m. Paul Finkleman
1:30 p.m. Winston Wuttunee
2:00 p.m. **Canada**
Luke Wilson & Lost in the Colonies, La Bottine Souriante, Spirit of the West, John Steins & Scott Sheerin
3:00 p.m. **Old Tyme Jamboree**
Gilbert Parent, La Bottine Souriante, Limited Edition, Reel World

String Band, Shuffle Creek Dancers
4:00 p.m. **Collage**
Randy Raine-Reusch, Anonymus, Ken Bloom, Julien Kytasty
5:00 p.m. Open Stage
Stage 3
11:00 a.m. **Strummin', Pickin', & Frailin' on the Ol' Ban-jo**
Sue Massek, Rich Bamman, Duncan Fremlin, Daniel Koulak, Denis Le Page, Luke Wilson
12:00 p.m. **Bellows & Buttons**
Queen Ida, Buckwheat, Dural Shayla Fink, Yves Lambert, David Raffenaud
1:00 p.m. Fun Country
1:30 p.m. Paddy Tutty
2:00 p.m. Anonymus
2:30 p.m. **They're Not Looney & I'm Not Jewish**
Finja, Al Simmons
3:00 p.m. **Swingin'**
Bob Brozman, Girls Who Wear Glasses, Gryphon Quintet, Iowa Rose
4:00 p.m. **All White & Feelin' Blue**
Ginni Clemmens, Bob Brozman, John Hammond, Linda Morrison
5:00 p.m. Open Stage
Stage 4
11:00 a.m. **Fiddle Fever**
Rollie La Pierre, James Hurley, Karen Jones, Shannon McDade, Martin Racine, Victor Schultz
12:00 p.m. **Something in Common**
Ken Bloom, Lost in the Colonies, John Steins & Scott Sheerin
1:00 p.m. Ken Bloom
1:30 p.m. Linda Morrison
2:00 p.m. **Emily's Front Porch Sessions**
Emily Friedman, Queen Ida, Jesse Colin Young
3:00 p.m. **Gotta Lotta Rhythm In My Soul**
David Amram, Queen Ida, Gwinyai & Sukatai Marimba Ensemble, k.d. lang & the Reclines
4:00 p.m. **Old Wave, New Time Music**
Jeff Rose with Iowa Rose, Finjan, Spirit of the West, Whiskey Jack
5:00 p.m. Open Stage
Tent I
12:00 p.m. **Mandolin Basics & Beyond**
Jack Tuttle
1:00 p.m. **The Dulcimer as a Solo Instrument**
Randy Raine-Reusch
2:00 p.m. **Appalachian Music: Past & Present**
Reel World String Band
3:00 p.m. **The Ukranian Bandura**
Ken Bloom, Julian Kytasty
4:00 p.m. **Bluegrass Banjo Techniques**
Denis Lepage
Tent II
12:00 p.m. **Improve Your Juggling**
Moshe Le Nuage, Roberto Morganti, We Juggle Till We Drop
1:00 p.m. **Finding Your Natural Voice**
Frankie Armstrong, Ginni Clemmens
2:00 p.m. **Vocal Arrangement**
Linda Morrison, Gryphon Quintent, Caitlin Hanford & Chris Whiteley, Whiskeyjack
3:00 p.m. **Let's Write a Song For Young Audiences**

Paulo
4:00 p.m. **Writing Songs With a Purpose**
Shingoose, Winston Wuttunee
Children's Stage
11:30 a.m. Doc Myles Snow
12:00 p.m. Ginni Clemmens
12:30 p.m. Gilbert Parent
1:00 p.m. Phuzz and Friends
1:30 p.m. McDade Family Band
2:00 p.m. Moz Wright & Roberto Morganti
2:30 p.m. Ma Fletcher
3:00 p.m. Kenuppets
3:30 p.m. Ian Johnstone
4:00 p.m. The Moon's a Rabbit
4:30 p.m. Paulo

5:30 to 10:30 p.m. **Main Stage**
Whiskeyjack, Ginni Clemmens, Finjan, Gwinyai & Sukatai Marimba Ensemble, Battlefield Band, Judy Small, Vasilios Papachristou with Kyklos, Jesse Colin Young and the Youngbloods, k.d. lang and the Reclines

AUGUST 11, 1985

Stage 1
11:00 a.m. **Songs to Raise Your Consciousness**
Ginni Clemmens, Ken Bloom, Bob Brozman, Vera Johnson, Paddy Tutty
12:00 p.m. **Women Singing About Women**
Ginni Clemmens, Vera Johnson, Judy Small, Faith Petric, Reel World String Band
1:00 p.m. Laughing Moon Theatre
1:30 p.m. Faith Petric
2:00 p.m. **Strong Women Remembered in Traditional Song**
Emily Friedman, Frankie Armstrong, Ginni Clemmens, John Hammond, Faith Petric, Paddy Tutty
3:00 p.m. **The All New Vaudeville Show**
Al Simmons, Moz Wright, Girls Who Wear Glasses, Laughing Moon Theatre, Moshe Le Nuage, Roberto Morganti
4:00 p.m. **I Had This Idea...**
Ken Bloom, Bob Brozman, Paul Finkleman, Leon Rosselson, Judy Small
5:00 p.m. Open Stage
Stage 2
11:00 a.m. **I Saw the Light**
Linda Morrison, Gryphon Quintet, Iowa Rose, Limited Edition, Whiskeyjack
12:00 p.m. **Hearing Double**
Girls Who Wear Glasses, Fun Country, Leon Rosselson & Frankie Armstrong, Chris Whiteley & Caitlin Hanford
1:00 p.m. Randy Raine-Reusch
1:30 p.m. **Juggling, Fire Breathing, & Sword Swallowing**
Roberto Morganti, Moz Wright
2:00 p.m. **Cloggin' Lessons**
Shuffle Creek Dancers, Reel World String Band
2:30 p.m. **Following Zorba's Footsteps**
Vasilios Papachristou with Kyklos
3:00 p.m. **Basically Bluegrass**
Mitch Le Page, Limited Edition, Gryphon Quintet, Iowa Rose, Whiskeyjack

4:00 p.m. **Celtic Influences**
J. Knutson, Spirit of the West, Paddy Tutty, Battlefield Band, Limited Edition
5:00 p.m. Open Stage
Stage 3
11:00 a.m. **So You've Got Laryngitis, Eh?**
John Steins & Scott Sheerin, Anonymus, Finjan, Randy Raine-Reusch
12:00 p.m. **Native Images**
Shingoose, David Amram, Winston Wuttunee
1:00 p.m. Girls Who Wear Glasses
1:30 p.m. Shingoose
2:00 p.m. **A Marriage of Musical Modes**
Randy Raine-Reusch, David Amram, Ken Bloom
3:00 p.m. **We Dance For You**
Vasilios Papachristou with Kyklos, Gwinyai & Sukatai Marimba Ensemble
4:00 p.m. **Cross-Cultural Blow-Out**
Myron Schultz, Finjan, Gwinyai & Sukatai Marimba Ensemble, Buckwheat Zydeco
5:00 p.m. Open Stage
Stage 4
11:00 a.m. **With Love, From Alberta**
Terry McDade with the McDade Family, Lost in the Colonies, Fun Country, Ma Fletcher, Paul Finkleman
12:00 p.m. **I Don't Normally Do This, But...**
Emily Friedman, Anonymus, Battlefield Band, John Hammond, k.d. lang, Al Simmons, Spirit of the West
1:00 p.m. John Steins & Scott Sheerin
1:30 p.m. Lost in the Colonies
2:00 p.m. **With Inspiration From Mother Earth**
Lost in the Colonies, McDade Family Band, Shingoose, John Steins & Scott Sheerin, Winston Wuttunee
3:00 p.m. **Let's Rock It!**
John Hammond, k.d. lang & the Reclines, Linda Morrison, Scott Sheerin, Chris Whiteley & Caitlin Hanford
4:00 p.m. **Goin' Up to the Country**
k.d. lang, Riders in the Sky, Al Simmons, Chris Whiteley & Caitlin Hanford, Linda Morrison
5:00 p.m. Open Stage
Tent I
12:00 p.m. **Basic Folk Guitar Workshop**
Ma Fletcher
1:00 p.m. **Slide Guitar Technique**
Bob Brozman
2:00 p.m. **Medieval Musical Instruments**
Anonymus
3:00 p.m. **Innovative Guitar Techniques**
John Steins
4:00 p.m. **Keeping the Tradition Alive**
Frankie Armstrong, Anonymus
Tent II
12:00 p.m. **All You Need to Know About Performance Sound & Lighting**
Clive Alcock, Ian Kerr
1:00 p.m. **Adapting Different Musical Styles to Bluegrass**
Whiskeyjack
2:00 p.m. **Writing Songs to Fan the Flames of Discontent**
Judy Small, Leon Rosselson

3:00 p.m. **Tips for Those Who Aspire to Teach Children to Make Music**
Ian Johnstone
4:00 p.m. **Writing Songs for Working People**
Vera Johnson, Faith Petric
Children's Stage
11:30 a.m. David Amram
12:00 p.m. Paulo
12:30 p.m. Kenuppets
1:00 p.m. Iowa Rose
1:30 p.m. Shayla Fink
2:00 p.m. Ian Johnstone
2:30 p.m. The Moon's a Rabbit
3:00 p.m. The Reel World String Band
3:30 p.m. Winston Wuttunee
4:00 p.m. Phuzz and Friends
4:30 p.m. Whiskeyjack

5:30 to 10:30 p.m. **Main Stage**
Limited Edition, Iowa Rose, John Hammond, Chris Whiteley & Caitlin Hanford, Buckwheat Zydeco, David Amram, Reel World String Band & The Shuffle Creek Dancers, Riders in the Sky, Finale

AUGUST 8, 1986

5:30 to 10:30 p.m. Main Stage
The Dixie Flyers, Prairie Oyster, Roy Bailey, Ellen McIlwaine, Ian Whitcomb & Dick Zimmerman, Lo Jai, Luther "Guitar Jr."Johnson & The Magic Rockers, Mimi Farina

AUGUST 9, 1986
Stage 1
11:00 a.m. **Old Wave, New Time**
Iowa Rose, The Mandolin Kid, The Dixie Flyers
12:00 p.m. **House Rent Party Piano Style**
Dick Zimmerman, Rusty Reed, Joan Besen & Gene Taylor, Stu MacDougal, Geoff Muldaur, Ellen McIlwaine
1:00 p.m. Gene Taylor & The Eh Team with Special Guest Lowell Fulson
3:00 p.m. Colin Linden with John Wynot & Guests
3:30 p.m. **Blues Workout**
Amos Garrett and The Eh Team, Ellen McIlwaine, Doug Sahm, Luther "Guitar Jr." Johnson, Geoff Muldaur, Gene Taylor
4:30 p.m. Murray McLauchlan, Ramblin' Jack Elliott
Stage 2
11:00 a.m. **Texas Cookin'**
Katy Moffatt, Guy Clark, Townes Van Zandt, Hugh Moffatt
12:00 p.m. **Country Jam**
The Chinook Arch Riders, Dennis Delorme, Russell DeCarle, Keith Glass, Mark French, John P. Allen
1:00 p.m. **Bluegrass Workshop**
The Dixie Flyers, Willie P. Bennett, Richard Greene, The Mandolin Kid, Iowa Rose, Tony Michael, John P. Allen
3:00 p.m.
Prairie Oyster, Ramblin' Jack Elliott, Willie P. Bennett, Richard Greene, Ian Tyson, Bim, Doug Sahm
4:15 p.m. **Queen Street Refugees**
Colin Linden, Mark Haines, Willie P. Bennett, Joe Hall

Stage 3
11:00 a.m. **Gospel Songs**
Ellen McIlwaine, Bill Bourne, Ted Crouch
11:45 a.m. **A Sense of Place**
Valdy, Bim, Bev Ross, Paul Hann, Lionel Rault, Rick Neufeld, Joe Hall, Richard White, The Smith Sisters
1:00 p.m. **Songs for Friends & Heroes**
Murray McLauchlan, John Stewart, Guy Clark, Townes Van Zandt, Ian Tyson, Hugh Moffatt
3:00 p.m. **We Normally Don't Do This But...**
Valdy, Original Balkan Jam, Spirit of the West, The Smith Sisters
4:00 p.m. **Front Porch Sessions**
Bruce Steele talks to Donovan
Stage 4
11:00 a.m. **Deep Feelings**
Bev Ross, Brenda Baker, Mimi Farina, The Smith Sisters, Katy Moffatt
11:45 a.m. Eileen McGann
12:00 p.m. **Human Condition Music**
Bim, Roy Bailey, Mimi Farina with Banana, Valdy, Willie P. Bennett, Colin Linden
1:00 p.m. **Anything Goes**
Paul Hann, The Dixie Flyers, Original Balkan Jam, McDade Family with Bob Shortt
4:00 p.m. **Novelty Songs & Stories**
Mark Haines, Bev Ross, Guy Delorme, Ian Whitcomb & Dick Zimmerman, Paul Hann, Ramblin' Jack Elliott, Joe Hall
Tent I
11:45 a.m. **Stephannson Poetry Put to Song**
Richard White, Gaye Delorme
12:00 p.m. **Mandolin Manoeuvres**
The Mandolin Kid, Ken Palmer
12:15 p.m. **Fiddle Technique**
Richard Greene
12:30 p.m. **Voice Technique**
Ellen McIlwaine, Geoff Muldaur
3:00 p.m. **Songs of Hard Times**
Roy Bailey, Cathal McConnell, Eileen McGann
4:00 p.m. **The North**
John Steins & Scott Sheerin
4:15 p.m. Open Stage
Tent II
11:45 a.m. Alpaka
12:00 p.m. **Spoon Workshop**
Gilbert Parent
12:15 p.m. **Music & Mime & More**
O.J. Anderson, Ted Crouch, Bruce Steele
3:00 p.m. **The Great Music Trivia Contest**
Moderators: Ian Whitcomb, Richard Flohil, Bruce Steele
Team One: Valdy, Mimi Farina, Norm MacPherson, Geoff Muldaur.
Team Two: Bim, Willie P. Bennett, Joan Besen, Rick Neufeld.
Team Three: The Audience
4:00 p.m. Open Stage
2:05 p.m. Main Stage, Jesse Winchester

5:00 p.m. **Main Stage**
Bev Ross, Iowa Rose, Lowell Fulson, Boys of the Lough, John Hiatt, Guy Clark, Doug Sahm, John Stewart

AUGUST 10, 1986

Stage 1
11:00 a.m. **Pipes, Whistles, Hurdy-Gurdies & More** Cathal McConnell, Guy Bertrand, Eric Montbell, Pierre Imbert, Geoff Kelly, Christy O'Leary, Dave Richardson, John Coakley
12:00 p.m. Original Balkan Jam
12:30 p.m. Joe Hall
1:00 p.m. **Three Approaches To Celtic Music**
Spirit of the West, Boys of the Lough, Lo Jai
3:00 p.m. Bill Bourne & The Jim Fitzgerald Band
3:30 p.m. **Acoustic/Electric Blues**
Colin Linden, Luther "Guitar Jr." Johnson, Ellen McIlwaine, Sunnyland Slim, Rusty Reed, Geoff Muldaur
Stage 2
11:00 a.m. **Songs That Showed Me How**
Bim, Hugh Moffatt, Joe Hall, Norm MacPherson, Rick Neufeld, Colin Linden
12:00 p.m. Willie P. Bennett, Colin Linden
1:00 p.m. **Cowboy Songs**
Ian Tyson, Townes Van Zandt, Guy Clark, Ramblin' Jack Elliott
3:00 p.m. **The Evolution of a Hit**
Hugh Moffatt
3:30 p.m. **Pure Country**
Hugh & Katy Moffatt, The Cowtones, The Mandolin Kid, Richard Greene, The Smith Sisters, Lionel Rault
Stage 3
11:00 a.m. **Fiddle Workshop**
Mark Haines, Aly Bain, Richard Greene, Tony Michael, John P. Allen, Bill Bourne, Christian Oller, Shannon McDade, Al Widmeyer
12:00 p.m. John Steins & Scott Sheerin
1:00 p.m. **Alberta Songs**
Lionel Rault, Bev Ross, Jim Serediak, Stu MacDougal, Richard White, Bill Bourne
3:00 p.m. Toonuniq Theatre Group
3:45 p.m. **Anxiously Awaited New Songs**
Ian Tyson, Townes Van Zandt, John Hiatt, Guy Clark, Jesse Winchester, John Stewart
Stage 4
11:00 a.m. **French Immersion**
McDade Family Band, Lo Jai, Gilbert Parent & Friends
11:30 a.m. **Unusual Instruments**
Lo Jai
3:00 p.m. **Topical Songs**
Spirit of the West, Roy Bailey, The Smith Sisters, Eileen McGann, Brenda Baker
3:30 p.m. **Changes - An Inuit Play**
Toonuniq Theatre Group
3:45 p.m. **French Country Dances**
Lo Jai
4:00 p.m. **Percussion Workshop**
Lo Jai, Jim Ross, Toonuniq Theatre Group
Tent I
1:00 p.m. **Write a Song**
Willie P. Bennett
3:00 p.m. **What Do We Do With It Now? The Music Biz** Richard Flohil, Colin Linden, Mark Moss, David McKerrell and special guests
3:30 p.m. **"Write What You Know" Questions & Answers** Guy

Clark, Townes Van Zandt
4:00 p.m. **Ballads**
Roy Bailey, Eileen McGann, Bill Bourne
4:30 p.m. Open Stage
Tent II
1:00 p.m. What Can Parents Do For Kids on a Rainy Day?
1:30 p.m. **T.A.L.E.S.**
Tigge-Anne Anderson, Marie Anne McLean, Diane Zinyk, Jonathan Dixon
3:30 p.m. **Tin Pan Alley - From Rag to Rock**
Ian Whitcomb & Dick Zimmerman
3:45 p.m. Alpaka
4:30 p.m. Open Stage
2:05 p.m. Main Stage Donovan

5 to 10:30 p.m. **Main Stage**
Katy & Hugh Moffatt with The Cowtones, The Mandolin Kid, Bim, Ramblin' Jack Elliott, Spirit of the West, The Robert Cray Band, Murray McLauchlan, Geoff Muldaur & Amos Garrett with Richard Greene, Ian Tyson

AUGUST 7, 1987

5:30 to 10:30 p.m. **Main Stage**
Rare Air, Diamond Joe White, Terry Garthwaite, The Romaniacs, Bill Bourne, Rory Block, Eric Anderson, Eric Bogle, John Sebastian, Ellen McIlwaine

AUGUST 8, 1987

Stage 1
11:00 a.m. **Whistles & Pipes & Percussion**
Geoffrey Kelly, Morris Goldberg, Rare Air
12:00 p.m. **Multi-Cultural Influences**
Ellen McIlwaine, Tony Bird & Morris Goldberg, Huara
1:00 p.m. **Country Blues**
Rory Block, Yank Rachell, Hans Theessink, Gene Taylor, Phil Alvin
3:00 p.m. **Party Music**
The Romaniacs, The Shuffle Demons
4:00 p.m. **Rhythm & Roots Workshop**
Ellen McIlwaine, Amos Garrett, Gene Taylor, Phil Alvin
Stage 2
11:00 a.m. **Stringing the Audience Along**
Shari Ulrich, Novi, Calvin Cairns, Bill Bourne, Tony Michael
12:00 p.m. James Keelaghan
12:30 p.m. Bob Carpenter
1:00 p.m. The Great Sneezy Waters Band with guest Doug Sahm
3:00 p.m. **Songs & Stories from the Road**
Danny O'Keefe, Townes Van Zandt, John D. Loudermilk, Bob Carpenter, Guy Clark
4:00 p.m. **The Songs of Hank Williams**
Sneezy Waters, Doug Sahm, Townes Van Zandt
Stage 3
11:00 a.m. **Prairie Songwriters**
Ian Tyson, Humphrey & The Dumptrucks, Lesley Schatz, Diamond Joe White, Paul Hann
12:00 p.m. **You're On Your Own**
John Mann, Danny Greenspoon, Michael Taylor, John Jones, Cindy Church & Nathan Tinkham
1:00 p.m. **The Hardest and Easiest Songs I've Ever Written**

Ferron, Eric Anderson, Bill Bourne, Rick Danko, Bob Carpenter
3:00 p.m. **N.Y.N.Y.**
Christine Lavin, Eric Andersen, Tony Bird, Rick Danko, Rory Block
4:00 p.m. **Celtic Highbred & Outside**
Spirit of the West, John Renbourn, Rare Air, James Keelaghan
Stage 4
11:00 a.m. **Songs From The Heart**
Ferron, Townes Van Zandt, Eric Andersen, Danny O'Keefe, Eric
Bogle
12:00 p.m. Tom Russell
12:30 p.m. Townes Van Zandt
1:00 p.m. **Native Rights**
Eric Bogle, Spirit of the West, Danny O'Keefe, Tony Bird & Morris
Goldberg
3:00 p.m. **Early Jazz & Blues**
Terry Garthwaite, Eugene Smith, Phil Alvin & Gene Taylor
4:00 p.m. **Cowboy Culture**
Ian Tyson, Guy Clark, Tom Russell, Diamond Joe White
Tent I
11:00 a.m. **Pickers Producing Each Other**
Danny Greenspoon, Bill Garrett & Curly Boy Stubbs, David Essig
12:00 p.m. **Folk, Blues & Beyond**
Ian Kearey, Alan Prosser, John Fahey, David Essig
1:00 p.m. **Songs of Northern Alberta**
Jacques Chauvin
1:30 p.m. **Songs of Southern Alberta**
Lesley Schatz
3:00 p.m. **International Acoustic Swing**
Morris Goldberg, Huara: Music of Clay & Concrete, Gaye Delorme
4:00 p.m. **The Mandolin**
David Essig, Yank Rachell, Jethro Burns, Steve Bengston, Dave
Wilkie
Tent II
11:00 a.m. Major Conrad Flapps
12:00 p.m. **Storytelling** T.A.L.E.S. The Alberta League to
Encourage Storytellers
1:30 p.m. **Unusual Instruments**
David Essig
3:00 p.m. **Guitar Improvisation by Example**
John Fahey
3:30 p.m. **Jam**
Hans Theessink & Rusty Reed, Bill Garrett & Curly Boy Stubbs
4:00 p.m. Open Stage
2 to 3:00 p.m. Main Stage Murray McLauchlan

5:00 to 10:30 p.m. **Main Stage**
Jethro Burns & The Great Western Orchestra, Danny O'Keefe,
Shari Ulrich, Yank Rachell, Christine Lavin, Humphrey & The
Dumptrucks, Phil Alvin, Tony Bird, The Shuffle Demons, The Amos
Garrett, Doug Sahm, Gene Taylor Band, with guests, The Oyster
Band

AUGUST 9, 1987
Stage 1
11:00 a.m. **Rhythm & Tunes**
Bruce Steele, Rare Air, Huara, Quammie Williams
12:00 p.m. Hans Theessink
12:30 p.m. Gene Taylor
1:00 p.m. **Acoustic Blues**

Colin Linden & Yank Rachell, Bill Bourne, Eugene Smith ,Terry
Garthwaite, Bill Garrett & Curly Boy Stubbs
3:00 p.m. **AmosBehavin'**
Amos Garrett, Gene Taylor, Phil Alvin, Big Miller
4:00 p.m. The Eddy Clearwater Band
Stage 2
11:00 a.m. **Piano Styles**
Shari Ulrich, Eric Andersen, Gene Taylor, Stewart MacDougall,
Ted Borowiecki
12:00 p.m. **The Incredible Al Simmons Show**
1:00 p.m. **Independent Women's Music**
Shari Ulrich, Christine Lavin, Rosanne Cash, Rory Block
3:00 p.m. **Jazz & Improvisation**
The Shuffle Demons, Terry Garthwaite, Morris Goldberg, Quammie
Williams, John Fahey, Ellen McIlwaine
4:00 p.m. **Old Time Country**
Doug Sahm, Diamond Joe White, Rick Danko, Sneezy Waters
Stage 3
11:00 a.m. **Gospel Singing**
Ellen McIlwaine, Cindy Church & Nathan Tinkham, Lesley Schatz,
Diamond Joe & Penny White, Big Miller
12:00 p.m. Colin Linden
12:30 p.m. Eugene Smith
1:00 p.m. **Master Class**
David Wilkie, Jethro Burns, Mark O'Connor, Jerry Douglas, Gaye
Delorme, John Renbourn
3:00 p.m. **Anxiously Awaited New Songs**
Ian Tyson, Rodney Crowell, Guy Clark, John D. Loudermilk
4:00 p.m. **Bluegrass & Shortgrass Music**
The Great Western Orchestra, Jethro Burns, Peter Rowan, Jerry
Douglas, Mark O'Connor
Stage 4
11:00 a.m. **A Sense of Place**
James Keelaghan, Tom Russell, Bob Carpenter, Danny O'Keefe,
Eric Bogle
12:00 p.m. **Human Condition**
Eric Bogle, Terry Garthwaite, Ferron, Tony Bird & Morris Goldberg,
Eric Andersen
1:00 p.m. **It Should Have Been a Hit!**
Murray McLauchlan, Peter Rowan, Danny O'Keefe, Eric Andersen
3:00 p.m. **The Character of the Canadian West**
Murray McLauchlan, Humphrey & The Dumptrucks, Spirit of the
West, James Keelaghan
4:00 p.m. **Dance** The Oyster Band
Tent I
11:00 a.m. **Songs I Wish I'd Written**
Sneezy Waters, Eugene Smith, Bill Bourne, Christine Lavin
12:00 p.m. Bill Garrett & Curly Boy Stubbs
12:30 p.m. **Asian/Ethno Music**
David Essig
1:00 p.m. John Fahey
1:30 p.m. **Accordion Styles**
John Malone & Friends, Ted Borowiecki, John Jones
3:00 p.m. **Comedy Workshop**
Christine Lavin, Al Simmons, Gaye Delorme, Eric Bogle, Jethro
Burns
4:00 p.m. **2nd Annual Folk Fest Quiz**
Quizmasters: Richard Flohil, Bruce Steele. Team One: J. Knutson,
Christine Lavin, Danny O'Keefe, Taras Ostashewsky. Team Two:

Geoffrey Kelly, Shari Ulrich, Tom Russell, Rosalie Goldstein.
Team Three: The Audience
Tent II
11:00 a.m. **Learn to Juggle**
J.J. The Juggling Fool
12:00 p.m. **How to Make Your Own Breaks in the Music Industry**
Richard Flohil, Bob Hunka, Franny Parrish, Paul Mills & Bill Garrett
1:00 p.m. **French Immersion**
Jacques Chauvin, Gilbert Parent
1:30 p.m. **Spoon Workshop**
Gilbert Parent
3:00 p.m. T.A.L.E.S. The Alberta League to Encourage Storytellers
2-4:15 p.m. Open Stage
2 to 3:00 p.m.
Main Stage Rick Danko

5 to 10:30 p.m. **Main Stage**
Huara: Music of Clay & Concrete, Spirit of the West, John D. Loudermilk, Peter Rowan, Mark O'Connor, Ian Tyson with Tom Russell & Jerry Douglas, John Renbourn, Rosanne Cash, Rodney Crowell, Gaye Delorme Quartet & Guy Clark, Finale

AUGUST 5, 1988

5:30 p.m. Main Stage
Butch Hancock & Marce Lacounture, Tamarack, Colleen Peterson, Jimmie Dale Gilmore, Ken Whiteley Band, Sylvia Tyson, Roy Forbes, Ian Matthews, Ponty Bone & the Squeezetones, Tom Russell Band

AUGUST 6, 1988

Strathcona Brewing Company Stage
11:00 a.m. **Affairs of the Heart**
Shari Ulrich, Bill Henderson, Jimmie Dale Gilmore, Bob Neuwirth, Tom Russell, Darden Smith
12:00 p.m. The Rault Brothers Band
12:30 p.m. Kelly Jay & Rusty Reed & guests
1:00 p.m. Dr. Ross The Harmonica Boss
1:30 p.m. Sonny Rhodes with the Rault Brothers Band
3:00 p.m. **Blues Jam**
Ellen McIlwaine, Dr. Ross, Sonny Rhodes, Mr. B, Long John Baldry with Dave Bjarnson & Brian Pollock & Ron Casat
4:00 p.m. **Rhythm & Roots**
Ken Whiteley, Richard Thompson, Colin Linden, Amos Garrett & the Eh Team, Maria Muldaur
CISN Stage
11:00 a.m. **The Hardest and Easiest Songs I've Ever Written**
Bill Bourne, Mike McDonald, Joan MacIsaac, Sunny Moser, Tim Williams
12:00 p.m. Slim Pickens Bluegrass Band
12:30 p.m. Mark Koenig
1:00 p.m. **Lonestar State of Mind**
Ponty Bone & the Squeezetones, Lyle Lovett, Butch Hancock & Marce Lacounture, Jimmie Dale Gilmore, Darden Smith
3:00 p.m. **More than Country**
Sylvia Tyson, The Tom Russell Band, Lyle Lovett, Roy Forbes
4:00 p.m. **Conjunto Workshop**

Doug Sahm, Flaco Jimenez, Ponty Bone, Louie Ortega, Fats Kaplin
K97 Stage
11:00 a.m. **What's a Folk Festival? An Introduction** David Amram, Roy Forbes, Uncle Bonsai, Ken Whiteley, Mr. B
12:00 p.m. Ken Whiteley & Friends
12:30 p.m. **Don't Touch That Dial**
The Grande Ol' Uproar with guests: Lesley Schatz, Tim Williams, Mark Koenig
3:00 p.m. **A Live Taping of CBC's "Simply Folk"**
Mitch Podolak, Stephen Fearing, Joan MacIsaac, Colleen Peterson, Lesley Schatz, Ken Whiteley
96 K-Lite Stage
11:00 a.m. **Contemporary Celtic**
Jim Keelaghan, Tamarack, Figgy Duff
12:00 p.m. Stephen Fearing
12:30 p.m. David Amram
1:00 p.m. **Hurtin' Songs**
Roy Forbes, Richard Thompson, Ian Matthews, Jim Keelaghan, Bob Neuwirth
3:00 p.m. **Sidewalk Mirage** Trickster
3:45 p.m. The Amazing Al Simmons
930 CJCA Stage
11:00 a.m. **Finding You**
Ellen McIlwaine, Alley Scatz, Big Miller, Ed McCurdy
12:00 p.m. T.A.L.E.S.
1:30 p.m. Ed McCurdy
3:00 p.m. **Cajun 2-Step**
Peter Jellard, Greg Hopper, Keith Burgess
3:30 p.m. **Old Time Dancin'**
Figgy Duff, Tamarack
4:30 p.m. **Open Stage**
QT 880 Stage
12:00 p.m. Bob Carpenter
12:30 p.m. Bill Bourne
1:00 p.m. **Banjo Workshop**
Peter Wernick, James Gordon, Terry Knutson
1:30 p.m. **Harmonica Workshop**
Rusty Reed & Kelly Jay, Butch Coulter, Frank Maher, Jeff Bird
3:00 p.m. **Mandolin Workshop**
David Wilkie, David Mansfield & Stephen Soles, Dave Panting, Cathy Cook, Shari Ulrich, Dave Wright
3:30 p.m. **Music from Open Spaces**
Mark Koenig, Tim Williams, Jimmie Dale Gilmore, Butch Hancock & Marce Lacounture
4:30 p.m. **Open Stage**
Kid's Stage
12:00 p.m. Nebulous Rebels
12:30 p.m. Ed McCurdy
1:00 p.m. Sun Ergos
1:30 p.m. Paul Hann
3:00 p.m. W.P. Puppeteers
3:45 p.m. Norman Foote
4:15 p.m. David & Loralee Amram
4:45 p.m. Parade

2 to 3 p.m. Main Stage Jane Siberry

5 p.m. Main Stage

Uncle Bonsai, Flaco Jimenez & Doug Sahm, James Keelaghan, Bobby King & Terry Evans, Darden Smith, Richard Thompson, Papa John Creach, Lyle Lovett, Hot Rize, Rick Danko & Garth Hudson with the Colin Linden Band

AUGUST 7, 1988
Strathcona Brewing Company Stage
11:00 a.m. **The Canadian Character**
Shari Ulrich, Bill Henderson, Jim Keelaghan, Michael Mitchell, Stephen Fearing, Sylvia Tyson
12:00 p.m. Mr. B
12:30 p.m. Colin Linden Band
1:00 p.m. **Rag Mama Rag**
Colin Linden Band, Rick Danko & Garth Hudson, Bob Neuwirth, Doug Sahm, Flaco Jimenez
3:00 p.m. **Country Blues**
Long John Baldry, Dr. Ross The Harmonica Boss, Mr. B, Kelly Jay & Rusty Reed, Ken Whiteley
4:00 p.m. **Ain't Nothing But The Blues**
Amos Garrett & The Eh Team, Doug Sahm Bobby King & Terry Evans, Snooks Eaglin, Papa John Creach,
CISN Stage
11:00 a.m. **Fiddle Workshop**
Shannon McDade, David Mansfield, Dan Burke, Fats Kaplan, Calvin Volrath, Tim O'Brien
12:00 p.m. Lesley Schatz
12:00 p.m. Tim Williams
1:00 p.m. **Honky Tonkin'**
Slim Chitlin ,Grande Ol' Uproar, Red Knuckles & The Trailblazers
3:00 p.m. **The Big Squeeze**
Ponty Bone & the Squeezetones, Flaco Jimenez, Garth Hudson, Fats Kaplin, Frank Maher
4:00 p.m. The Legendary Blues Band
K97 Stage
11:00 a.m. **Acoustic Guitar Styles**
Roy Forbes, Gary Koliger, John King, Charles Sawtelle, Steven Soles, Mark Hallman
12:00 p.m. Ed McCurdy
12:30 p.m. Michael Mitchell Band
1:00 p.m. **And Now For Something Completely Different**
Colleen Peterson, Darden Smith, Snooks Eaglin, Butch Hancock & Marce Lacounture, Bill Henderson, Ken Whiteley
3:00 p.m. **Rhythm Clinic**
David Grisman Quartet
3:45 p.m. **Anxiously Awaited New Songs**
Sylvia Tyson, John Prine, Mickey Newbury, Jane Siberry, Butch Hancock, Rick Danko
96 K-Lite
11:00 a.m. **Gospel Singing**
Maria Muldaur, Ken Whiteley, Big Miller, Alley Scatz, Bobby King & Terry Evans, Ellen McIlwaine
12:30 p.m. Joan MacIsaac
1:00 p.m. **No Borders Here**
Roy Forbes, Jane Siberry, Stephen Fearing, Uncle Bonsai, Al Simmons
3:00 p.m. **Sidewalk Mirage**
Trickster
3:45 p.m. **This Last Laugh**

Slim Chitlin, Al Simmons, Uncle Bonsai, Ed McCurdy, The Lumberjack Show, J.J. The Juggling Fool, Colin Linden
930 CJCA Stage
11:00 a.m. **How to Make Your Own Breaks in the Music Industry**
Diane Sward, Richard Flohil, Ian Matthews, Colleen Peterson, Bob Hunka & Franny Parrish
12:00 p.m. T.A.L.E.S. with special guest Grant MacEwan
3:00 p.m. **The Last Chance Ceilidh**
Figgy Duff, Michael Mitchell, Jim Keelaghan
4:00 p.m. **Learn to Juggle**
J.J. The Juggling Fool and Mugs Mullen
QT 880 Stage
11:30 a.m. **Spoons & Bones, Jigs & Reels**
Les Bucherons
12:00 p.m. Sunny Moser
12:30 p.m. Mike McDonald
1:00 p.m. **Songs of the Sea**
Jim Keelaghan, Ed McCurdy, Pamela Morgan, Michael Mitchell, Bob Carpenter
3:00 p.m. **Prairie Songwriters**
Cindy Church, Nathan Tinkham, Lionel Rault, Bill Bourne, Tim Williams, Mike McDonald
4:15 p.m. **Open Stage**
Kid's Stage
11:30 a.m. Doc Myles Snow Travelling Show
12:30 p.m. Mugs Mullen
1:00 p.m. Lesley Schatz
1:30 p.m. Sun Ergos
3:00 p.m. Nebulous Rebels
3:30 p.m. Joie de Vivre - The Lumberjack Show
4:00 p.m. Paul Hann & Parade

2 to 3 p.m. Main Stage John Prine

5 p.m. Main Stage
Figgy Duff, Mickey Newbury, Snooks Eaglin, Maria Muldaur with Amos Garrett, Grande Ol' Uproar, David Grisman Quartet, Bill Henderson, Bill Monroe & the Bluegrass Boys, Bob Neuwirth, Finale

AUGUST 11, **1989**
5:30 p.m. to 12:30 a.m. Main Stage
Patsy Montana and The Great Western Orchestra, Bob Neuwirth, Capercaillie, Heather Bishop, James Keelaghan, Garnet Rogers, Sarah McLachlan, Guy Clark, Christine Lavin, Ellen McIlwaine, Doug Sahm and Flaco Jimenez

AUGUST 12, 1989 Stage 1
11:00 a.m. **Riverside Blues**
Rusty Reed, Bobby King and Terry Evans, Gene Taylor Rory Block, Joe Louis Walker
12:20 p.m. Lionel Rault, Jamie Kidd, Jeremy Sagar, Ken Chalmers
3:00 p.m. **Guitar City Limits**
Tim Koslo, Ellen McIlwaine, Eddie Patterson, Lester Quitzau, Gaye Delorme, John Logan, Farley Scott
4:00 p.m. **Blues Jam**
Rusty Reed & the Southside Shuffle, Pinetop Perkins, Amos

Garrett
Stage 2
11:00 a.m. **A Tight Squeeze**
Ponty Bone and the Squeezetones, Doug Sahm, Flaco Jimenez,
Louis Ortega, Ted Borowiecki
12:00 p.m. Joan MacIsaac, John Towill
12:40 p.m. The Grievous Angels
3:00 p.m. Colleen Peterson with Gary Koliger, Kit Johnson,
Bohdan Hluszko, Shari Ulrich
4:00 p.m. **West Coast Song Writers**
Rick Scott, Joe Mock, John Mann, Geoffrey Kelly, Louis Ortega,
Lucinda Williams
Stage 3
10:30 a.m. McDade Family
11:00 a.m. **We Love to Laugh**
Hot Free Lunch, Christine Lavin, The Chenille Sisters
12:00 p.m. **A Sense of Place**
Bob Neuwirth, Lesley Schatz, Lucinda Williams, Rufus Guinchard,
R.C. Banks, Robert Earl Keen Jr.
3:00 p.m. Pierre Bensusan
4:00 p.m. **Voices**
The Chenille Sisters, Show of Hands, Jane Siberry and Ken Mhyr
Stage 4
11:00 a.m. Slim Pickens Bluegrass Band
11:30 p.m. **Celtic Heartbeat**
Spirit of the West, Alan MacLeod, James Keelaghan, Jim Payne,
Margaret Christl
12:30 p.m. **Noteworthy**
Gary Koliger, Oscar Lopez, Preston Reed, Ken Mhyr, Edgar Meyer
3:00 p.m. **All in the Family**
McDade Family, Deighton Family
4:00 p.m. Robert Earl Keen Jr.
Tent I
11:00 a.m. **Stand Up Bass**
Edgar Meyer, Dr. John, Ciambotti
11:30 a.m. Hal Ketchum
12:30 p.m. Gaye Delorme, Ted Borowiecki
3:00 p.m. Preston Reed
3:40 p.m. **Let Love Begin**
Rory Block, Bobby King Terry Evans
4:20 p.m. Rufus Guinchard, Jim Payne
Tent II
11:00 a.m. **Flamenco Concert**
Oscar Lopez, Manuel Jara
11:30 a.m. **Homegrown**
Guy Clark, Colleen Peterson, Patsy Montana, Peter Case
12:30 p.m. **Change**
Jennifer Berezan, Bill Bourne, Heather Bishop, Connie Kaldor
3:00 p.m. Emile Benoit, Jim Payne
3:40 p.m. **Anything Goes**
Bob Neuwirth, Peter Case and Friends
4:20 p.m. Amelia Kaminsky, Denise Whithnell
Kid's Area
11:00 a.m. Izzi, Amelia Kaminsky
11:30 a.m. Heather Bishop
12:00 p.m. Norman Foote
12:30 p.m. Le Circus Bop et Zezelle
1:30 p.m. MAINSTAGE
3:00 p.m. Paul Hann, Surprise Guest

3:30 p.m. Paul Hann
4:00 p.m. Mugs Mullen and Foo Ling Lou
4:30 p.m. McDade Family Band
5:00 p.m. J.J. the Juggling Fool
ALL DAY Alberta Wildlife Park Petting Zoo

1:30 to 3 p.m. Main Stage Rory Block, Roger McGuinn

5 p.m. to 12:30 a.m. Main Stage
The Chenille Sisters, Free Hot Lunch, Deighton Family, Jerry
Douglas, Edgar Meyer, Connie Kaldor and Russ Barenberg,
Michael Hedges, Timbuk 3, Amos Garret and The Eh Team, Joe
Louis Walker, Bobby King and Terry Evans

AUGUST 13, 1989
Stage 1
11:00 a.m. Juba
12:00 p.m. **Gospel**
Ellen McIlwaine, Big Miller, Joe Louis Walker, Rory Block, Bobby
King Terry Evans, Gene Taylor, Kit Johnson, Bohdan Hluszko
3:00 p.m. Sugar Blue
4:00 p.m. **Return of the Formerly Brothers**
Amos Garrett, Doug Sahm, Gene Taylor, Kit Johnson, Bohdan
Hluszko
Stage 2
11:00 a.m. **All You Need Is Love**
Jennifer Berezan, Hal Ketchum, Sarah McLachlan
12:00 p.m. **One World**
Gaye Delorme, Russ Barenberg, Martin Simpson, Pierre
Bensusan, Oscar Lopez
3:00 p.m. **Canadian Airs**
Garnet Rogers, Grievous Angels, James Keelaghan Trio, Jim
Payne, Don Freed
4:00 p.m. **Texas Gold**
Ponty Bone and the Squeezetones, Timbuk 3, Guy Clark
Stage 3
11:00 a.m. **They Often Call Me Speedo**
Gaye Delorme, Preston Reed
11:30 a.m. **War and Peace**
Garnet Rogers, Timbuk 3, Show of Hands, Heather Bishop
12:35 p.m. **This Land is Our Land**
James Keelaghan, Peter Case, Lucinda Williams, Bob Neuwirth
and Friends
MAIN STAGE
3:00 p.m. **Celtic Ray**
Spirit of the West, Capercaillie
4:00 p.m. **Still Crazy After All These Years**
Bob Neuwirth, T Bone Burnett, Loudon Wainwright III, Roger
McGuinn, Steve Forbert
Stage 4
11:00 a.m. McDade Family
11:30 a.m. **Zydeco Concert**
Fernest and the Thunders
12:30 p.m. **Porch Songs**
Guy Clark, Robert Earl Keen Jr,. Hal Ketchum, Colleen Peterson,
Patsy Montana
3:00 p.m. Martin Simpson
4:00 p.m. **Harmony**
Free Hot Lunch, Show of Hands

Tent I
11:00 a.m. Margaret Christl, Mike Johnson
11:45 a.m. Bill Bourne, Alan MacLeod
12:30 p.m. **Generations of Fiddling**
Peter Jellard, Kathleen Deighton, Rufus Guinchard, Emile Benoit, Shannon McDade
3:00 p.m. **All the Bells and Whistles**
Rick Scott, Randall Kirsch, Joe Mock, Dave Deighton, Alan MacLeod
4:00 p.m. **Masters**
Jerry Douglas, Edgar Meyer, Pierre Bensusan, Emile Benoit
Tent II
10:30 a.m. Open Stage
11:30 a.m. Peter Case
12:30 p.m. **Ten Years After**
Margaret Christl, Connie Kaldor, Joan MacIsaac, Bill Bourne
3:00 p.m. Lesley Schatz, Gary Koliger, John Hyde
4:00 p.m. Jennifer Berezan, Chris Webster
Kid's Area
11:00 a.m. Izzi, J.J. The Juggling Fool
11:30 a.m. Lesley Schatz
12:00 p.m. Mugs Mullen and Foo Ling Lou
12:30 p.m. Rick Scott
1:00 p.m. Surprise Guest
1:30 p.m. MAINSTAGE
3:00 p.m. Paul Hann, Les Bucherons
3:30 p.m. Les Bucherons
4:00 p.m. Paul Hann
4:30 p.m. McDade Family Band
5:00 p.m. J.J. The Juggling Fool

1:30 to 3:00 p.m. Main Stage
Pinetop Perkins, Steve Forbert, Rusty Reed & the Southside Shuffle

5 to 11:30 p.m. Main Stage
Show of Hands, Jane Siberry, Lucinda Williams, T Bone Burnett, Pied Pumpkin, Spirit of the West, Loudon Wainwright III, Jerry Jeff Walker, Finale

AUGUST 10, **1990**

5:30 p.m. Main Stage
Juba!, Grievous Angels, Women in the Round, Ranch Romance, Metamora with Martin Simpson, Altan, Crash Test Dummies, Hans Theessink with Jon Sass, Loreena McKennitt, Beausoleil with Michael Doucet

AUGUST 11, 1990

Stage 1
11:00 am. **Double Trouble**
Gaye Delorme, Davey Graham
12:00 p.m. **Ceilidh**
Altan Battlefield Band, Rawlins Cross, Peter Rowan, Metamora
3:00 p.m. **New Kids on the Block**
Grievous Angels, Crash Test Dummies, Boiled in Lead
4:00 p.m. **Blues Jam**
Amos Garrett, Ron Casat, Larry Lever, Rusty Reed, Bohdan

Hlusko, Kit Johnson, Hans Theessink
Stage 2
11:00 am. **North and South**
Mark Koenig, Pam Tillis, Laura Vinson, Tricia Walker, Danny Mack, Karen Staley
12:00 p.m. Fred Koller
12:30 p.m. Oscar Lopez
1:00 p.m. **Celtic Mystique**
Davey Graham, Daithi Sproule, Alistair Russell, Anton Drennan, Davy Spillane
3:00 p.m. Lennie Gallant, Janet Munson, Brian Bourne
4:00 p.m. **Styles**
Gaye Delorme, Davey Graham, Kafala Brothers, Frank Sibanda, 5:00 p.m. Mark Koenig, Jeff Bradshaw, Derek Stremel, Tim Lent
Stage 3
11:00 am. **Turner Valley Gold**
Amos Garrett, Oscar Lopez, Ron Casat, David Wilkie,
12:00 p.m. Jerusalem Ridge
1:00 p.m. James Keelaghan, Gary Bird, Bill Eaglesham
3:00 p.m. **As the World Turns**
James Keelaghan, Ranch Romance, Shawn Colvin, Peter Rowan
4:00 p.m. Laura Vinson, Dave Martineau, Paul Martineau, Randy Hillman, Tony Michael
5:00 p.m. **Lucky in Love**
Fred Koller, Laurie Lewis, Shawn Colvin, Carmen Campagne, L.J. Booth
Stage 4
11:00 am. **No Fiddle, No Guitars**
Artis the Spoonman, Jon Sass, Stewart MacDougall, Faith Nolan
12:00 p.m. **Travelling Songs**
Grievous Angels, L.J. Booth, James Keelaghan, Lynn Miles, Jennifer Berezan
1:00 p.m. **Tradition with a Twist**
Lennie Gallant, La Bottine Souriante, Loreena McKennitt, Crash Test Dummies
3:00 p.m. **Airs and Graces**
Loreena McKennitt, Davy Spillane, Battlefield Band, Metamora
4:00 p.m. Rawlins Cross
5:00 p.m. **Maple Spirit**
Jennifer Berezan, Brad Roberts, Mike McDonald, Mae Moore
Family Stage
11:00 am. Juba!
11:30 am. Ranch Romance
12:00 p.m. Tom Kubinek
1:00 p.m. Artis the Spoonman, Jim Page
3:00 p.m. **Amaize Theatre Presents**
The Tale of Four Directions
4:00 p.m. Holly Graham
5:00 p.m. Les Bucherons
Tent 1
11:00 am. Ashley Cleveland
12:00 p.m. **Cajun History & Demonstration**
Michael Doucet & guests
1:00 p.m. Karen Staley
3:00 p.m. **Old Songs, New Songs**
Carmen Campagne, Laura Vinson, La Bottine Souriante, Tricia Walker
4:00 p.m. **Acapella & Yodel**
Juba!, Michelle Rumball, Jo Miller & Lisa Theo, Jessica Simpson,

Mairead Ni Mhaonaigh
5:00 p.m. **Just for Laughs**
Faith Nolan, Lynn Miles, Tom Kubinek, Oscar Lopez
Tent 2
11:00 am. **Flute & Whistle**
Frankie Kennedy, Davy Spillane, Ian McKinnon, Grey Larsen
12:00 p.m. **Open Stage**
1:00 p.m. **Ask a Master**
Fred Koller, Jerry Douglas
3:00 p.m. **Hour at the Improv**
Fred Koller, Jim Page, Wyckham Porteous
4:00 p.m. **Open Stage**
5:00 p.m. **Home**
Danny Mack, Dave Brown, Pam Tillis, Great Western Orchestra

2 to 3 p.m. Main Stage
Emmylou Harris and The Nash Ramblers

6 p.m. Main Stage
Peter Rowan and Jerry Douglas, The Kafala Brothers, Laurie
Lewis and Grant Street, The Four Brothers, Davy Spillane, Michael
Hedges, Koko Taylor and the Blues Machine, Solomon Burke

AUGUST 12, 1990

Stage 1
11:00 am. **Around the World in 60 Minutes**
Boiled in Lead, Kafala Brothers, Juba!
12:00 p.m. **The Slide Area**
Gaye Delorme, Amos Garrett, Ted Borowiecki, Ron Casat, Kit
Johnson, Bohdan Hlusko, Hans Theessink, Roger Stanley, David
Bromberg and guests
3:00 p.m. 3X the Blues
4:00 p.m. **Brothers**
Panting Brothers, Four Brothers, Kafala Brothers
5:00 p.m. **Out of Africa**
Fatala, Four Brothers
Stage 2
11:00 am. Mae Moore
12:00 p.m. L.J. Booth
1:00 p.m. Jennifer Berezan, Chris Webster
3:00 p.m. **Something Old, Something Newgrass, Something
Borrowed, Something Bluegrass**
Jerusalem Ridge, Peter Rowan, Tony Michael, Laurie Lewis &
Grant Street, Jerry Douglas
4:00 p.m. **Open Tuning**
Martin Simpson, Mae Moore, Gaye Delorme, Hans Theessink,
Oscar Lopez
5:00 p.m. **Atlantic Crossing**
Loreena McKennitt, Maura O'Connell, Jerry Douglas, Altan
Stage 3
11:00 am. **Sea to Shining Sea**
Rawlins Cross, Wyckham Porteous, Mark Koenig, Crash Test,
Dummies
12:00 p.m. **Gospel Hour 1**
Jerusalem Ridge, Faith Nolan, Karen Staley, Juba!, Stewart
MacDougall
1:00 p.m. **Gospel Hour 2**
Solomon Burke & Band
3:00 p.m. **Bon Temps Roulez**

Michael Doucet with Beausoleil, La Bottine Souriante, Metamora,
David Bromberg
4:00 p.m. Jr. Gone Wild
5:00 p.m. Great Western Orchestra, David Wilkie, Stewart
MacDougall
Stage 4
11:00 am. **Reeds**
Rusty Reed, Dougie Pincock, Yves Lambert, Grey Larsen
12:00 p.m. **Close, But No Guitar**
Loreena McKennitt, Jerry Douglas, Davey Graham, Lisa Theo
1:00 p.m. Danny Mack, David Wilkie, Stewart MacDougall, Oscar
Lopez
3:00 p.m. Wyckham Porteous
4:00 p.m. Faith Nolan
5:00 p.m. Lynn Miles
Family Stage
11:00 am. **Clownin' Around**
Norman Foote, Tom Kubinek, Artis the Spoonman
12:00 p.m. Jacques Chauvin
1:00 p.m. Norman Foote
3:00 p.m. Carmen Campagne
4:00 p.m. **Tout Dans Le Meme Bateau**
Jacques Chauvin, Carmen Campagne, Les Bucherons
5:00 p.m. Les Bucherons
Tent 1
11:00 am. **Promoting Your Own Work**
Fred Koller, James Keelaghan, Carmen Campagne, Mike
McDonald
12:00 p.m. Pam Tillis
12:30 p.m. Tricia Walker
1:00 p.m. **Country Celtic Fiddle**
Brian McNeil, Peter Sutherland, Mairead Ni Mhaonaigh, Barbara
Lamb, Laurie Lewis
3:00 p.m. **Mandolin Wind**
David Wilkie, Hans Theessink
4:00 p.m. **Heartbeats**
Artis the Spoonman, Lennie Gallant, Alberta Parent, Billy Ware
5:00 p.m. **Song Collecting**
Lennie Gallant, Shawn Colvin, Jim Page, Jennifer Berezan
Tent 2
11:00 am. Martin & Jessica Simpson
12:00 p.m. **Open Stage**
1:00 p.m. **East Meets West**
Mae Moore, Lynn Miles, Mark Koenig, Lennie Gallant
3:00 p.m. **Just For Laughs, Too**
Norman Foote, Ranch Romance, L.J. Booth, Danny Mack
4:00 p.m. **Open Stage**
5:00 p.m. **Women in the Tent**
Karen Staley, Pam Tillis, Tricia Walker

2 to 3 p.m. Main Stage
Fatala

6 p.m. Main Stage
Gaye Delorme and Davey Graham, The Battlefield Band, Shawn
Colvin, Boiled in Lead, Maura O'Connell, David Bromberg, La
Bottine Souriante, Finale

AUGUST 9, 1991

5:30 p.m. Main Stage
Jane Hawley and The Cranky Brats, Clive Gregson and Christine Collister, Cheryl Wheeler, Mari Boine Persen, Patty Larkin Rossy, Capercaillie, Bobby King and Terry Evans, Saffire - The Uppity Blues Women

AUGUST 10, 1991

Stage 1
11:00 a.m. Lindi Smith
11:45 a.m. Crystal Plamondon
12:30 p.m. Paul James
1:15 p.m. Jr. Gone Wild
3:00 p.m. **Tribute to Robert Johnson**
John Hammond, Paul James, Johnny Shines, Kent DuChaine
4:00 p.m. Acoustically Inclined
5:00 p.m. Violent Femmes
Stage 2
11:00 a.m. **Lots of Strings**
Jim Rooney, Eric Weissberg, Kenny Kosek, Oscar Lopez, David Schnaufer, Bill Keith Rossy
12:00 p.m. **The Funny Farm**
Bob Bossin, Calvin Cairns, Saffire - The Uppity Blues Women, Patty Larkin, Cheryl Wheeler
1:00 p.m. **Old Time Music**
Jim Rooney, Bill Keith, Ken Kosek, Eric Weissberg, Acoustically Inclined
3:00 p.m. **Wild Roses**
David Wilkie, Oscar Lopez, Dove, Jane Hawley, Jennifer Gibson
4:00 p.m. **Accompanying Yourself**
Steve Young, Clive Gregson, Patty Larkin, Bill Bourne
5:00 p.m. **Squeeze Box**
John Jones, Ted Borowiecki, Donald Shaw, "Fats" Kaplin, Zachary Richard
Stage 3
11:00 a.m. Mark Holmgren
11:45 a.m. Dale Ladouceur
12:30 p.m. Great Western Orchestra
1:15 p.m. David Schnaufer
3:00 p.m. Cindy Church and The Rhythm Rangers
3:45 p.m. Jann Arden
4:30 p.m. Johnny Shines, Candy Martin Shines, Kent DuChaine
5:15 p.m. Steve Young
Stage 4
11:00 a.m. **Puirt-A-Beul (Gaelic Singing)**
Capercaillie, The Rankin Family, Pamela Morgan
12:00 p.m. **Dance and Celebrate**
Figgy Duff, The Rankin Family, Toto, La Momposina y sus Tambores
3:00 p.m. **A Voice of One's Own**
Ferron, Cheryl Wheeler, Patty Larkin, Saffire - The Uppity Blues Women
4:00 p.m. **Prairie Songs**
Bob Bossin, Calvin Cairns, Cindy Church and The Rhythm Rangers, Jane Hawley, Great Western Orchestra
5:00 p.m. **You Play What?**
David Schnaufer, Dale Ladouceur, Rossy, Mark Holmgren

Tent I
11:00 a.m. **Songs of Doom and Gloom**
Bill Bourne, Jann Arden, Steve Young, Katy Moffatt
12:00 p.m. **West Coast**
Stephen Fearing, Allen Dobb, Ferron
1:15 p.m. **W.O.M.A.D. Presents**
Marie Boine, Persen Rossy, Joji Hirota
3:00 p.m. **For the Record (You've written your song, now what?)**
Richard Flohil, Stephen Fearing, Raylene Rankin, Tom Russell, Mike McDonald, Jim Rooney
4:00 p.m. **Fiddle Tunes (With a Twist)**
Ken Kosek, Bill Keith, David Schnaufer, Alain Lamontagne
5:00 p.m. **Cultural Survival**
Michael Asch, Mari Boine Persen, Bill Miller, Ian Telfer, Alain Lamontagne
Tent II
11:00 a.m. Open Stage
1:00 p.m. **Vocalizing**
Christine Collister, Karen Matheson, Cindy Church, Bobby King and Terry Evans
3:00 p.m. Open Stage
4:00 p.m. **Pied Pipers (Flutes and Whistles)**
Pol Brennan, Guo Yue, Bill Miller, Carlos Zamata, Quispe, Marc Duff
5:00 p.m. **Hit Men (Inside the Music Business)**
Richard Flohil, Jim Rooney, Katy Moffatt, Alan MacLeod
Family Stage
11:00 a.m. Charlie Brown
12:00 p.m. Fred Garbo & Drue Franklin
1:00 p.m. **Storytelling**
Anne Andersen, John Marsh, Liz Dorman, Gail De Vos, Paul Hann
3:00 p.m. Fred Garbo
4:00 p.m. Paul Hann
5:00 p.m. The Great Main Stagecoach Parade

2 to 3 p.m. Main Stage Violent Femmes

6 p.m. Main Stage
Pol Brennan, Guo Yue, Joji Hirota, Figgy Duff, The Rankin Family, The Oyster Band, John Hammond, Zachary Richard, Toto La Momposina y sus Tambores, Bourne and MacLeod

AUGUST 11, 1991 Stage 1

11:00 a.m. **Gospel**
Cindy Church and The Rhythm Rangers, Stewart MacDougall, Bobby King and Terry Evans, Johnny Shines, Candy Martin Shines, Kent DuChaine
1:00 p.m. **Country Blues**
Bill Bourne, John Hammond, Johnny Shines, Kent DuChaine, Saffire - The Uppity Blues Women
3:00 p.m. **Slide**
Paul James, Johnny Shines, Kent DuChaine, John Hammond, Lester Quitzau
4:00 p.m. Sons of the Blues
5:00 p.m. **Jammin'**
Amos Garrett and Friends, Bobby King and Terry Evans, Los Lobos, Long John Baldry
Stage 2

11:00 a.m. **In the Spirit of Gram Parsons**
Tom Russell, Mike McDonald, Steve Young
12:00 p.m. **Stony Plain 15th Anniversary 1**
Holger Petersen, Tom Russell Band, Katy Moffatt, Jr. Gone Wild
1:00 p.m. **Stony Plain 15th Anniversary 2**
Holger Petersen, Amos Garrett and The Eh Team, Paul James, Bobby King and Terry Evans, Long John Baldry
3:00 p.m. **The First, Best, and Last Song I Wrote**
Patty Larkin, Great Western Orchestra, Jann Arden, Bill Miller
4:00 p.m. **Everything You Always Wanted to Know About the Guitar** (Now's the time to ask)
Alan Prosser, "Fats" Kaplin, Andrew Hardin, Oscar Lopez, Dave Hamilton, Nathan Tinkham
5:00 p.m. **Collaborations**
Tom Russell, Katy Moffatt, Steve Young, Clive Gregson, Christine Collister
Stage 3
11:00 a.m. Oscar Lopez
11:45 a.m. Bob Bossin, Calvin Cairns
12:30 p.m. 3X The Blues
1:15 p.m. Katy Moffatt
3:00 p.m. Bill Keith, Eric Weissberg, Jim Rooney, Kenny Kosek
3:45 p.m. Bill Miller
4:30 p.m. Dobb and Dumela
5:15 p.m. Alain Lamontagne
Stage 4
11:00 a.m. **Celtic Music and Beyond**
Alan MacLeod, Figgy Duff, Pol Brennan, Guo Yue, Joji Hirota Martin Swan, Mairi MacInnes,
12:00 p.m. **Traditional Music From the East Coast**
The Rankin Family, Figgy Duff
1:00 p.m. **Both Sides the Tweed**
The Oyster Band, Mouth Music, Alan MacLeod
3:00 p.m. **For the Cause**
Stephen Fearing, The Oyster Band, Bob Bossin, Mark Holmgren
4:00 p.m. **Folk Festival Quiz**
Richard Flohil, Holger Petersen, Mitch Podolak, Cindy Church, Pamela Morgan, Cheryl Wheeler, Jann Arden, David Wilkie, Bill Bourne, John Lomax III, John Jones
5:30 p.m. **Ceilidh**
Capercaillie and guests
Tent I
11:00 a.m. Open Stage
12:00 p.m. **Acousticity**
Acoustically Inclined, David Schnaufer
1:00 p.m. **French Immersion**
Alain Lamontagne, Crystal Plamondon
3:00 p.m. Open Stage
4:00 p.m. **The Producers (Questions and Answers)**
Jim Rooney, Steve Berlin, Clive Gregson
5:00 p.m. **New Nashville Cats**
Cheryl Wheeler, David Schnaufer, Bill Miller
Tent II
11:00 a.m. **A Cappella**
Raylene Rankin, Carol Jean Rankin, Heather Rankin, Dale Ladouceur
12:00 p.m. **The Hardest and Easiest Songs I've Written**
Stephen Fearing, Patty Larkin Ferron
1:00 p.m. **Fiddle Styles**

Kenny Kosek, Calvin Cairns, Richard Moody, Jane Hawley
3:00 p.m. **Harp Attack**
Rusty Reed, Alain Lamontagne, Billy Branch
4:00 p.m. **Banjo Styles**
Bob Bossin, Bill Keith, Eric Weissberg
5:00 p.m. **Open Story Event**
T.A.L.E.S., John Marsh, Gail De Vos
Family Stage
11:00 a.m. T.A.L.E.S. Liz Dorman, Anne Andersen
12:00 p.m. Charlie Brown, Fred Garbo
1:00 p.m. Paul Hann
3:00 p.m. Fred Garbo
4:00 p.m. Charlie Brown, Drue Franklin
5:00 p.m. The Great Main Stagecoach Parade

2 to 3 p.m. Main Stage Inner Circle

6 p.m. Main Stage
Johnny Shines, Tom Russell, Mouth Music, Los Lobos, Stephen Fearing, Ferron, Finale

AUGUST 7, 1992

5:30 p.m. to 12:30 a.m. Main Stage
Tom Jackson, Shingoose, Dave Cramer, Four Bitchin' Babes, Mark Koenig Trio, Arcady, Pete Morton, Maria Muldaur, Lucinda Williams, The Holmes Brothers, Dick Gaughan

AUGUST 8, 1992

Stage 1
11:00 a.m. **More**
Four Bitchin' Babes1
12:00 p.m. **Master Class**
Alan MacLeod, Mike Auldridge, Pat Alger, Jackie Daly and Johnny McDonough
1:00 p.m. **White Warbly Voiced Crooners Who Sound Sort of Black,** Geoff Muldaur, Bill Bourne, Amos Garrett, Chris Smither
3:00 p.m. The Hard Rock Miners
4:00 p.m. **Red Hot Blues**
Amos Garrett & the Festival House Band, Maria Muldaur, Geoff Muldaur,The Holmes Brothers, Jackson Delta
Stage 2
11:00 a.m. **Songs From the Public Domain**
Lesley Schatz, Cindy Church, Nathan Tinkham, Chris Smither
12:00 p.m. **On the Calgary Trail**
Mark Koenig, Triple Threat, Eileen McGann, Cathy Miller, Ron Casat
1:00 p.m. **Duets**
Tom Russell & Andrew Hardin, Open Mind, Cindy Church & Nathan Tinkham, Martin & Jessica Simpson
3:00 p.m. **Prisoners of Conscience**
Pete Morton, Dick Gaughan, Ron Kavana, Ani DiFranco
4:00 p.m. **Brand New (Future Classics)**
Tom Russell, Lucinda Williams, Dave Alvin, Pat Alger
5:00 p.m. **Tribute to Ewan MacColl**
Dick Gaughan, Kate and Anna McGarrigle, Peggy Seeger and Irene Scott
Stage 3
11:00 a.m. **Guitar Town**

David Essig, Andrew Hardin, Gurf Morlix, Oscar Lopez
12:00 p.m. **Lives of Girls and Women**
Peggy Seeger, Kate and Anna McGarrigle, Colleen Peterson, Ani DiFranco
1:00 p.m. Manigance
3:00 p.m. **A Chording to the Gospel I**
The Seldom Scene, Cindy Church and Nathan Tinkham, Charlie Louvin and Charles Whitstein
4:30 p.m. **Oh, Oh Canada**
Lennie Gallant Band, Colleen Peterson, Tom Jackson, Lionel Rault, Shingoose
Stage 4
11:00 a.m. Kathleen Yearwood
11:45 a.m. Geoff Muldaur
12:30 p.m. David Broza
1:15 p.m. Eileen McGann
3:00 p.m. Lesley Schatz and Lost in the Labels
3:45 p.m. Chris Smither
4:30 p.m. Open Mind
5:15 p.m. David Essig Family
Stage1
11:00 a.m. Cathy Miller, O.J. Anderson
12:00 p.m. **Dance**
Red Thunder Cultural Society
1:00 p.m. Judy Anderson-Hansen, Steve Hansen
3:00 p.m. Al Simmons
4:00 p.m. **Story-telling**
Watson Smarch, Tommy McGinty
Tent "A"
11:00 a.m. **Canadian Fiddle Styles**
Janet Munson, Jane Hawley, Karl Roth, Tony and Gene Michael, Claude Methe
12:00 p.m. **A Sense of Place**
Pete Morton, Shingoose, Paul Ubana Jones
1:00 p.m. **With a Banjo On My Knee**
Lesley Schatz, Gerry O'Connor, Ben Eldridge
3:00 p.m. **The Deep South**
Oscar Lopez, Apurimac
4:00 p.m. Three Dead Trolls in a Baggie
5:00 p.m. **Take a Bow: Fiddling Workshop**
Karl Roth, Brendan Larrissey, Joel Zifkin, Daniel Lemieux and Claude Methe
Tent "B"
11:00 a.m. **Blowin' in the Wind**
Nicholas Quemenar, Daniel Roy, Maurice Gallardo and Marco Cerda
12:00 p.m. **Tickling the Funny Bone**
Lynn Miles, Meryn Cadell, Lionel Rault
1:00 p.m. Holger Petersen interviews Charlie Louvin and Dave Alvin
3:00 p.m. **Festival Quiz**
Rosalie Goldstein, Richard Flohil. Team (USA). Christine Lavin, Sally Fingerett, Megon McDonough, Julie Gold. Team (Canada). Bill Bourne, Tim Williams, Alan MacLeod, Johnny V.
4:45 p.m. **Short Concert**
Ani DiFranco
5:00 p.m. **Poetry Into Song**
David Broza, Meryn Cadell, Acoustic

Open Stage 11:00 a.m
2 to 3 p.m. Main Stage
Kate & Anna McGarrigle
6 p.m. to 12:30 a.m. Main Stage
Charlie Louvin & Charles Whitstein, David Lindley, Martin Simpson, Oscar Lopez, The Seldom Scene, Lennie Gallant, Dave Alvin, Thomas Mapfumo & The Blacks Unlimited, Alias Ron Kavana

AUGUST 9, 1992
Stage 1
11:00 a.m. Colleen Peterson
12:00 p.m. **Landslide**
Martin Simpson, Tim Williams, Johnny V., Gary Peeples
1:00 p.m. Bourne and MacLeod
3:00 p.m. **Dance Traditions**
Edward II, Manigance
4:00 p.m. **Country Blues**
Geoff Muldaur, Lucinda Williams, Robert Jr. Lockwood, Bill Bourne
5:00 p.m. **Sounds of Zimbabwe,**
Members of Thomas Mapfumo & The Blacks Unlimited, The Bhundu Boys
Stage 2
11:00 a.m. **The Human Condition**
Tom Russell, Mark Koenig, Laurie Lewis, Charlie Louvin
12:00 p.m. Dan Ar Bras
1:00 p.m. Tom Russell, Andrew Hardin
3:00 p.m. **First Nations**
Tom Jackson, Shingoose, Watson Smarch, Tommy McGinty, Red Thunder
4:00 p.m. Pat Alger
5:00 p.m. **"Dave? Dave's Not Here"**
David Essig, David Lindley, David Broza
Stage 3
11:00 a.m. **Influences**
Lennie Gallant, David Broza, Lucinda Williams, Dick Gaughan
12:00 p.m. **Love Songs For the 90's**
Christine Lavin, Julie Gold, Open Mind, Meryn Cadel
1:00 p.m. **A Chording to the Gospel II**
The Holmes Brothers, Maria Muldaur
3:00 p.m. **Nothing to Fret About**
Amos Garrett, David Lindley, Martin Simpson, Dan Ar Bras
4:30 p.m. **Ceilidh**
Jackie Daly, Ron Kavana, Alan MacLeod
Stage 4
11:00 a.m. Jackson Delta
11:45 a.m. **Music of the Andes**
Apurimac
12:30 p.m. Lynn Miles
1:15 p.m. Meryn Cadell
3:00 p.m. Peggy Seeger, Irene Scott
3:45 p.m. Paul Ubana Jones
4:30 p.m. Cathy Miller
5:15 p.m. Lionel Rault
Family Stage
11:00 a.m. Judy Anderson-Hansen, Steve Hansen
12:00 p.m. Cathy Miller
1:00 p.m. O.J. Anderson
3:00 p.m. **Something's Fishy at Camp Wiganishie**

Al Simmons
4:00 p.m. **Vaudeville**
Al Simmons, O.J. Anderson, Three Dead Trolls in a Baggie
Tent "A"
11:00 a.m. Tony Michael & the Foggy Minded Mountain Boys
12:00 p.m. **And Justice for All**
Peggy Seeger, Kathleen Yearwood, Sally Fingerett, Megon
McDonough
1:00 p.m. **To the Beat of a Different Drummer**
Johnny McDonough, Hani Naser, Paul Ubana Jones, Tom Roach
3:00 p.m. **A Cappella**
Lynn Miles, Frances Black, Kathleen Yearwood, Eileen McGann,
Ani DiFranco
4:00 p.m. **Irish Genes**
Eileen McGann, Dick Gaughan, Irene Scott
5:00 p.m. Triple Threat
Tent "B"
11:00 a.m. Jane Hawley, Mike McDonald
12:00 p.m. **Making a Living in Music (Panel)**
Richard Flohil, Chris Smither, Rosalie Goldstein, Holger Petersen,
Dave Bulmer
1:00 p.m. **Lonesome Songs**
Mark Koenig, Colleen Peterson, Lesley Schatz, Jane Hawley
3:00 p.m. Cindy Church, Nathan Tinkham
4:00 p.m. **40 Shades of Blue**
Jackson Delta, David Essig, Lionel Rault, Paul Ubana Jones
5:00 p.m. **A Little Bit of Country**
Laurie Lewis, Jane Hawley, Mike McDonald, Tom Jackson,
Acoustic
Open Stage11:00 a.m.
3:00 p.m. Holger Petersen interviews Robert Jr. Lockwood
3:30 p.m.
2 to 3 p.m. Main Stage Ry Cooder and David Lindley

6 p.m. to 12:30 a.m. Main Stage
Robert Jr. Lockwood, Ani DiFranco, Edward II, The Bhundu Boys,
Ron Kavana and the House Band, Laurie Lewis and the Grant
Street Band, Finale: Amazing Grace, Imagine, Four Strong Winds

AUGUST 5, **1993**

6:30 to 11:00 p.m. Main Stage
Ismael Lo, Baaba Maal, Angelique Kidjo, J.J. Cale

AUGUST 6, 1993

5:30 p.m. to 12:00 a.m. Main Stage
Els Trobadors, Bad Livers, Roy Harper, Topp Twins, John
Bottomley, Roy Forbes, Mary Coughlan, Moxy Fruvous

AUGUST 7, 1993

Stage 1
11:00 a.m. **A Sense of Place**
Andy Irvine, Topp Twins, Iris DeMent, Els Trobadors
12:00 p.m. Jerusalem Ridge
1:00 p.m. Mary Coughlan Band and special guests
3:00 p.m. **Blues Jam - Part I**
Amos Garrett, House Band, Doug Sahm, Colin Linden
4:00 p.m. **Blues Jam - Part II**
Honeyboy Edwards, Ellen McIlwaine, Lester Quitzau

5:00 p.m. Bourbon Tabernacle Choir
Stage 2
11:00 a.m. Great Western Orchestra
11:45 a.m. Jennifer Berezan, Nina Gerber
12:30 p.m. **In the Tradition**
Rawlins Cross, Santiago Jimenez Jr.,.Laura Smith, Chris Wood
and Andy Cutting, Bad Livers
3:00 p.m. Wyckham Porteous
4:00 p.m. **Rave On**
Rory MacLeod, Brenda Kahn, Steve Forbert, Don Ross
5:00 p.m. **The Country Beat**
Roy Forbes, Iris DeMent, Kevin Welch, Jennifer Gibson
Stage 3
11:00 a.m. **Je Me Souviens**
Ad Vielle Que Pourra, Chris Wood and Andy Cutting, Les
Bucherons
12:00 p.m. **Manchester Songwriters "United We Stand"**
Clive Gregson, Roy Harper, Keith Hancock
1:00 p.m. **Southern Fried Blues**
Colin Linden, Hans Theessink, Honeyboy Edwards, Nina Gerber,
Ken Hamm
3:00 p.m. June Tabor, Mark Emerson, Huw Warren, Mark
Lockheart
4:00 p.m. **Sing Out!**
Fairfield Four, Tuva Ensemble, Moxy Fruvous
5:00 p.m. Ani DiFranco
Stage 4
11:00 a.m. **The Canadian In Me**
James Keelaghan, Laura Smith, Wyckham Porteous, The Wyrd
Sisters, Don Ross
12:00 p.m. **Open Minds**
Nancy White, Roy Forbes, Randy Newman, Steve Forbert
1:15 p.m. Nickel Finger
3:00 p.m. **Bonaparte's Retreat**
Maighread and Triona Ni Dhomhnaill, Donal Lunny, Paddy Glackin,
Ad Vielle Que Pourra, Chris Wood and Andy Cutting
4:30 p.m. Holger Petersen interviews Charles Brown
5:15 p.m. Richard Flohil interviews Randy Newman
Tent A
11:00 a.m. Brenda Kahn
11:45 a.m. Dave Moore
12:30 p.m. The Wyrd Sisters
1:15 p.m. Rory MacLeod
3:00 p.m. **A Change is Gonna Come**
Keith Hancock, Roy Harper, Jennifer Berezan, Ani DiFranco
4:00 p.m. **Influences**
Johnny Cunningham, Andy Irvine, Ken Hamm, Hans Theessink
5:00 p.m. Laura Vinson and Free Spirit
Tent B
11:00 a.m. Lester Quintzau
12:00 p.m. **It's a Hit**
Moxy Fruvous, Wyckham Porteous, Robert Earl, Keen John
Bottomley
1:00 p.m. **Take a Bow**
Johnny Cunningham, Paddy Glackin, Calvin Volrath, Victor Schultz
3:00 p.m. Laura Smith
3:45 p.m. Danny Greenspoon
4:30 p.m. **Sibling Rivalry**
Topp Twins, Dave and Geoff Panting

5:15 p.m. **Prairie Home Companions**
James Keelaghan, The Wyrd Sisters, Great Western Orchestra
Family Stage
11:00 a.m. Kaetz and Glover
12:00 p.m. Topp Twins
1:00 p.m. Les Bucherons
3:00 p.m. **Dance**
White Braid Society
4:00 p.m. Dave Moore
4:45 p.m. Parade
5:00 p.m. Open Stage

2 to 3 p.m. Main Stage Randy Newman

6 p.m. to 12:00 a.m. Main Stage
Finjan, Keith Hancock Band, Hans Theessink & Jon Sass, Charles Brown, Tuva Ensemble, June Tabor, Kevin Welch Nashville Bluegrass Band, Donal Lunny, Paddy Glackin, Maighread & Triona Ni Dhomhnaill

AUGUST, 8, 1993
Stage 1
11:00 a.m. **Sideman Serenade**
Colin Linden, Lee Collinson, Jon Sass, Clive Gregson
12:00 p.m. Rawlins Cross
1:00 p.m. Ken Hamm & Tony Trischka
3:00 p.m. **A Virus Called the Blues**
Roy Forbes, Charles Brown, Hans Theessink, Lester Quitzau
4:00 p.m. Ellen McIlwaine, Kit Johnson, Bohdan Hluszko
5:00 p.m. **Something Wild**
Judy Mowatt, Frank Carroll, Sister Carol Anthem
Stage 2
11:00 a.m. **A New Generation**
Wyckham Porteous, Laura Smith, Chris Brown, Sue Hodge & Kevin Smith
12:00 p.m. **Storytellers**
Rory MacLeod, John Bottomley, Brenda Kahn
1:00 p.m. Jennifer Gibson
3:00 p.m. **Celtic Connections**
Rawlins Cross, James Keelaghan, Laura Smith, John Bottomley
4:00 p.m. Santiago Jimenez Jr.
5:00 p.m. **Brand New Songs**
Rory McLeod, Robert Earl Keen, Dave Moore, The Wyrd Sisters
Stage 3
11:00 a.m. **Ancient Heartbeats**
Ad Vielle Que Pourra, Els Trobadors
12:00 p.m. **Free Trade**
Great Western Orchestra, Iris DeMent, Kevin Welch, Mark Koenig
1:00 p.m. **World Out of Time**
Ellen McIlwaine, Tuva Ensemble, Finjan
3:00 p.m. **One From the Heart**
Wyckham Porteous, Iris Dement, Great Western Orchestra
4:00 p.m. **All the Right Moves**
Don Ross, Nina Gerber, Lee Collinson, Tony Trischka
5:00 p.m. **Men's Issues**
Ani DiFranco, Sister Breeze, Brenda Kahn, Jennifer Berezan
Stage 4
11:00 a.m. **Gospel Hour (and a half)**

Fairfield Four, Jerusalem Ridge, Nashville Bluegrass Band, Ellen McIlwaine
12:30 p.m. **Celtic Karaoke**
Johnny Cunningham, Donal Lunny, Paddy Glackin, Maighread & Triona Ni Dhomhnaill, Liam O'Flynn, Andy Irvine
3:00 p.m. **Anything Goes**
Nancy White, Tuva Ensemble, Topp Twins, Bourbon Tabernacle Choir
4:30 p.m. Fairfield Four
5:15 p.m. Tuva Ensemble
Tent A
11:00 a.m. Andy Irvine
12:00 p.m. **Don't Mess With Texas**
Bad Livers, Santiago Jimenez Jr., Robert Earl Keen
1:00 p.m. **Hard Pressed**
Keith Hancock, Santiago Jimenez Jr., Andy Cutting, Dave Moore
3:00 p.m. Chris Wood and Andy Cutting
3:45 p.m. Johnny Cunningham
4:30 p.m. Honeyboy Edwards
5:15 p.m. Colin Linden
Tent B
11:00 a.m. **Sex, Money and the Music Business**
Richard Flohil, James Keelaghan, Jennifer Gibson, Ani DiFranco
12:00 p.m. **Love Me Tender**
Jennifer Berezan, The Wyrd Sisters, Ani DiFranco
1:00 p.m. Don Ross
3:00 p.m. **With a Banjo on My Knee**
Tony Trischka, Danny Barnes, Daniel Koulack, Craig Korth, Alan O'Bryant
4:00 p.m. **Fiddle Quartet**
Chris Wood, Stuart Duncan, Alain Leroux, Ralph White III
5:00 p.m. **Great Set of Pipes**
Ian McKinnon, Liam O'Flynn, Gilles Plante
Family Stage
11:00 a.m. Les Bucherons
12:00 p.m. Nancy White
1:00 p.m. Members of Els Trobadors
3:00 p.m. Major Conrad Flapps
4:00 p.m. Kaetz and Glover
4:45 p.m. Parade
5:00 p.m. Open Stage

2 to 3 p.m. Main Stage
Women of Reggae

6 p.m. to 12 a.m. Main Stage
Ad Vielle, Que Pourra, Robert Earl Keen, Iris DeMent, Liam O'Flynn, Fairfield Four, Steve Forbert, James Keelaghan, Finale